C000186865

MINISTERS AND MANDARINS

INSIDE THE WHITEHALL VILLAGE

JOCK BRUCE-GARDYNE

SIDGWICK & JACKSON
LONDON

First published in Great Britain in October 1986
by Sidgwick & Jackson Limited

Reprinted December 1986

ISBN 0–283–99415–0

Phototypeset by Cambrian Typesetters
90 High Street, Frimley, Camberley, Surrey
Printed and bound in Great Britain by
Biddles Ltd., Guildford and King's Lynn
for Sidgwick & Jackson Limited
1 Tavistock Chambers, Bloomsbury Way,
London WC1A 2SG

CONTENTS

Bibliography

Barnett, Joel *Inside the Treasury* André Deutsch, 1982.
Beloff, Max, and Gillian Peels *Government of the UK* Weidenfeld, 1985.
Bridges, Lord *Portrait of a Profession* CUP, 1950.
Brittan, Samuel *The Treasury Under the Tories* Penguin, 1964 (revised as *Steering the Economy* Pelican, 1970).
Bruce-Gardyne, J. *Whatever Happened to the Quiet Revolution?* Charles Knight, 1974.
Mrs Thatcher's First Administration Macmillan, 1984.
Bruce-Gardyne, J. and Lawson, N. *The Power Game* Macmillan, 1976.
Burton, J. *Why No Cuts?* Hobart Paper, Institute of Economic Affairs, 1985.
Butler, E. and Pirie, Dr M. *Freeports* Adam Smith Institution, 1983.
Castle, Barbara *The Castle Diaries* Weidenfeld, 1965.
Chapman, L. *Your Disobedient Servant* Penguin, 1979.
Chester, D. N. and Wilson, F. *The Organisation of British Central Government* Allen & Unwin, 1968.
Clarke, Sir R. *Public Expenditure Management and Control* Macmillan, 1978.
Crossman, R. H. S. *Diaries of a Cabinet Minister* H. Hamilton and J. Cape, 1975–78.
Inside View Cape, 1972.
Dell, Edmund *Political Responsibility and Industry* Allen & Unwin, 1973.
Galloway, D. *Public Prodigals* Maurice Temple-Smith, 1969.
Gilmour, I. *Body Politic* Hutchinson, 1971.
Goldman, S. *Developing a System of Public Expenditure Management and Control* HMSO, 1973.
Gordon Walker, P. *The Cabinet* Collins, 1972.
Griffiths, B. *Inflation* Weidenfeld, 1976.
Haines, J. *Politics of Power* Cape, 1977.
Headey, B. *British Cabinet Ministers* Allen & Unwin, 1974.
Heclo, H. and Wildavsky, A. *Private Government of Public Money* Macmillan, 1974.
Henderson, N. *The Private Office* 1985.
Howell, D. *Blind Victory* Hamilton, 1986.
Hurd, D. *An End to Promises* Collins, 1979.
Institute of Directorss *Re-skilling Government: Report of Conference* April, 1986.
Jay, D. *Sterling* Sidgwick & Jackson, 1985.
Jennings, Sir I. *Cabinet Government* CUP, 1959.
Kaufman, G. *How to be a Minister* Sidgwick & Jackson, 1980.
Keegan, W. *Mrs Thatcher's Economic Experiment* Allen Lane, 1984.
Kellner, P. and Crowther-Hunt, N. *The Civil Servants* Macdonald, 1980.
King, Antony (ed) *The Prime Minister* Macmillan, 1969.
Mackintosh, P. *The British Cabinet*(3rd ed) Stevens, 1977.
Government & Politics of Britain Hutchinson, 1970.
Maudling, R. *Memoires* Sidgwick & Jackson, 1978.
Pliatzky, D. *Getting and Spending* Blackwell, 1982.
Pryke, R. *Nationalised Industries* Martin Robertson, 1981.
Redwood, J. *Going for Broke* Blackwell, 1984.
Riddell, Peter *The Thatcher Government* Martin Robertson, 1983.
Sedgemore, B. *The Secret Constitution* Hodder & Stoughton, 1980.
Stewart, M. *The Jekyll & Hyde Years* Dent, 1977.
Treasury & Civil Service Select Committee *Civil Servants & Ministers* HC 92 of Session 85/86
The Future of the Civil Service Dept HC 730 or 79
Wass, D. *Government and the Governed* 1984.
Young, H. and Sloman, A. *No, Minister* BBC Publications, 1982.
But, Chancellor BBC Publications, 1984.

INTRODUCTION

A Travelogue

Ten years ago I wrote a book with Nigel Lawson, the genial tourist, who resides in Peckham where he writes Italian guides. We called it *the Power Game*. It consisted of four case histories[1] of how individual decisions appeared to be reached in Whitehall. We attempted to track down the genesis of each of them; the influences which shaped their formulation; the rocks and shoals around their path; the relative significance of the input of ministers, civil servants, Westminster, the City, the press. Our modest conclusion was that 'there is only one certainty, and that is that both the true nature of power and influence in the British polity, and our understanding of it, are constantly evolving'. All we had aimed to do was to 'shed some light upon the processes at work and interplay of men and institutions at a particular moment in the recent past'.

Subsequently both of us crossed the footlights to take on speaking roles in the Whitehall theatre. Nigel Lawson entered the Government immediately after the 1979 Election, as Financial Secretary to the Treasury, and rose via the Energy Department to his present eminence as Chancellor. I had more of a bit part. But I did serve as Minister of State and then Economic Secretary in the Treasury from the autumn of 1981 until the Boundaries Commission removed my constituency, and hence my mandate, in the 1983 Election.

One day, we must hope, Nigel Lawson will compose his

[1] The four case-histories were Concorde; the approach to the Common Market; the abolition of resale price maintenance; and devaluation.

memoirs. He can be relied upon to do so with elegance and distinction. For the time being he is otherwise engaged. I, on the other hand, am, in the Gladstonian sense, 'unbound'.

This book is not an attempt to weigh up the estimates of where power and influence are to be found, and how they are exerted which we made in *The Power Game* from outside, against the reality I discovered once inside Whitehall. For one thing, precisely because of constant evolution any attempt at such comparisons would inevitably distort both sides of the equation. For another, I can only speak from experience of one department – admittedly the one that occupies the centre of the Whitehall web – and although I have sought to relate my experience to contemporary events in other sectors of the Government, the Treasury slant would not permit a balanced reassessment of our perceptions of the participants in the process of decision-making in the late fifties and early sixties (with regard to issues some of which were fairly marginal to the Treasury). But above all I wished on this occasion to range rather wider than the business of decision-making. For crucial though that business is to Government, there is more to Whitehall's lifestyle than this.

A classic study of at least a corner of that lifestyle is still *The Private Government of Public Money* (Heclo and Wildavsky, Macmillan, 1974). The authors' theme was the management of public expenditure by the Treasury. But in the course of their exposition they developed the concept of 'the Whitehall Village': a close-knit community of introspective, sparring, and occasionally gossipy mandarins who owed allegiance to the corporate entity, but in particular to the departments to which they happened, at any given time, to be attached. Like the faculties of one of our ancient Universities, they were displayed shoulder to shoulder against the outside world, yet at the same time eager for competitive advancement of their own foundation. This seemed to me, when we were writing *The Power Game*, a perceptive interpretation; and it is one that has stood well the test of personal experience.

The politicians are the tourists in the village. They come, and go. Their habits are not always to the taste of the villagers, who do their best to educate them in village ways.

Since the village lives on tourism, it has no choice other than to accommodate the visitors. Fortunately they are guaranteed eventually to depart. Some contrive to shift the villagers around. Some successfully impose new religions. Some are so uncouth that the villagers manage to evict them, or at least to lock them up in the village tolbooth. But the villagers know they will outstay them all.

So this is essentially a travelogue. In the concluding chapter I have hazarded a few suggestions concerning ways in which, it seems to me, the visitors might be more gainfully diverted, and the villagers more gainfully employed. But it does not set out to be another textbook on the British polity, still less to present a blueprint of a better way of Government for the twenty-first century. I never cease to marvel at the courage of those who embark on the latter task. For I suspect we are a sluggish people, who instinctively resist implanted tissues.

In recent years Whitehall's (and Downing Street's) favourite soap opera, 'Yes, Minister', has presented to the television audience an entertaining picture of scheming mandarins and scared, self-seeking ministers, whom both the civil servants and the politicians can easily recognise. If much of its material has not fallen off the back of departmental lorries it has certainly given that impression. As a result the watching audience has probably learned more about the manner of its government than it ever will from libraries of constitutional exegesis. But while Minister Hacker and Permanent Secretary Sir Humphrey are equal butts for ribaldry, the viewpoint – or so it seems to me – is essentially that of the permanent residents in Whitehall. I have attempted to compose a contrasting viewpoint: that of the transient – and not infrequently embarrassed – visitors from Parliament. If there are occasional resemblances to the television caricature, they are strictly unintentional.

For caricature exaggerates: that is how it transmits its message. I never encountered a real-life Sir Humphrey in Whitehall (even if I have heard rumours of his existence), any more than I can believe that a Parliamentary colleague quite as gormless, and spineless, as Jim Hacker would be selected for ministerial office – let alone, as most recently envisaged in the television series, for the Premiership. Leaving aside the sheer grind, and the penury, which are the inescapable concomitants of preferment nowadays, it remains an immensely rewarding privilege, and certainly all one is told about the intellectual calibre and genuine devotion to the public service of those who staff the permanent Treasury turned out to be true. I would not wish anything in the ensuing pages to leave a contrary impression.

The politicians are always bound to be intruders, strutting around in their suits of self-importance. But most of them, I think, depart when their time is up with gratitude for the tolerance and hospitality they enjoyed from the villagers. I certainly did. The villagers also have wisdom to impart – though whether I absorbed any of it is not for me to judge. At least I like to think that I have returned to my former place in the stalls to watch the continuing performance with a better understanding of the 'business' occurring on the other side of the footlights. That is what this book is all about.

1

Paths to Office

For young men and women with ambition to stroke one day the levers of political power, the world offers a diversity of ladders. In many parts of Africa, Asia and Latin America the military cadet carries a Presidential baton in his cartridge-pouch. In Eastern Europe the first rung on the ladder is entry to the Party, followed by the acquisition of a *patron*. In France there is no substitute for the achievement of the ultimate accolade of that most elitist of educational systems, the *Inspectorat des Finances*[1]. In the United States a law degree, followed by attachment to the coat-tails of a rising Congressman, or – better still – a rising Senator, is strongly indicated. In Britain, and in the Old Commonwealth, the almost indispensable preliminary is the acquisition of a winnable, and preferably a keepable, Parliamentary constituency.

It was not always so. For much of our history a golden ticket to political office was delivered at birth – along with so much else – to the heirs to hereditary peerages. The career was open to talent, as Prime Ministers from Disraeli to Bonar Law remind us. But a coronet in the cradle gave a flying start. Those were the days when the House of Lords supplied the preponderance of the Ministry. As the twentieth-century advanced, and clout slipped from the Lords to the Commons, the indispensability of the constituency base emerged. For perhaps a couple of generations thereafter the Party managers

[1] Party allegiance in France is wonderfully irrelevant. Some years ago one of the most brilliant of young Inspectors of Finance, Jean Deniau, fresh from a stint as France's youngest Commissioner in Brussels, told me he was going into politics at home. 'Which party?' I asked. 'I'm not sure', was the reply. 'I haven't done my sums yet'.

could usually provide an electoral nest for those they needed. Today they have no guarantees to offer. There is still the House of Lords, to which the candidate of talent can be elevated – like the current Secretary of State for Employment, Lord Young – by Prime Ministerial whim. But the large preponderance of the portfolios must be filled from those who have earned the electoral qualification.

Given the dominant role of Trades Union finance and patronage in reliable Labour constituencies, a Labour Prime Minister may still be able to arrange a Parliamentary vacancy for imported talent. Even here recent experience suggests great caution.

Tory managers have no such faithful henchmen to rely on. Since the so-called Maxwell-Fyfe reforms at the end of the 1940s, secure Tory Parliamentary seats are required to be self-financing. They have shown themselves increasingly resistant to centralised choice of standard-bearers. Winston Churchill, wanting Oliver Lyttleton for his Government, could endow him with a seat on command. Ted Heath, similarly choosing John Davies from the CBI, had to watch him run the gauntlet of one constituency selectorate after another, until finally – in the nick of time – he came uneasily to rest in Knutsford. Mrs Thatcher might not even try. Grahame Turner, writing in the *Daily Telegraph* as the shires were limbering up for her second Election victory in 1983, recorded the deliberations of one safe Tory selection committee confronted with one applicant (among several others) recommended by his supporters as a future Chancellor. 'In that case', commented one of the assembled ladies acidly, 'he's not at all the type we want for Barsetshire.'

So first catch your constituency. This is a lottery. In the Labour Party it is a matter of lining up the block votes of the Unions, and it seems that skill and perseverance can work wonders.

Towards the end of the 1970s it was reported, for example, that Mr (later Lord) Charles Williams, who belonged to that endangered species the Socialist merchant banker, had almost succeeded in securing enough pledges from Trades Union representatives on the Committee of Management of the Vauxhall constituency Labour Party to be assured of selection. This was to replace the retiring Labour MP with the only solid Labour constituency within a stone's throw of the House of Commons. In the end, though, skill and perseverance were not quite enough. An approach was made on his behalf to a single lady representative of the National Union of Mineworkers who, it seemed, held the balance of power, notwithstanding the fact that coal-mining is not an activity normally associated with Vauxhall. Unfortunately it turned out that this lady was in touch with left-wing elements in the local Party, to whom she blew the gaff. Mr Williams was accused of right-wing 'entryism' and was banished from the scene, having to find eventual consolation in the House of Lords.

For would-be Tory travellers to the Whitehall village skill and perseverance, though essential, are nothing like enough. Luck is a great deal more important. I was chosen for what was then the safe Tory seat of South Angus in 1962, by a majority of one on the first and only ballot from a field of three. This was against all the ground-rules for these contests. But the sitting MP's wife had scrutinised the list of applicants, and being terrified lest her husband should go back on his decision to retire, chose me (whether rightly or wrongly) as the applicant he was least likely to object to. She then convinced the local Party chairman – the key figure in the Tory, though not the Labour, grassroots organisation – that it was his duty to secure my selection. Which he did.

About the only prediction that can be made with any confidence about the Tory selectorate is that they usually choose the opposite of what they have had to date. If the retiring member is the scion of an ancient landed family, they are liable to pick an advertising account executive to succeed him, and vice versa. One person they are unlikely to pick is a lady. The female members of the selectorate can usually be relied upon to put paid to the chances of their own sex.

The acquisition of a winnable constituency constitutes our traveller's base camp. But like that of the mountaineer, even the base camp is much exposed to the elements. It may be instantly demolished at any time by electoral defeat. It may be eroded and eventually destroyed by neglect or by personal, financial or sexual aberrations. In the Labour Party it may be sabotaged by 'entryism' from the far Left or by political conflict between the member and his selectorate. Tory Members are more secure in this respect. Because the Tory Party has something far more akin to a mass grassroots membership than any of its rivals, a member who is threatened by a radical take-over of his local constituency machine can always demand a head-count of the faithful. His re-selection to fight the constituency he holds is normally a formality,[1] as it is not today in the Labour Party; and should he encounter trouble for idiosyncratic views (even those in conflict with the Party line) the Party machine, guided from the centre, will swing in behind him. Local constituency Parties which showed an inclination to ditch Tory MPs who had opposed our accession to the European Community in the early 1970s, in defiance of Party policy, were swiftly told to mind their manners by headquarters. Thirty years have passed since the last sitting Tory Member – Nigel Nicolson in Bournemouth – was evicted on straightforward political grounds by his local Party, and that eviction was performed in defiance of the pressures from the Tory Central Office.

There is no such thing, though, as a 'safe' constituency. Indeed, the safer it may look on paper, the more vulnerable it may be in fact. This is because the best recruiting sergeant for the two major Parties is the terror of its rival. Paper-thin majorities survive because sceptics turn out to vote lest the alternative ticket should triumph by default, whereas the champion who earns the applause of his supporters by depriving his opponents of their deposit is most vulnerable to the threat of elimination at the hands of a third party next time round. I know. In 1966 I had the biggest pro-Tory swing nationwide (in a bad year for the Party) and was one of but a handful of MPs nationwide to secure the votes of more than half the electorate. Eight years later I was out. Labour had ceased to represent a credible champion for its local supporters, or a credible threat to locals disillusioned by the performance of the Edward Heath Government.

That is not all. Once in every decade the Boundaries Commission applies its terrible swift sword to existing base-

[1] Or at any rate has been: deselection by Tory constituencies is becoming rather less of a rarity.

camps. Some constituencies lose a toe or gain a finger; and life goes on as usual. Even that degree of redistribution can, however, provide sufficient reason to advertise a vacancy – certainly in the Labour Party. Many more constituencies experience substantial surgery. In the Tory Party every effort is made to secure a chair for each of those who had one, but it does not always work. Sometimes the Boundaries Commission is not content with judicious redistribution. It tears constituencies apart. When that happens (as once again I know to my cost) then sitting Members are thrown into the maelstrom.

Until the passage of the Reelection of Ministers Act, in 1919, would-be travellers to the Whitehall village faced an extra hurdle. Appointment to ministerial office necessitated endorsement by the local electorate at a by-election. Had this obligation not been struck off the Statute Book after the First World War, modern Prime Ministers would have found it impossible to construct an administration, since by-elections caused by advancement of existing Members (for example to the House of Lords) are nowadays more often lost than saved, regardless of majorities.

Admittedly base-camps can be relocated, sometimes seemingly with effortless ease. But not always. Kenneth Baker, the current Education Secretary, elected to speak for Acton in 1968 and lost his base in June 1970, notwithstanding his Party's nationwide return to office. Within three months he was back again for Marylebone. When Marylebone succumbed to the scissors of the Boundaries Commission before the 1983 election, he passed comfortably to an impregnable-looking patch in Surrey commuter-land in good time. Patrick Gordon-Walker, by contrast, picked by Harold Wilson as his Foreign Secretary in October 1964, had the misfortune to lose his Birmingham constituency even though there was a national swing in his Party's favour. A vacancy was swiftly contrived for him in a safe Labour seat in East London. Alas! he lost it in the arranged by-election in early 1965. His portfolio was forfeited, and although he eventually recovered the East London constituency for his Party in 1966 he was never heard of again.

So those who contrive eventually to reach a lofty position in the Whitehall village must not forget to cultivate their grassroots gardens. Mrs Thatcher may be the 'Iron Lady' with whom her counterparts around the globe negotiate, and love or hate. Back in Finchley she remains the local MP who is expected to sort out a plague of rats at No 14b. Couve de Murville, a distinguished (and very upper-crust) French diplomat whom de Gaulle selected as his Foreign Minister in the 1960s was subsequently ordered by his master to prove his worth by contesting a deeply bourgeois Parliamentary seat in the 7th *arrondissement* of Paris. He was asked for his views about the local car parking arrangements, and brusquely responded that he had higher things to think about. Nevertheless he was duly elected. Christopher Soames, fresh from our Embassy in Paris and the European Commission in Brussels, was confronted by the Tory selectorate in the equally bourgeois London bailiwick of Kensington with a similar enquiry, and gave a similar answer. He was not even given the opportunity to fight the election. That is the difference between our systems.

Yet the forces which control the destinies of political bases in our system are largely elemental. The most assiduous cultivator of the grassroots can be swept away by electoral tides or redistribution, forces over which he or she can have little or no influence. By the same token survival may be easily compatible with neglect. I once shared a secretary with a Glasgow MP whose demands upon her services appeared to be so minimal that I eventually asked whether she ever saw him. 'Oh yes', she told me, 'I saw him last week. He had a pile of letters from constituents, but he threw them out unopened. He had one urgent letter, to the local authorities responsible for the locality of his flat in Westminster. It was a protest about the fouling of the pavement outside his door by local dogs.' He survived election after election to the moment of his death.

So the would-be traveller to Whitehall must contrive to progress while he may. The late John Mackintosh once likened backbench MPs to the children in a nursery of days gone by, who stared through the bannisters at the glittering assemblies of the grown-up Ministers as they gathered down below, and dreamed of the time when they would be summoned to join in. For they had joined the club from which the masters of Whitehall are chosen. Traditionally Parliament has contained a large ballast of MPs without ambition for office: the knights of the shires on the Tory benches and, more recently, the Trades Union veterans on the other side. Both groups have almost disappeared. Today the only MPs who do not dream of Ministerial red boxes are the champions of extra-Parliamentary action on the Labour benches, and the Tories who constitute the 'Court in exile', defying the present Party leadership – and they dream instead about the Restoration.

Most at least arrive at Westminster with expectations of an early start upon Disraeli's 'greasy pole'. How to set about it? The late Richard Crossman records the advice of Aneurin Bevan that 'there are only two ways of getting into Cabinet. One way is to crawl up the staircase of preferment on your belly. The other way is to kick them in the teeth. But for God's sake don't mix the two methods'.[1] That must be Westminster folklore. For I was given remarkably similar advice by one of Harold Macmillan's Ministers soon after I arrived in 1964. 'Only two ways to get on in this place', he advised me. 'Make a bloody nuisance of yourself. Or crawl up every arse in sight. No half-measures'.

Such is the conventional wisdom. Like most conventional wisdom, it is a gross over-simplification. It ignores the enduring role of Westminster as theatre. Disraeli commanded preferment, notwithstanding a most improbable background for a Victorian Tory, by the brilliance of his oratory. More recently, Iain Macleod was reputed to have forced his way to his Party's front bench on the strength of a single Parliamentary demolition job on Aneurin Bevan at the height of Bevan's ministerial ascendancy. More recently still, Norman St John-Stevas was not a much less exotic bird of paradise in the Tory Party of the 1970s than Disraeli had been in the 1840s; yet like Disraeli his thespian talents were not to be ignored.

Nor is it accurate to equate the effectiveness of toadyism and rebellion regardless of party labels. In the Labour Party, rebels earn campaign medals: in the Tory Party they are more

[1] *Inside View*

likely to be sent to Coventry. Among Tories, 'clubability' still ranks high in the catalogue of virtues; whereas among Labour politicians clubs are places where the members plot to cut each others' throats.

Very few of us possess the brilliance to enforce preferment. For the rest – on both sides of the Chamber – there is much to be said for either a patron or a worried Party manager. Labour Governments may be particularly prone to take on board the backbench snipers. But Tory Governments do not ignore the homespun wisdom of President Lyndon Johnson, who commented about one particularly disputatious member of his Cabinet that he would rather him 'inside the tent and pissing out than outside pissing in'. John Peyton was widely believed to have owed his place in the 1970 Tory Government (as Minister of Transport) to his possession of both a sharp tongue and an independent spirit; and Peter Walker, having ostentatiously declined to remain a member of the Shadow Cabinet when Mrs Thatcher dislodged Mr Heath in 1975, was nevertheless deemed indispensable when the new Tory Cabinet was formed in 1979, and has been found indispensable ever since.

Where Labour and Tory Parties do differ is that in the Tory Party rebellion is not enough. Camp followers are also called for. Harold Wilson may have spotted exceptional abilities in David Owen when he gave him his first step on the ladder in the late 1960s; the impression at the time was that Dr Owen's merits were no more obvious than those of his close allies, Professor Mackintosh, David Marquand and Brian Walden, but that his sharp tongue had scared his leader. What is certain is that he had no substantial backbench claque behind him, and therefore that he would have been most unlikely to have sniped his way to preferment in the Tory Party. A maverick like Robin Maxwell-Hyslop, who did not hesitate to suggest to Ted Heath at a full meeting of the Tory backbenchers that he should resign when he introduced legislation to control wages and prices in 1972 in defiance of manifesto commitments to the contrary, has never had a following and therefore in Tory terms has never required placating with promotion. Men like Jim Prior and Peter Walker, by contrast, have had backbench acolytes, and therefore could not safely be passed over, in spite of the well-advertised incompatibility of their views with those of the Party leadership.

Camp-followers are all very well. But new boys at Westminster will, by definition, be them rather than have them. So whether the path preferred is that of obsequiousness or that of trouble-making, there is nothing like a patron. On both sides of the Chamber patronage comes essentially in two forms. One is the backing of a senior and influential Parliamentary godfather or two: the other is the Whips' Office.

The Whips are the stakhanovites of the British Parliamentary system. They are on parade at the Commons around the clock. Bound to a collective vow of silence (which is by no means always observed in Opposition – the present Chancellor earned the reputation of being the most talkative Whip on record in the 1976 Parliament, but in truth his loquaciousness was far from unprecedented) their formal task is to shepherd their flock into the appropriate lobby when the votes are called. Their true role is much more extensive. They are the eyes and ears of the Party leadership, and expected to know what all their colleagues are getting up to. Plots and private peccadilloes are equally their *métier*. They are the secret service of their Parties. It is an essential element in the functioning of Parliament, mostly humdrum, sometimes sordid, seldom seen. But it has one precious attribute. No Party leader in his or her senses makes promotions to the Front Bench without consultation with the Whips' Office. It does not have an absolute power of veto, although its blackball is not lightly to be overruled. But its entitlement to more than a fair share of the spoils of office is broadly recognised. Of the fourteen Tory Commons whips in the summer of 1981, seven had achieved departmental office within two years. It has to be so: for who would take up such a thankless task unless the expectation of reward were high? Indeed those who come to office without apprenticeship in the Whips' Office are regarded with something approaching resentment by that formidable institution.

A second formal stepping-stone to Office, appointment as a Parliamentary Private Secretary, can turn out to be a snare and a delusion. There is in reality but one PPS who enjoys near-automatic reversion to Ministerial office, and that is the PPS to the Prime Minister (or leader of the Opposition – providing he is still *in situ* when his Party eventually takes the helm).[1] For the rest it is a largely decorative duty which may – but often does not – pave the way to real office.

In days gone by entitlement to a Parliamentary Private Secretary was confined to Cabinet Ministers. His task is to act as the private bagman of his Minister, promoting his interests, listening to his critics among the troops at Westminster, and finding him a 'pair' from the Opposition Parties when he wants – or is obliged by ministerial duty – to be absent when a vote is called. In return he is allowed to sit in on meetings at his boss's department (so long as nothing significant or confidential is under discussion). He is unpaid and mostly unconsulted. In modern degenerate times he has proliferated, because the Whips can treat him as automatic lobby-fodder: he must vote the Party ticket, on pain of instant dismissal, and he is banned from speaking on his master's topics. So it suits the Whips to have more of him. Nowadays Ministers outside the Cabinet – in other words anybody apart from the lowest grade of office-holders, the Parliamentary Under-Secretaries – are entitled to a PPS. Even that distinction seems to be passing.

Those who get the call to carry round a Ministerial bag succumb almost unfailingly to the illusion that they are on their way. The late 'Chips' Channon described in euphoric terms his emotions on being appointed as PPS to Rab Butler, then a junior Foreign Office Minister, in the 1930s. Attitudes have not changed. I still cringe with embarrassment at the memory of the response of my own PPS to the invitation to serve.

Happily for the system, the ambitious backbencher sees the Minister who invites him to serve as his PPS as the patron that he needs. Sometimes it may be so. But the Minister has been presented – by the Whips' Office, naturally – with a list of permissible candidates. Trouble-makers and originals have

[1] The present incumbent, Michael Alison, is something of a case apart. He surrendered middle-rank Ministerial office to take on the job. But it would be surprising if he did not revert to at least his former rank when his time is up.

been censored out in advance, although the list makes curious reading – the one that I was offered, I recall, included the name of Norman St John-Stevas, sacked from the Cabinet not long before. I was tempted to give him a ring. For the most part a Minister feels no commitment to advance the prospects of his PPS, even if he is in a position to do so, and only Cabinet Ministers are likely to be capable of furthering careers. So while there may be a case for accepting service as a bagman to a senior Cabinet Minister – the Chancellor, for example, or the Home Secretary – the only possible benefit conferred by acceptance of a PPS-ship to a lesser mortal is the acquisition of an unpaid sincecure from which to resign in a blaze of high profile principle.

Even that is not so easy. I was recruited to serve as PPS to the Secretary of State for Scotland in 1970 (I have no doubt that, being a well-trained former civil servant, he cheerfully accepted instructions to keep me out of mischief). By the spring of 1972 I was becoming deeply disillusioned with the drift of public policy. When rumours circulated that the Government was about to surrender to a sit-in in the Glasgow dockyards, producing brand new subsidies which had been hitherto refused, I warned my master that if these rumours should prove true I would have to say farewell. They did prove true. But my master begged me not to 'rock the boat', to carry on till Easter, and then, with the Commons in recess, announce that after two years I felt the time had come to give someone else a chance. Because I was fond of my master, I agreed to fall in with his request. I was a fool. There is no point in being a PPS unless you are prepared to exploit the position for the only purpose of advancement that it can be made to serve – by resigning to a public fanfare.

In any case you do not have to serve as PPS to find a patron. In days gone by family connections always came in useful. The first Tory Government of this century was dubbed the 'Hotel Cecil' in tribute to the proliferation of members of that great aristocratic family which it contained. More recently Harold Macmillan's backbench critics complained that preferment seemed to come easily to his in-laws, the Cavendishes (in fact his taste in aristocracy was a good deal less eclectic); and eyebrows were raised when Jim

Callaghan chose his son-in-law, Peter Jay, for the Embassy in Washington. By all accounts that choice was actually pressed upon a reluctant Prime Minister by his newly elevated Foreign Secretary, David Owen, whose own elevation was said to have been recommended by the son-in-law. Nevertheless it was the father-in-law who took the flak. Modern Prime Ministers are liable to be sensitive to allegations of nepotism which their eighteenth- and nineteenth-century predecessors would have taken in their stride.

Besides, the upwardly mobile modern MP does not need relations or a PPS-ship to acquire a patron. The hitching of a wagon to a star is often achieved in the backrooms, before Parliament is reached. Gerald Kaufman began his rise to fame as press secretary to Harold Wilson in 10 Downing Street in the 1960s; Chris Patten became a close *protégé* of Jim Prior while he was running the Conservative Research Department in the 1970s, and his patron was subsequently able to carry him to his first Ministerial preferment at the Northern Ireland Office in spite of the fact that Patten's distaste for 'monetarism' was, if anything, more outspoken than Prior's own.

Perhaps the most instructive example of the value of a patron – in this case two – in the present Government, however, was that of Leon Brittan. Brittan, a brilliant libel lawyer, took his time to find his base-camp. Nevertheless his academic background and early success at the bar had no doubt marked him out as 'ministerial timber' by the time he finally reached the House of Commons in 1974. But he did not prove a star debater; he was certainly no rebel; and he never served his passage in the Whips' Office. Yet as soon as his Party returned to power in 1979 he moved straight to middle-ranking office as Minister of State at the Home Office; within two years he had reached the Cabinet, and two years later had become the youngest Home Secretary since Winston Churchill.

He had achieved a remarkable patronage double. He had been a close friend of Sir Geoffrey and Lady Howe from the days in the 1960s when he and Sir Geoffrey were working at the Bar; and when Sir Geoffrey decided to throw his hat into the ring for the Tory leadership contest following Ted

Heath's defeat in early 1975, Brittan acted as his campaign manager. So Sir Geoffrey's support for his younger colleague's aspirations was assured. The more remarkable coup was also to achieve the enthusiastic backing of Willie Whitelaw. For the clever, industrious lawyer with a central European background and the bluff, golf-playing Tory squire had nothing obviously in common. But as his Minster of State he swiftly made himself so useful – indeed indispensable – to Home Secretary Whitelaw that he too became an ardent fan. With two such formidable sponsors Brittan's progress was assured.

There are those who resort to self-promotion. Most politicians will jump at invitations to air their views and talents in the public prints, and still more on television.[1] But some go further than this. They hire PR agents to get their names before the public, although they risk exposure by malicious journalists. In the early 1980s one prominent Tory backbencher wrote to the City Editor of the *Sunday Telegraph* to commend him on a comment he had written, pointing out that it coincided precisely with unsolicited advice the backbencher had himself been offering in recent speeches to the Government, and suggesting that the City Editor might therefore profitably advise the Government to employ him as Chancellor. The City Editor, a kindly man, failed to report this proposition to his readership. Some go further still. One Tory backbencher is reputed to carry around with him ready-written letters to the Prime Minister, advancing his exceptional claims to preferment, and deploring the absence of recognition for them, which admiring members of his audiences up and down the country are urged to top and tail and post. Alas! the call has never come.

Last, but by no means least, there is advancement by election. In the modern Labour Party, indeed, observers might conclude it was the only path available. For when that Party is in opposition its Leader's Shadow Cabinet is selected

[1] Enoch Powell is said to insist – as a fervent believer in the market – on negotiating a fee for his performances before agreeing to appear. Most of his colleagues would happily pay for the privilege. The BBC has, in recent years, struck a judicious mean by declining, in the normal course of business, to pay a fee to politicians – or, for that matter, to be paid.

for him by the Parliamentary Party. Fortunately for him and his Party, attempts to extend the system of election to the real – as opposed to the Shadow – Cabinet have so far been resisted. Nevertheless, when a Party is in opposition its members stand a far better chance of impressing their colleagues and the watching newspapers and television viewers, and thus of positioning themselves for appointment to office when the moment comes, if they are entitled to address the Commons from the Front Bench. So the annual elections to the Labour Shadow Cabinet are not to be ignored by those with aspirations.

The Tory Party has wisely refrained from seeking to dictate its leader's choices thus. When the Party is in opposition the appropriate member of the Shadow Cabinet, chosen by the Leader, invariably presides over meetings of the backbench committee devoted to his, or her, zone of responsibility. Nevertheless the annual elections of the other officers of these committees (of the chairmen as well when the Party is in Government) are closely contested and rightly seen as potential stepping-stones to office. For when the Tories languish in opposition it is considered good PR for the appointed spokesman to enlist the aid of elected officers to open or reply to debates from time to time; and in power or out those officers are deemed to have a claim to speak in prime time in debates related to their chosen subjects. So they, too, have a chance to shine and make their reputations.

Over the past ten years, indeed, the annual elections of these backbench officers have been seen within the Tory Party and outside as pointers to the balance of opinion in the Party. Rival 'lists' are drawn up by left-wing and by right, and unofficial whips are organised: in this respect at least the Tory Party has become much more like its rival, with its 'Tribune' and 'Campaign' groups. Almost forgotten are the days when backbench officers were picked on grounds of character or popularity, with a cheerful disregard for their real or supposed opinions.

This limited respect apart, however, within the Tory Party (and even to some extent within the Labour Party, it would seem) identification with a particular doctrine or philosophical stance does not demonstrably either advance or retard the chances of the hopeful. Flexibility of attitude is often said to be essential in a Party which has always espoused Pope's dictum that 'for forms of Government let fools contest – what's best administered is best'.

We are regularly reminded that several members of the present Administration – Douglas Hurd and Ken Baker and departed stars like Jim Prior and David Howell – made their names originally as courtiers at the Court of Edward Heath, and certainly an obstinate adherence to a banished monarch would smack of masochism. Few Tories would care to indulge publicly in the awful frankness of Mr Hattersley's pledge to support whatever might happen to be the policies of his Party; most would privately agree with him. A judicious 'flexibility' has never done the aspiring politician any harm: Peter Walker, for example, first attracted notice in politics for his rousing crusade, in the late 1950s and early 1960s, against the Common Market. Ten years later he displayed no qualms as a Minister when his leader took us in.

Consistency, on the other hand, while it may be, in Winston Churchill's phrase, 'the hobgoblin of little minds', often comes right in the end. The so-called 'monetarists' were a bunch of heretics in the Tory Party of the early 1970s – 'the awkward squad', as Ted Heath used to call us – and not over-popular with the mass of Government backbenchers, who though they might occasionally have wondered whether we might be on to something, profoundly (and understandably) hoped we weren't. No sooner had Ted Heath fallen than 'monetarism' suddenly became the flavour of the season. One of our coterie reported with glee overhearing Christopher Tugendhat, Willie Whitelaw's campaign manager in the ensuing leadership contest, grooming his champion for the Paddock: 'And another thing, Willie. They are worried that you don't understand about monetary policy'. 'They're right: I don't' was the disarming reply. 'Neither do they – but they just think it *matters*'. No doubt the time will come when the Keynesians and Corporatists in the Tory Party will, in their turn, come in from the cold.

So the ambitious jostle on the paths to Whitehall. But while many travel hopefully, relatively few of them can arrive. How are the lucky ones selected? According to constitutional theory the Prime Minister has absolute discretion. There is a legal limit on the permissible total of 'Ministers' (i.e. Cabinet members plus Ministers of State). But that can always be adjusted by persuading Parliament to pass the necessary legislation. The Chancellor of the Exchequer must be in the House of Commons, and the Lord Chancellor must be a lawyer as well as in the House of Lords (until recently also not a Catholic). Otherwise the Prime Minister can indulge his – or her – untrammelled fancy.

That is the theory. Practice is a vastly different matter. Some colleagues impose themselves by Party status and/or following, regardless of their empathy, or lack of it, with the Leader: in particular those whom the Leader vanquished to achieve the Crown (Mrs Thatcher was criticised for not offering a suitable billet to Mr Heath in 1979, though the critics showed scant imagination if they seriously envisaged the former Premier seated comfortably at her table). Counsel must be taken with the Chief Whip and one or more of the Party's elder statesmen – Lord Whitelaw is said to have had at least as significant a role in selecting the members of the Governments of 1979 and 1983 (and the intervening reshuffles) as the Prime Minister herself. The Prime Minister is advised to ensure that her Government reflects 'all shades of opinion' in the Party.

Then there are the geographical priorities. The Scottish Office must be staffed with incumbents of Scottish constituencies (or Lords); the Welsh Office likewise – although Peter Thomas served as Welsh Secretary under Ted Heath notwithstanding his migration to Hendon. The Northern Ireland Office, is by contrast, the preserve of those who do *not* represent the Province. Barristers are *de rigueur* for the Law Offices, and at least one for the Home Office. The Ministry of Agriculture is deemed to need a practising farmer somewhere (and furthermore he is allowed to keep his farm: an interesting potential conflict of interests which would be quite unacceptable for any other trade or business). The Northern Ireland Office must have at least one statutory Catholic. No self-respecting modern Prime Minister would fail to give preferment to at least a few of the ladies. There must be at least some Lords – a minimum of three in Cabinet

– though not too many. Finally, custom dictates that those chosen as Cabinet Ministers should have some say in the selection of their departmental subordinates. In 1979 Sir Keith Joseph let it be known that he would be only too happy with whomsoever the Prime Minister saw fit to appoint to help him at the Department of Industry. This was considered eccentric – indeed downright foolish.

So it is probably nearer the mark to see the modern Prime Minister as enjoying a limited number of 'bisques'. Thus it was claimed that when Mrs Thatcher formed her first Administration she had insisted on inserting at least one of those who came to be known as 'one of us' in each department (and there were many) presided over by one of the dissenters, to keep an eye on his superior, particularly the purse-strings. If so, it did not always work out: one Minister appointed to the Foreign Office with instructions from 10 Downing Street to keep a close watch on spending was breezily informed by the patrician Foreign Secretary Lord Carrington that no such role existed.

The actual allocation of the seals is often almost wondrously haphazard. For the process of Government-making is a jigsaw, in which all the pieces must somehow be made to fit. Legend has it that King George VI blackballed Hugh Dalton for the Foreign Office, so he had to be shifted to the Treasury at the last moment. The last-minute blackballing (by Lord Whitelaw and Chief Whip John Wakeham) of Mr Cecil Parkinson's planned return to the Department of Trade and Industry in the summer of 1985 is no legend. It resulted in the wholly unexpected movement of Leon Brittan to Trade and Industry, and of Douglas Hurd to the Home Office. Some MPs who have specialised in particular subjects from the back benches are given the chance to put their talents to the test – Nigel Lawson is a prominent current example. And other things being equal (which they rarely are), Shadow Spokesmen are reckoned to have a claim to the reversion to the substance of their subject. It is not always honoured. The backbencher who is genuinely relaxed about the charms of office may be in a position to insist on a department of his choice, or nothing. Likewise – *a fortiori* – those who have already climbed to the Cabinet Table. Yet even they may turn out to be bluffing. Thus in the summer of 1981 Jim Prior left few newspaper readers in any doubt that he would withdraw to the back benches rather than vacate the Department of Employment (apparently because he had learned that his chosen successor would be Norman Tebbit). In the end, however, he went to Ulster like a rather sore-headed lamb. But most MPs are only too grateful to take what they are given. Francis Pym, interviewed before the 1979 Election, when asked what post he aimed to serve in, insisted that he would be delighted to serve wherever the Prime Minister might direct him. Most of his colleagues would say 'amen' to that.

So those to whom the call to penetrate the Whitehall Village eventually comes are likely to have circumnavigated successfully the electoral shoals en route; to have impressed at least some of their Parliamentary colleagues and the commentators (and preferably not to have alienated too many others); but above all, perhaps, they are likely to have contrived to manoeuvre themselves into the right place at the right time. The late Randolph Churchill liked to claim that he had trapped the future Lord Eccles when his father was forming the 1951 Tory Government (he had no doubt tried to trap some others). On the third evening of Government-making he rang David Eccles at dinner-time. He announced himself as 'Mr Churchill'. The butler summoned his master, who picked up the phone saying 'Eccles here, good evening Sir'. 'It's Randolph, David. Were you expecting someone else?' A cruel jape, assuredly. But eventually the call did come. Better to receive a false alarm than to miss the real call completely.

2
Trial by Glory

Those marked out for greatness – the Cabinet appointees – receive a formal call to Downing Street. For the lesser Minister and Under-Secretaries, a telephone call must suffice. For many it poses quite a dilemma.

In other walks of life 'a title on the door', in the words of the old US carpet ad, 'rates a Bigelow on the floor' – and a substantial salary uplift in addition. In politics, at least for most Tory MPs, it rates a cut in income. Backbenchers are at liberty to pursue an extra-Parliamentary occupation (although they are liable to find that the demands of politics diminish their attractiveness to outside employers except as lobbyists – a role which can easily involve them in conflicts of interest and responsibility). Most fortunate are the lawyers. The bar is so well represented at Westminster that the 'learned' MPs (as they are traditionally labelled) can nearly always pair off with their colleagues in the rival parties whenever Courtroom duties necessitate their absence from Westminster. Others may have complaisant partners in their offices as solicitors or estate agents, who will cover for their absences *at* Westminster. Others still have directorships or columns in the newspapers. The lucky ones have farms.

The farmers are privileged since they – and they alone – are allowed by custom to retain their outside interest on elevation to the Ministry. The rest must abandon all their other occupations. Basil de Ferranti was actually driven to abandon Westminster in the early 1960s on learning that if he wished to retain – let alone ultimately progress from – the junior Ministerial office to which he had been appointed he would have to dispose of his substantial holdings in his family business: a condition which, since it was then a private company, he found he could not fulfil. Sometimes the rules are carried to absurd lengths. Nicholas Ridley, the present Transport Minister, and a highly talented water-colourist, was sternly ordered by the Treasury to abandon a one-man show of paintings his agent had arranged when he was serving as a Junior Industry Minister in the Heath Administration. Would-be customers for departmental favours, it was pointed out to him, might drop by and buy a painting or two, not out of respect for his artistic skills, but out of ambition for his Ministerial support.

It was not always thus. Soon after I was appointed to the Treasury in 1981, when I was bemoaning to a friend my doubled workload for an income cut in half, he assured me that when F. E. Smith, the first Lord Birkenhead, was asked in the early 1920s to accept promotion to the Woolsack, he replied that he had just entered into a contract to write a weekly column for Lord Beaverbrook's *Sunday Express* for the impressive sum – by the standards of those days – of £5,000 a year, and could not afford to give it up. The Prime Minister readily agreed that he should not do so: he would write his articles, and sign them, from the Lord Chancellor's chambers. Such a proposition would get short shrift today.

So the majority of appointees to a modern Tory Government (and no doubt a substantial minority of appointees to a modern Labour one as well) must make up their minds to take a large cut in income. There is little time to ponder it. In the business world, the rising young executive who is summoned to the Managing Director's office and invited to take on the running of the Wigan pier subsidiary can always – indeed is expected to – go home and consult the wife and probably the older children as well. Portfolios in politics are offered on a take-it-or-leave-it basis. Greatly daring, I asked for an hour for consideration, on the grounds that acceptance would almost halve the family housekeeping money. 'Jock, you are so well paid' was the stern response. Still, I was given my hour – no more.

Yet the answer was foredoomed. If a backbencher is offered office of a kind for which he is vain enough to think that he is qualified, and turns it down, he has to ask himself why he is in politics. If, like the knights of the shire or the

Trades Union stalwarts of a bygone age, he is there for service and for ballast, he may prefer to keep his outside income. But if, like most of us these days, he regards the House of Commons as the stepping-stone to office, then rejection of the invitation when eventually it comes makes a nonsense of his vocation. So the sums are done. They do not add up. But the offer is accepted.

Not that the hour need be wholly wasted on back-of-the-envelope accountancy. Time spent in reconnaissance, as the Army used to teach us, is seldom wasted. The appointment to which I had been summoned, that of Minister of State at the Treasury, covers a multitude of sins. It is always worth enquiring which of them one would be dealing with.

The modern Treasury contains anything from four to six Ministers. The Chancellor, by definition, covers the waterfront. The Chief Secretary is responsible for public spending. The Financial Secretary has constitutional responsibility for the Treasury's relationship with the Parliamentary auditors, the Public Accounts Committee. But the allocation of first-line responsibility for the rest of the Treasury workload is determined on an ad hoc basis between the Financial Secretary and one, two, or three Ministers of State.

Peter Rees, whom I was summoned to replace, had been responsible for virtually the whole tax-gathering system, both Inland Revenue and Customs and Excise. This was not a role which had much appeal to me. However swift enquiries revealed that the patch earmarked for me, while it did include the Customs, also covered (instead of Inland Revenue) monetary policy and the Treasury's relations with the financial institutions. This was the gilt on the gingerbread, and put a term to any lingering doubts. The die is cast. The trial by glory has begun.

Even the second and third degree appointments may attract a line of comment. *The Times* carried the news of my appointment in its first edition even before I had accepted it. One journalistic wellwisher advised his readers that I was so 'dry'[1] that the Treasury would need to renew its fire-extinguishers.

[1] This is the terminology of the popular division of the Tory Party into 'wets', who opposed the 'monetarist' orthodoxy, and 'dries' who supported it.

First call for the newly elevated Junior Minister is upon his departmental boss. 'This', says the Chancellor, 'is my assistant private secretary, Henry Bloggs'. 'Welcome, Minister', says Henry Bloggs. The new arrival straightaway feels 'his blushing honours thick upon him'.

By Whitehall convention the civil servants formally address the politicians by their titles: 'Chancellor', 'Financial Secretary', 'Economic Secretary', as the case may be. On informal occasions, officials – who in turn are always addressed by their Christian names – will descend to 'Geoffrey', or 'Nicholas', or 'Jock'. But at meetings the constitutional proprieties are rigidly observed. It helps the Ministers to know their place.

Henry Bloggs will then conduct the neophyte to his Private Office. Awaiting him will be two private secretaries, an archivist, a typist and a clerk. He is shown into his sanctum, an imposing room with imposing desk, long table for departmental conferences, and a set of easy chairs for the reception of less formal visitors.

As soon as Henry Bloggs has made the formal introductions and departed, the senior Private Secretary says 'Minister, we have your car and driver.' At this point I had a difficulty. 'But I go round London', I explained, 'by bicycle'. 'Around Sloane Square, Minister?' (the Private Office will have done its homework, and located where their new charge has his London base). 'No. Around Hyde Park Corner'. The blood drained from the faces of the Private Office. But they did not give up easily. 'But what about your boxes, Minister?' 'What about them?' 'Well, Minister, if you took them on your bicycle, you might be stopped by the police'. 'So what? You would know, and I would know, that I was in proper possession of my boxes, so what have the police to do with it?'

They withdrew. But not for long. Two days later they were back. 'Minister, will you see your driver? He's afraid he's going to be redundant.' Their timing was impeccable. Two days of pedalling back and forth to Kensington had taught me that the lead-lined red boxes play havoc with the brakes of a pedal-cycle; and furthermore that the workload of reading I had to keep abreast with was such that even the twenty minutes of reading-time which could be gleaned in a chauffeur-driven car should not be sneered at.

So a compromise was reached. The car and driver collected Minister and boxes in the morning, and delivered both home at night. But during the day the faithful bicycle reposed in the Treasury courtyard. As my Ministerial colleagues clambered into their limousines for the short trip to No 11 Downing Street for the regular meetings which the Chancellor preferred to hold at home, I got upon my faithful steed. When the Governor of the Bank of England was of the party he would drive up in his Rolls as I dismounted from my ancient Raleigh. It was never clear to me who won on points.

Ministerial carmanship does not come easily. Towards the end of my first week of office I had promised to attend a farewell party with my former colleagues at the City office of the *Sunday Telegraph*, from which I had been unceremoniously abducted by the Prime Ministerial summons. When the moment for this party came I found myself awaiting delivery of an urgent – and highly secret – message to the Chancellor, who was currently in Washington for the annual meeting of the International Monetary Fund. This precious document arrived for my signature just as I was about to leave for the *Sunday Telegraph*. I had to take it with me to study en route. I reached the party belatedly. When the time came to leave, my colleagues from the *Daily Telegraph* asked if I had an official car and could take them back (from the City office) to Fleet Street. Thinking of my precious secret document I had to tell them that I had – but couldn't. They left me in no doubt about their opinion of ministerial *hubris*.

Nevertheless I persevered with the bicycle. One afternoon not long after my arrival in the Treasury I was summoned to luncheon with the top brass of ICI, just down the road on Millbank. I said I would take the 'bike. As I was about to leave the Treasury courtyard I was accosted by the Security Guard, who required my pass. I had left it in my office. I would go and fetch it. 'Hold on,' he said. 'I recognise you.' 'You're one of the Messengers, aren't you?' Well, no, I explained, I was one of the Ministers. 'Oh well, I knew I knew your face.' I sometimes thought in the months ahead that he'd got it right first time anyway.

At nights, though, the car was indispensable. It sometimes occurred to me that my driver might be in the wrong profession. Prior to my arrival he had been driver to Sir Ian Gilmour who, as a Cabinet Minister, had ranked a Rover. As a Minister of State I ranked a modest Princess. I feared he might resent the demotion. Not at all. 'You see,' he assured me, 'Mr Atkins took Sir Ian's job, and I was scared stiff I'd get him. For coming from Northern Ireland he'd have had a hit-man. And I've had them before. Even when your Minister has a night off the hit-man expects you to take him to the flicks.'

Now to most of Whitehall's Ministerial drivers a hit-man requiring attendance at the cinema when the Minister has gone home to bed would be treated as a bonus. For the essence of the Ministerial driver's life is overtime. Bill was an exception. A bachelor, without ambition to boost his income, he could never wait to get home to bed. He did not share his colleagues' joy in waiting round the clock as the overtime ticked up.

This had its drawbacks. It meant that a premium was placed on precision of the hour at night for collection and delivery. On one occasion my colleague Leon Brittan, the Chief Secretary, and I and our respective wives were bidden to dine with the American Ambassador in Regent's Park. We had to vote at the House of Commons at 10 pm, afer which it was agreed that I should take Leon's car back to the Ambassador's Residence, and my driver would collect our wives and myself to drive us home at 11 pm. I got back to the Residence at 10.25 to find that – notwithstanding the fact that the party had not sat down to dinner until 8.45 – the Ambassador and his lady were already off to bed. We, alas! were not.

Rank and car are but part of the 'blushing honours' which await to turn the head of the newly elevated Minister. The ritual of the boxes enhances the sense of self-importance. Wherever the Minister may be (within the United Kingdom) the boxes follow him. Wrapped in padlocked hempen sacks, they are delivered every morning by the postman, who if necessary undertakes an individual delivery, much to the edification of a weekend host. In next to no time the Minister is provided with a large Chubb safe, complete with combination lock, for each one of his homes. These safes prove invaluable for the storage of the family silver during absences.

Constituents bask in reflected glory from the new appointment. It does not last. Inability to attend the Piddletrenthide Tory branch's annual cheese and wine owing to Ministerial engagements soon begins to rile. But while the honeymoon endures it also does wonders for the new Ministers self-esteem. And then – for Ministers of State and better – there is the biennial haunch of venison from the Royal Parks. The bill for delivery makes a dent in the shrunken Ministerial purse. But constituents invited to partake are undoubtedly impressed.

Meanwhile the official car is waiting to collect the minister as the train from his constituency decants him at the London terminal on Monday morning, while neighbouring backbenchers queue up for a taxi, or to drive him home after the last division in the Commons late at night while his colleagues push and shove to extract their cars from the communal garage.

There are the late-night confidential conversations ('do you have somewhere private and secure where I can telephone?'); even occasionally recourse to the 'scrambler' telephone to be found at County police headquarters. It is all calculated to impress the watching world and puff out the feathers of the budding statesman.

The consequential temptation to settle for the pomp and forget about the substance may be – no doubt is – entirely coincidental. But it exists. If the political visitor to Whitehall should choose to warm himself in his little blaze of passing glory and snooze, the residents will manage very well without him.

Like most developed cultures, Whitehall has a clearly-defined pecking-order. At the apex of the pyramid, the list of Cabinet precedence is regularly up-dated. After the Prime Minister come the Lord President, Lord Whitelaw – sometimes, quite unconstitutionally, described as 'Deputy Prime Minister' -- and the Lord Chancellor, Lord Hailsham. After that the order is a matter of discretion, and often used by Prime Ministers as a balm for injured pride. Thus when Leon Brittan was unexpectedly shifted from the Home Office to the Department of Industry in the late summer of 1985 his place at number five was ostentatiously reasserted.

Whitehall villagers are not deluded. They know who, within the Cabinet, is up or moving up, and who is down or moving down. Nicholas Ridley, as Transport Secretary, for example, might have sat humbly near the bottom of the list. Whitehall knew that did not reflect his standing in the Cabinet, or his rating with the Prime Minister.

The villagers' own pecking-order is a good deal more significant. Among the different departments the Treasury is *primus inter pares*. It hardly needs saying that a meeting attended by the Prime Minister takes place at No 10. But in the absence of the Prime Minister a meeting attended by the Chancellor takes place at the Treasury (or, if the Chancellor so chooses, at No 11); similarly a meeting of Permanent Secretaries attended by the Treasury's top mandarin will take place in his parlour. And so on down the scale. Other departments have Parliamentary Under-Secretaries as their lowest grade of Minister. Treasury Ministers below the two Cabinet participants, the Chancellor and Chief Secretary, are all Ministers of State.[1] In consequence, inter-departmental gatherings at second Ministerial level (i.e. without Cabinet participation) where a Treasury Minister is present also take place on his home ground. The Treasury, always encircled by the predatory spenders, believes strongly and perhaps with justice that the host on these occasions starts with an edge over the guests.

Within departments there is a matching pecking-order.

[1] In 1983 there was a rare exception. The Government had run out of available Ministries of State, and shrank from asking Parliament to sanction an increase. As a result Ian Stewart was appointed Economic Secretary, an intermittent Treasury appointment which has invariably carried Minister of State rank. Nothing more was said. It required a careful reading of the small print to discover that he was ranking as a Parliamentary Under-Secretary. Treasury-watchers (and the mandarins) were appalled. Fortunately within months a reshuffle provided a vacancy for another Minister, and Ian Stewart was discreetly upgraded.

Most of it is self-evident: Chancellor takes precedence over Chief Secretary, who in turn takes precedence over Financial Secretary (who ranks traditionally as Whitehall's senior politician outside the Cabinet); all Ministers – even the humble Paliamentary Private Secretaries – take formal precedence over all civil servants; and the mountain always comes to Mohammed.

Shortly after my arrival at the Treasury, on the occasion of the drafting of the urgent despatch to Geoffrey Howe in Washington (to which reference has been made already), a point occurred to me which had not been covered in preliminary discussions with the senior mandarin, Peter Middleton, who was to do the drafting. Rather than disturb his drafting when time was very short, I told my Private Office that I would go in search of him.

Consternation. 'But Minister, we'll call him round'. I told them not to worry: it would not take a moment, and I only required directions to locate his office. These were grudgingly supplied, but even so I was pursued down the corridor by my anxious 'Bernard',[1] begging me to come home to base so that Peter Middleton could be sent for. The shock of my arrival made me feel like a school headmaster erupting into the boys' locker-room. I never dared repeat the experiment.

Occasionally the demarcation-lines become confused. At the time of my arrival in the Treasury there was one other Minister of State, Lord Cockfield.[2] Shortly afterwards the Civil Service Department was abolished (after an epic rearguard battle by the mandarins led by Sir Ian Bancroft, Head of the Civil Service) and for the most part reabsorbed into the Treasury whence it had originally emerged. With it came another Minister of State, Barney Hayhoe.

It was decided that three Ministers of State was one too many. So the title of Economic Secretary, which had fallen into abeyance for several years, was revived for me. There

[1] 'Bernard' is the name of the Private Secretary in the television series 'Yes, Minister' – Whitehall's favourite soap opera. Hence the soubriquet.

[2] Lord Cockfield's appointment to the Treasury in 1979 had broken new constitutional ground. Traditionally Treasury Ministers have always sat in the Commons. There was some shaking of heads. But the earth did not open up and swallow Arthur Cockfield.

was no change in my functions (although one of my elderly relations reacted with dismay: she logically deduced that from Minister to Secretary must imply demotion), nor, alas!, in my remuneration. But all my red boxes, though but a month old, had to be sent back to the box factory to be exchanged for a new set marked 'Economic Secretary'.

Thenceforward a stately minuet took place at each meeting called in the Chancellor's study at No 11. For these occasions the chairs were laid out in an unchanging pattern. On each side of the fireplace were two large arm-chairs: facing them a ring of a dozen or more upright chairs. The Chancellor invariably occupied the arm-chair to the left of the fireplace, with the Chief Secretary facing him, and the Financial Secretary on his right. That left one arm-chair vacant. If only four Ministers were present, no problem arose. But when more than four were in attendance, somebody was bound to be demoted to an upright.

So long as there had been but two of us to contest the spare arm-chair we had taken pot luck. But our new recruit from the Civil Service Department was leaving nothing to chance. However early the meeting might be called, he would contrive to get in first and ensconce himself safely in the fourth arm-chair. Nothing was ever said: but the claim to a particular precedence was delicately asserted. Ministers, at heart, are just like lesser mortals.

Whitehall departments, like the titles which they carry, are frequently relocated. The current *logement* of the Treasury includes the whole of the front of the building occupying the corner site in the north-west corner of Parliament Square, plus about half of the two wings stretching back along Great George Street and King Charles Street. Many other departments – the Department of Industry on Victoria Street, for example, or the Department of Education beside Waterloo, are all modernistic glass and steel. Internally the Treasury contrives to display something of the appearance of a Victorian poorhouse. Tiles and lino constitute the prevailing decor. The atmosphere is one of earnest frugality which seems perfectly appropriate to the Treasury's *métier*. The Chancellor enjoys a lift: I never found another one. The loos (marked 'men' and 'women') are reputed to be Spartan.

The hub of the machine is located on the second floor. It is easily identified since it – and it alone – is laid out with red lino, polished to a high gloss every evening. Here the top-most mandarins and all the Ministers have their offices. These, too, are shifted round according to the whims of Chancellors. For the present, the Chancellor looks out north towards the Foreign Office. The office I was allocated looked out over Parliament Square. It was panelled in dark brown wood, and sombre; and because of its location the windows could only be opened to the accompaniment of deafening traffic noise. But it has two unusual perquisites. It was the only one (apart from the Chancellor's) to have its own private loo. And it was the only one with direct access to the passage. All my colleagues could only come and go via the security of private secretaries.

That is the way that Whitehall prefers to have it. Sir Nicholas Henderson, long-time Private Secretary to successive Foreign Secretaries, and eventually Ambassador in Washington, describes the Private Secretaries as 'the impresarios of Whitehall . . . in their Private Offices the drama and friction between politics and the machine are theatrically audible' (*The Private Office*, Weidenfeld, 1984, p. 1). That is not exactly how it feels from the Ministerial desk. To the Minister, the Private Office has some of the attributes of a prison warder.

The Private Office is the sole channel of communication permitted with the outside world. The Minister is admittedly provided with a private outside telephone line, but he is not encouraged to make use of it. Otherwise all calls are filtered through the Private Secretaries, whose duty it is to listen in and take note of what transpires.[1] They are the keepers of the Ministerial diary, and all communications – whether from within or without the department – are filtered through their hands. They are the arbiters of what is and is not included in the precious nightly boxes. They sit in on all their Minister's meetings; they accompany him wherever he may go on duty.

[1] They are apparently trained to replace their receivers at the signal of personal endearments.

They work inordinately long hours: as I scurried to the House of Commons for the regular votes at 10 pm I often used to see the lights still blazing in my Private Office. They are on call night and day, obliged to ensure that their 'master' always knows where they may be contacted. Yet a Private Secretaryship is a coveted position. The young men and women (usually in their late twenties) selected for the task are recognised by their colleagues as 'high flyers' of the future. Thereby hangs a complication.

Nico Henderson quotes with approval Disraeli in *Endymion*: 'the relations between a Minister and his Secretary are, or at least should be, among the finest that can subsist between two individuals'. Disraeli was thinking of his faithful Monty Corrie. Many of his successors have had their hand-picked amanuenses: Churchill's Eddie Marsh, for example, or Macmillan's John Egremont. But in today's Whitehall it is the machine that makes the selection.

The Treasury was still humming when I got there with the remarkable tale of Nigel Lawson's Private Secretary. On his appointment as Financial Secretary in 1979 Nigel Lawson, like many new arrivals, was presented with a carefully selected short-list of candidates to choose from. But it so happened that in the years in opposition he had had a very bright young research assistant who had subsequently passed into the Treasury as a career civil servant. That was the young man he wanted. He was firmly told the young man was not available. He insisted. He was told that appointment of his former research assistant would smack of political preferment which conflicted with the *mores* of the civil service. He was unrepentant. Eventually the issue was deemed sufficiently momentous for upward reference to the Head of the Civil Service, Sir Ian Bancroft. Nigel Lawson got his way.

Many Ministers, however, do not have a choice at all. Their predecessors have recently approved a new appointee: they are expected to take what they are given. Most often, no doubt, that works very well. In my case it didn't. I rapidly decided that the 'chemistry' between my Principal Private Secretary and myself was unlikely to be comfortable. Since the relationship is so crucial to the ministerial lifestyle, I naively assumed that one had but to pass the word and a change would be forthcoming.

I swiftly learned my error. More experienced Ministers had advised me that I should call in the Treasury's Establishment Officer and explain my needs. So I asked for an appointment with that gentleman. Weeks passed. Nothing happened. I gently repeated my request (not rendered any easier by the fact that it had naturally to pass through the Private Secretary in question). I was told the Establishment Officer was on holiday. Eventually a date was fixed.

My Private Secretary, who no doubt saw the way the wind was blowing, expressed the assumption that she should sit in on the meeting. I demurred. So finally I had the Establishment Officer to see me *tête-à-tête*. I told him my requirement. 'Oh dear', was his reaction: 'that *is* awkward.' Early eviction from a Private Office so soon after appointment would be a black mark on the official's record; and it mattered not the least that I insisted that the fault was entirely mine. Perhaps I could have a word with the Financial Secretary, and arrange a straight swap with his incumbent. I agreed to try, although since his Private Secretary was the very bright young man whom Nigel Lawson had forcibly promoted, I couldn't see my colleague acquiescing. Nor did he. Finally the move was made. But it had involved long months of tension. Nor was it lightly forgiven. Months afterwards I was sternly advised by one senior mandarin that I had blighted my former Private Secretary's career. Had I known what I was embarking on I never would have started.

Yet the Private Secretary is supposed to be the Minister's Man – or Woman – Friday. Other mandarins may owe their first allegiance to the department. The Private Secretary, in Whitehall folklore, owes his first allegiance to his Minister.

Up to a point, Lord Copper. Some years before I made my sortie through the Whitehall village I fell into conversation at a party with a highly articulate young civil servant who had recently, he revealed to me, done service as Private Secretary to Tony Wedgwood Benn.

Few Ministers in modern times have proved a greater shock to the Whitehall system than Tony Wedgwood Benn. He insisted on installing his two personal political advisers,

Francis Cripps and Frances Morrell, virtually on bunks in the doorway to his office. When his Permanent Secretary had returned – in Court dress – from a visit to the Palace to receive the insignia of his elevation as a GCB, Wedgwood Benn had insisted on having him photographed in front of a banner of the National Union of Mineworkers which hung proudly in his Ministerial office. Whitehall was not amused.

So I was not altogether surprised when my young informant catalogued the sins of his former 'master'. But when he had detailed them for all of ten minutes, I ventured to suggest to him that the constitutional duty of the civil servant – and *a priori* the Ministerial Private Secretary – might indeed be to warn his Minister of potential pitfalls on the course he wished to follow; but also to back the Minister to the best of his ability once the Minister had laid down his decision.

'Not at all', my informant replied. 'That's a mis-reading of the constitution. Our duty is to support and execute the policies of the *Government*. If our Minister's policies are in conflict with those of the Government, then it's the Government we must back.' Not – I hasten to add – that I had any personal experience in the Treasury of such conflicting loyalties.

Back to the Office. An early date in the new Minister's diary is a visit to the morgue where Whitehall keeps its stock of pictures and other artefacts to decorate the Ministerial offices. The prize exhibits are reserved, quite properly, for the greatest of the visitors. No. 10 Downing Street gets first pick, followed by the members of the Cabinet in broad ranking order. The choice awaiting a new Minister of State half-way through a Government's term of office is inevitably somewhat circumscribed. But we did our best.

I added a less conventional piece of furniture. A typewriter. I am used to working at a typewriter. My Private Office were, I think, mildly shocked, but took it in their stride. I found it more indispensable than I had realised. For while the Private Office is equipped with a shorthand typist, she is absolutely *not* 'Ministers, for the use of'. If the Minister has a vision of the future to dictate, then one or other of his Private

Secretaries will step in to take it down, regardless of the fact that neither is remotely likely to have shorthand.

Another innovation was less readily absorbed. Some months after my arrival I informed my Private Office one evening that the following day I would be obliged to bring my black labrador bitch in with me, since there was no-one else to look after her. My Private Office did not look amused. 'It's OK,' I assured them, 'she's signed the Official Secrets Act'. That did not cheer them up.

Nevertheless she came, and all went well. She sat peacefully beneath my desk. But around five in the evening I had a conference with senior officials. 5 pm is the bitch's teatime. So she became somewhat restless. Leaving the shelter of my desk she toured the assembled mandarins, licking their hands. At this point my second Private Secretary came in with a sheaf of papers. The bitch started to follow her out, and I had visions of her straying in the passage, or worse. I shouted at her to return. Unfortunately the most senior of the mandarins, and he alone, was blissfully unaware that we were overlooked. He thought I was shouting at my official colleagues, and almost fell off his chair.[1] My Private Secretary looked reproachful.

It would be wrong to leave the impression, though, that the Treasury is other than a friendly place. The natives are hospitable. Underneath the formalities there is precious little savouring of pomposity. The officials from the lowliest to the Permanent Under-Secretary address each other by their Christian names, and do not hesitate to contradict each other cheerfully. On the second evening of my sojourn there was a farewell party for Nigel Lawson, who had been elevated, in the reshuffle that had wafted me to office, from Financial Secretary to running the Energy Department. Permanent Secretary Douglas Wass (whom, like many of the other senior

[1] This was not the only occasion on which I was instrumental in shocking this particular mandarin rigid. There was also a meeting at the office of the Financial Secretary. The Financial Secretary was in the middle of a detailed explanation of his plans to the Inland Revenue. I sneezed. It was, I admit, a loud sneeze: my sneezes are. The Financial Secretary roared 'SHUT UP, Economic Secretary'. The mandarins were aghast. They could hardly be expected to know that the Financial Secretary and I were long-time buddies, or to appreciate our private joke.

mandarins I had got to know already when I was on the back benches) came up to me. 'I hope you'll be happy here', he said. 'I think most people are. There's not much "Yes, Minister" syndrome about the Treasury'. I did not find it difficult to believe the first part of his assessment. As to the second, time would show.

3

The Grindstone

Whitehall works odd hours. Legend has it that the Foreign Office, in its golden age, before Sir Edward Grey watched 'the lamps going out all over Europe' from his office overlooking St James's Park, did not assemble until 10.30 am to give time for the stage-coach to come up from Dover with the despatches. Sir John Colville has revealed, in his published diaries, that as a junior secretary he clocked in at 11 am on the morning after the Second World War was declared. Things had moved forwards there by the 1950s, when I served briefly as a junior clerk. 10 am was clock-in time. Today the village comes alive by 9.30 am. But it still seems to be the case, in my experience, that if a civil servant, an industrialist, and a priest of Mammon from the City are entertained to lunch, it is the priest of Mammon from the City who leaves the table first, and the civil servant last. But long after the industrialists and the City gentlemen have departed to the bosoms of their families, the midnight oil will be burning bright in Whitehall.

Ministers have to be early birds and late owls as well. Two or three times a week their first assignment is their 'morning prayers'. This is a comparatively recent innovation. The first known reference dates back only to the Heath Government of the early 1970s, when Peter Walker, as overlord of the newly amalgamated Department of Trade and Industry, let it be known to the watching world that he gathered together regularly all his subordinate ministers, and their respective Parliamentary Private Secretaries, to plan their departmental strategy.

His spiritual predecessor was Tony Wedgwood Benn, who celebrated his promotion to a super-Ministry of Technology in the late 1960s by summoning his cloud of Junior Ministers to a working lunch on the day of their appointments. Arriving himself at 8.30 am, he sent his yawning secretaries around the ministerial private offices to alert his colleagues, and to tell them that he had ordered a sandwich meal for the occasion from the departmental canteen. Harold Lever, statutory sybarite of Socialism in the Wilson era, did not turn up for some time. When eventually his new patron's minions caught up with him, and informed him of the luncheon arrangements, he promptly replied that he would order lunch for all concerned from The Savoy. Which he did. A graphic report appeared in *The Times* next morning. So far as is known, the experiment was not regularly repeated by Mr Wedgwood Benn.

'Prayers' at the Treasury did not run to take-away meals from The Savoy. Coffee of an unusual colour and an even odder flavour was the sole refreshment. Sometimes it took place in the Chancellor's office at the Treasury; more often at No 11. The coffee was marginally better in the Treasury. The hour was almost invariably 9 am. This was the one occasion in the week when Ministers foregathered in the absence of the civil servants. The political advisers were also of the party (in both senses). Occasionally our Parliamentary Private Secretaries were invited to attend to cheer them up: but only on the strict understanding that there would be nothing serious to discuss.

Commentators might assume that this would be the moment at which Ministers would co-ordinate the 'politics' of what they were about, in the absence of the mandarins: when the political advisers would drag them back to the paths of party rectitude from which the Whitehall natives had been trying to distract them. It didn't seem to work that way. Indeed the agenda frequently contained items of almost breathtaking triviality: who was to be delegated to put in a Treasury presence at a social occasion organised by an influential Government backbencher, perhaps; or the phraseology to be used in response to an awkward letter from the fearsome Executive of the Tory backbench 1922 Committee. Occasionally tasks would be delegated to individual ministers. The fortunate – or more often unfortunate – nominee would subsequently hurry to inform his Private Office. The Private Office usually seemed to be forewarned. Such is the power of the Whitehall grapevine.

This might be the first item on the daily diary of the Ministers. But before that they would have been well advised to catch up with the morning papers. Newspapers ordered from the local newsagent would have to be paid for from the shrunken ministerial pocket. So there was an incentive to arrange to have them delivered in the car which collected Minister and boxes at 8.30 am. The journey into Whitehall then had to suffice to identify the storms and rocks ahead.

Whether or not morning 'prayers' were on the agenda, the day would be swiftly blocked in with meetings. An efficient Private Office would ensure that the Minister was kept fully occupied and out of mischief. There would be conferences with officials of the Minister's own cabbage-patch; meetings with the Chancellor and up to fifteen senior mandarins; meetings with the Financial Secretary or Chief Secretary and a troupe of officials; meetings with the Bank of England; delegations to receive; visiting VIPs to offer tea, or something stronger, to (according to significance and religion).

Yet the Minister is oddly isolated. The House of Commons is (or was: it seems to be changing drastically) a gregarious institution. Backbenchers spend many of their mornings processing legislation through small committees selected for the purpose; and many of their afternoons attending committees of their Party to discuss the departmental subjects of their preference. Ministers are drafted on to the legislative committees when legislation for which they are responsible is under scrutiny. But they are in the firing-line. Opportunities to swap the sort of gossip on which the Commons, like any other closed society, thrives are limited. The pressure is too great.

As to the Party Committees, the Minister may not (in the Tory Party, at any rate) attend unless he is invited. Nor will he be invited except to explain himself and the peccadilloes of his department. He has to rely on second-hand reports from his Parliamentary Private Secretary, who is supposed to cruise around the corridors of Westminster to tell him what is going on.

One consequence of this isolation is that Ministers outside the Cabinet are prone to tunnel vision. They may know all there is to know about the storage of Europe's grain mountains, or housing grants for the disabled, as the case may be. But they are liable to be no better informed about the thrust of public policies outside their own departmental territory than the average newspaper reader (indeed perhaps less well informed, since the pressure of work discourages general reading).

When a crisis arises, from the coalfields to the Falklands, Government backbenchers will enjoy the benefit of extensive briefing by the Ministers concerned. They may not avail themselves of the opportunities, but the opportunities are there. Similar briefing is provided for the Opposition leaders (indeed on 'privy council terms' – for those who happen to be Privy Councillors – the briefing may be a good deal more profound than that offered to the Government's own backbenchers). Cabinet Ministers must be assumed to be constitutionally aware of all that is afoot, even though there have been numerous occasions, of which Suez was only the most celebrated modern instance, when Prime Ministers have found it more convenient to work in a more restricted circle. But Ministers outside the Cabinet are in limbo. They see Cabinet minutes, but in a form so censored that even Dr Bowdler would have called for greater detail. They are barred, in the Tory Party, from the Party meetings. They have no time to listen in on emergency debates about the burning topic of the moment – not that they would be any better informed if they did.

Rarely Prime Ministers recognise this isolation, and the need to reduce it. During the drama of the Falklands campaign, the Prime Minister held two special meetings for her junior Ministers to bring them up to date. These were a special benison, for the lower tiers of office still have constituents to answer to, and they do not want to sound like ignoramuses before them.

For the relationship with the constituency is unchanged by elevation to Ministerial office. The flow of letters from constituents continues unabated, and continues to demand response. So several times a week a time-slot is allocated in the Ministerial diary for a visitation from the Minister's Parliamentary Secretary. This is one occasion when the Private Office does not obtrude: politics are beyond its ken. However official business always takes priority. The Commons secretary whose employer comes to glory soon acclimatises herself to sitting in the Minister's Private Secretaries' outer office while departmental work is overrun, and not infrequently to unceremonious eviction from the Minister's office when matters of state too delicate for her ears have urgently to be processed.

Yet the Minister is at a disadvantage in the search for satisfaction of his voters. The backbencher dissatisfied with a Ministerial response to his representations on behalf of constituents can always raise their grievances at Question Time, or in an Adjournment debate, on the floor of the House of Commons. He may rarely obtain a satisfaction which he failed to obtain by letter, but his valiant efforts will (if he knows his job) be well reported in the local press.

The Minister has no such options. He is still at liberty to write to his Ministerial collegues on behalf of his constituents. Convention allows him to display silent concern by sitting on the Commons backbenches (not the front, where he normally belongs) when a neighbouring MP is raising a problem related to his locality, as a gesture of silent solidarity. But he is debarred from speaking,[1] and (unlike his vociferous neighbour) he is likely to be ignored by his all-important local press.

Ministers may, however, be in a position on occasion to guide a slice from the pork-barrel in the direction of their constituents, or to save one that's already in position. Soon after Peter Rees was returned to the backbenches from the Chief Secretaryship in the summer of 1985, it was alleged that he had contrived, from the Treasury, to ensure that when the Army musical establishments were being cut from three to one, the one that survived was the one at his constituency of Dover. When Jim Callaghan was Prime Minister, the

[1] There was an apparently unprecedented occasion in 1980 when Adam Butler, then a Junior Minister in the Department of Industry, turned up for a debate about hospital provision in Leicestershire (his constituency location) and joined the criticism of his Ministerial colleague who had to answer for the Health Department. That he was not sacked on the spot caused raised eyebrows.

energy and (taxpayers') money he expended to attract Ford Motors to South Wales – where they were minded to go anyway – was felt to be not wholly unconnected with the proximity of the site Ford had selected to the Prime Minister's Cardiff baliwick.

I recall a vigorous discussion in the Treasury over a remarkable clause which had been inserted (before my arrival) in the 1981 Finance Act. This had been put in, at the insistence of the Scottish Office, to provide a special and unique tax concession for the benefit of Shell and Esso, which had contracted, on the strength of massive *douceurs* from the public purse, to build a petrochemical plant at Mossmorran in Fife. Since the products from this plant were promising to be something of a glut upon the market, Shell and Esso had threatened to pack it in unless they were given the concession.

The concession was a – justifiable – subject of outrage to ICI and BP, who were in competition with Mossmorran without benefit of tax break. I had a (small) BP chemical plant in my Knutsford constituency; Leon Brittan, the Chief Secretary, had the (vast) ICI plant at Billingham on his constituency doorstep. Unfortunately, while they were united in opposition to the 'Mossmorran clause', BP and ICI did not see eye to eye about the appropriate remedial action. Inevitably Leon Brittan campaigned for the ICI solution, and I for the BP one. We both lost.

But in any case, Ministers can only do good for their constituencies by stealth. They will hope that the achievements of their powers of in-house advocacy will not pass unnoticed locally. But they cannot, like their backbench brethren, crow about them.

For these reasons the system is supposed to compensate for the Miniserial disadvantages, by according preferential consideration to representations from one Minister to another. I saw no sign that this worked out in practice. There were, so far as I could tell, but two MPs whose letters on behalf of their constituents were reckoned to deserve special favours. One was the Prime Minister, for obvious reasons. The other was the Speaker, since civil servants like to think that by giving pleasure to the Speaker they will encourage him to give their Ministers the easy break when the classroom at Westminster has become unruly at those Ministers' expense. There was never any evidence that their expectations were fulfilled. But since the Speaker is more disabled in the public pursuit of constituents' satisfaction than any Minister, the civil servants' eagerness to please him is probably just as well.

Correspondence is a crucial part of the Minister's enduring duty to his local voters. But it is only a part. Every Friday evening he will have the round to make of constituency branch functions – the wine-and-cheese, the bring-and-buy, the barbecue – interlarded with the local Mayoral dinner or Rotary dinner-dance. These are all part of the life-cycle of the MP and his wife, and they constitute essential points-of-contact between him and his grassroots. But at the end of an exhausting Ministerial week they take their toll. After four nights at Westminster averaging four-and-a-half hours' sleep it is not always easy to display the interest and concern that is expected when tackled by a local farmer with his tribulations over gypsies or a right-of-way at midnight on the Friday. But our Ministers – unlike those of France, for example, who are constitutionally exonerated from constituency responsibility – should never be in danger of losing touch with those who chose them.

Weekends are fully occupied with the constituency round. Throughout the week the ubiquitous boxes always lurk in wait. As normal folk are digesting evening newspapers on the homeward tube or commuter train, the Whitehall Private Offices are gathering in the homework. By 7 pm, or thereabouts, the boxes and attendant despatch cases will be safely stuffed. The Minister will have been escorted off to represent the collective wisdom of the Government at the annual dinner of the National Association of Mousetrap Manufacturers ('this Government recognises the *essential* role that mousetrap manufacture plays in our national progress'). Eventually he makes his farewells and climbs gratefully into the waiting car to contemplate the workload prepared for him. On good nights it may be but one red box. On bad nights it is two, plus a briefcase. He soon learns that each one represents a solid hour of work, or more. On one occasion when I had been recruited to assist the Prime Minister with a speech she was preparing, we achieved agreement on the text as Big Ben across Parliament Square struck midnight. I rose swiftly to my feet. 'If you will forgive me, Prime Minister, I must get on with my boxes'. 'And what about *my* boxes?' was the sharp response. 'Yes, Prime Minister', I couldn't resist replying, 'but *you* don't seem to need to sleep'.

The boxes are rather like the traditional Christmas stocking, writ large. At the top are the oranges: fat folders of letters, mostly to MPs, some to outside interests deemed deserving of a Ministerial answer to their representations, each requiring topping-and-tailing. They seem encouraging, since the time-to-weight ratio is much more favourable than it will be with the departmental submissions which follow them. Yet they must be read with care. For each letter can be passed to the press, whether local or national, and used in evidence against the Minister. To the civil servant one MP is no doubt like another. But to a Minister they need individual thought. A dismissive tone may be fine for a barrack-room lawyer on the Opposition benches; for a similarly awkward cuss from amongst the Government supporters it can be dynamite. The Minister who signs away his correspondence without bothering to read it is riding for a fall.

The next layer below the folders of correspondence – the equivalent of the diaries and knick-knacks in the Christmas stocking – consists of more peripheral matter: those Cabinet papers, much bowdlerised, already mentioned; letters from the Secretary of State for the Administration Department to the Chancellor about the allocation of responsibility for garbage collection in Whitehall; for Treasury Ministers there will be market reports to explain that the dollar has gone stronger in expectation of bad monetary figures from the US central bank (how odd, you reflect, when excessive monetary growth is supposed to be bad for the currency). These are fairly swiftly digested, but – unlike the correspondence files – do not make much of a dent in the contents of the box.

Then comes the heavy stuff. Fat files containing detailed submissions from the mandarins regarding current policy and future plans. Many of these will concern the other aspects of departmental activity for which the Ministerial colleagues have primary responsibility. They can be ignored without much hazard. On the other hand if the Minister wants to seize the opportunity given him by his elevation to influence the overall policies of the department to which he happens to be attached (and is the sacrifice of income and the burden of responsibility worth having if that opportunity is spurned?) then these dossiers must be read and commented upon.

Finally, at the toe of the stocking, are the prizes or the horror stories. Here lie the submissions calling for the Minister's decision. Legend has it that Whitehall keeps the shockers for last. Legend turns out to be correct. There, nestling coyly at the bottom of the second box, designed to be reached at 2.30 or 3 am, when Ministerial resistance is likely to be low, and Ministerial wife or concubine exasperated, will be the 12-page file concluding with the message that 'we would be grateful for your decision on this proposition by 12 noon on February 31st at the latest, since a public statement should be made by then'. Suddenly it dawns upon you that February 31st is already three hours old. The wise Minister scrawls across the message 'I will not be bounced. This must be discussed'. He may be wise. He is not thanked.

Another claim on ministerial diaries is the Cabinet Committee, that offshoot of the parent body which has proliferated in recent years to the point at which it attracts from time to time the charge of usurpation of the Cabinet itself. Owing, perhaps, to the nature of my private cabbage patch, I had relatively little experience of these instruments of delegated Cabinet responsibility. My Customs hat produced one memorable inter-departmental Whitehall assignment (see Chapter 10); but funding and monetary policy were both too arcane and too 'sensitive' to be discussed with others than the Bank of England (see Chapter 6).

Soon after my arrival, however, I was told to report on behalf of the Treasury to 'L' Committee. This is the Cabinet Committee which, under all modern Governments, maps out the Parliamentary legislative programme. It meets once a week when Parliament is sitting, and several times during the recesses as well, under the chairmanship of the Lord President of the Council. I owed my attendance – of which I had been notified belatedly by my Private Office – to the detention of the Financial Secretary, who would normally have represented the Treasury, on other duties.

There were, as I recall, seven items on the agenda. None of them, I gathered, required the Treasury to 'lead'. But the first item concerned the attitude the Government was to adopt towards an awkward Private Member's Bill, promoted by a Labour backbencher who was hoping to score marks for 'compassion' – at the taxpayers' expense – by imposing costly and superfluous new obligations on the Department of Health and Social Security. My brief advised me that the DHSS was reckoned to be vastly unenthusiastic; neverthless it was essential that I should make it plain (for the avoidance of doubt – as if any doubt could have existed) that the Treasury was not prepared to buy the Bill at any price. The second item concerned a Bill which the DHSS itself was anxious to promote. Here, too, the Treasury was unhappy about the spending implications; but here too, fortunately, my brief advised me that I should not need to do more than murmur a ritual reservation, since the Bill was in contention between several other Whitehall departments, and a long way from the legislative slipway. There followed three or four more minor items to which, I was advised, I could safely wish 'God speed' on the Treasury's behalf, if I felt it necessary to open my mouth. The last dish on the menu was an exotic affair entitled The Duchy of Cornwall Bill: something, so my briefing note informed me, to do with the Prince of Wales' finances, which had run into trouble with that stage republican on the Labour benches, Mr Willie Hamilton. My briefs had been duly supplemented by a conference with the officials concerned with items one and two, to make sure that I would leave my colleagues on 'L' Committee in no doubt about the Treasury's unyielding opposition to both.

Clutching my smart blue folder containing the agenda and my briefs, I pedalled one hundred yards up Whitehall to the entrance to the Cabinet Office. I was shown into a ground-floor room in which was set out a green baize-topped table constituting the four sides of a quadrilateral, with an empty space in the middle. The baize was prepared with place-cards for each of those attending, the Lord President's in the centre of one side. Around the walls of the room sat a score of mandarins-in-attendance. I found my card marked Minister of State, Treasury (this was before I had been transformed into Economic Secretary), sat down; opened my folder; and awaited play.

On Item 1 (the Private Member's Bill) I was asked in due course to give the Treasury opinion. Fortunately it was already apparent that almost everyone was against it, the only faint note of dissent coming from the Leader of the House of Commons, who feared that the Government might be presented in a poor light. When my turn came I did my best to sound appropriately stern. On Item 2 I intervened briefly to confirm 'for the record' that the Treasury would have serious reservations if anything were to materialise. On Items 3, 4, 5 and 6 I held my peace and felt I'd had an easy passage for a first experience.

'Item 7', Francis Pym intoned (for he was then Lord President). 'Duchy of Cornwall Bill. Minister of State?' Silence. I looked around me to see who claimed this baby. Suddenly, to my horror, I realised that one and all around the table were looking back at me. I gulped. It began to dawn upon me that the Prince of Wales was, that morning, in my hands. I hastily looked down and read out the briefing note from the folder, reckoning that if, when I had finished, any of my colleagues were to murmur 'arising out of that reply' I should be tempted, like Hilaire Belloc's Lord Lundy, to burst into tears. Fortunately they didn't. Lunchtime was drawing on, and the Lord President remarked that 'that all seems to be in hand', and adjourned the meeting. So far as I was aware nobody had even noticed that the Duchy of Cornwall Bill was a far off country of which I knew nothing. I pedalled back to the Treasury to have a word or two with my Private Office.

Then there was the steady stream of individual visitors. A courtesy call from the current Chairman of the Committee of London Clearing Banks, anxious no doubt to size up the new political animal with whom they might be called upon to deal, was an early item on my agenda. The Chief Economic Adviser to the current *patron* of Nigeria was another. He was on a visit to London to explain that while his Government was not just at that moment in a position to settle any bills, exporters and investors need not fear that all would, eventually, be well. He assured me that his reception in the City of London had been all that he could have wished for, and that the Square Mile was packed with merchants eager – indeed ravenous – to add fresh credits to his country's unpaid bills. One major project for which he had found many volunteers offering financial packages, he told me, was a smart new steel complex upon which his leader's heart was set. Since steel was, at that time, a glut upon the international market, I wondered where they planned to sell it once they'd built their complex. 'Oh, in Nigeria', I was told. 'All of it?' I asked. 'Oh no', I was told, 'all over Africa too'. I hoped they'd get a decent price.

One day I was told that the British Ambassador to Washington, over for 'consultations' or some leave, I know not which, sought some moments of my time. A date was fixed. When the day arrived I asked my Private Secretary to find out to what precisely I owed this honour. My Private Secretary rang the Foreign Office, but reported back none the wiser. The Ambassador arrived, and we discussed the weather and the traffic. Eventually, since he did not seem to be in any hurry to broach whatever subject he might have in mind, I asked him about the 'supply side' strategy – involving substantial tax cuts unmatched by cuts in spending programmes – on which the Reagan Administration was, at the time, embarked. The Ambassador turned out to be a fan. Indeed I finally got the message – or at least I thought I did – that the purpose of his visit was to tell me that it was high time for us to adopt the American example. I expressed scepticism, suggesting that the resulting Budget deficit seemed likely to land the US Government in trouble eventually; and that if we accepted similar risks they would rebound upon us rapidly. We agreed to differ. Six months later I ran into the Ambassador again. He cheerfully assured me that 'supply side economics' were a load of rubbish. Or words to that effect. So what our chat had really been about eludes me.

Visitors, constituencies, committees and boxes do not complete the Ministerial schedule. There is also voting in the House of Commons. For the self-opinionated, and those prone to agonising about the way to cast their votes, elevation to Ministerial office is akin to conversion to the Catholic Church for a Protestant. The private conscience is abandoned. You vote the Party ticket, or resign. There is, however, a flip side to this blessed simplicity of conduct. Ministers are treated by the Party Whips as the ultimate in lobby fodder. They may have Parliamentary Private Secretaries to search out for them, when needed, a 'pair' from the Opposition benches to balance their absences at voting time when they are called away from Westminster on official business (and the PPS is expected on occasion to make the ultimate Parliamentary sacrifice by surrendering his own Opposition 'pair', if – as some do – he has a regular 'arrangement', to cover for his Minister). But on major votes a Ministerial absence will not be excused at any price. The Minister will be ordered back from Tokyo in the midst of international negotiations; he may find himself obliged to shuttle back from Brussels in the middle of a lengthy wrangle in the European Community to vote all night at Westminster before going back to Brussels once again to sit up all night in a Ministerial Council. His Parliamentary colleagues are accorded a 'free vote' to indulge their fancies without recrimination from their Whips on matters ranging from car seat-belts to abortion. Ministers are often refused such luxuries. Ministers were, for example, required to present themselves to vote in favour of compulsory seat belts in 1982; a proposition about which their backbench colleagues were at liberty to take a view without pressure from the Whips. Since the Tory Chief Whip had consistently himself opposed compulsory seat-belts, the doubters amongst us were permitted, as a special privilege, to go home unvoted. But we were expected to report in the pro-seat-belt-lobby in case our votes were needed.

The pressure of departmental business is not to be regarded as any excuse for Ministerial absence. When, in early 1971, Parliament was kept voting constantly at ten-minute intervals on the ill-fated Industrial Relations Act, throughout the night from midnight until 10 in the morning, Willie Whitelaw, then Government Chief Whip, invited us to marvel at the stamina displayed by the octogenarian backbench MP for Tynemouth, Dame Irene Ward. The comparable stamina displayed by Sir Alec Douglas Home, then Foreign Secretary, was not thought worthy of comment. It occurred to some of us that the octogenarian lady could always have withdrawn from the kitchen if she did not like the heat; whereas spending a night on the treadmill might not be the best preparation for the conduct of our international relations. Such considerations cut no ice in the Whips' Office.

4

The Village Culture

In most advanced industrial countries the civil service has its own distinctive culture. Thirty years ago, when I was the correspondent for the *Financial Times* in Paris, I owed the only real scoop of my journalistic career to the unique culture of the Japanese civil service.

I had received a call one morning from head office in London. Could I, they asked, find out what was going on at a special meeting of COCOM, the Nato committee which arranged and supervised controls over the sales of 'strategically sensitive' materials and components to Eastern Europe, and which, in those days, met in Paris? I politely suggested that head office must be joking. Delegates to COCOM, I explained, attended its meetings in false beards and funny noses. One might as well seek access to the nuclear codes. I promised to do my best: and promptly forgot the request.

That evening a Japanese journalist acquaintance of mine dropped by. He wanted an 'up-date' on the goings-on at what was then called the Organisation for European Economic Co-operation (now OECD). I was not infrequently consulted by my journalist colleagues about the operations of this esoteric organisation, since they were of more abiding interest to the FT than to more generalist newspapers.

I filled him in as best I could. As he was leaving my office I suddenly recalled the morning call from London. By way of *quid pro quo*, could my Japanese visitor by any chance shed any light on COCOM?

He could, and did. The British, he told me, had that day demanded a major relaxation in the range and severity of the controls on East-West trade; and the Americans had not been best amused. He clearly knew in detail what he was talking about. I sent a brief and cautious story back to London.

The next morning – an exceptional event – my editor was on the 'phone. My story, he told me, had attracted a good deal of interest. Could I produce some more? I rang my Japanese friend, and asked to drop by. When I reached him, I asked whether he had any further information. He had indeed. He had the complete transcript of the previous day's conversations at COCOM (each page marked 'NATO TOP SECRET' in red ink). I had a ball.

Others were not so fortunate. Months later I was accosted at a party in Paris by a stranger who informed me that I had almost cost him his job. He was, he revealed, the British representative on COCOM.

My informant was a former Japanese diplomat, son of an erstwhile Japanese ambassador in London, who had been obliged to abandon 'the career' following a bigamous marriage with a citizen of Switzerland. Although he was thereafter but a journalist, it would not have occurred to his former colleagues to deny him access to their papers.

In other countries, *esprit de corps* would not conceivably be carried to such lengths. Not even in France, arguably the most 'Japanese' of western countries in its style of Government. French civil servants are notably the most sophisticated and most highly educated of the international fraternity. The French education system, with its apex, the '*grandes écoles*', from which the future managers of France emerge to filter back and forth between the public and the private sectors, equip the elites with minds that lesser mortals cannot hope to match. High-flying *fonctionnaires* are entrepreneurs within the system. They pursue their individual fancies, and back their individual favourites in the commercial sector with the taxes of the citizens, without a backward glance towards the changing aspirations of their governments. (In Fifth Republican France the ministers are themselves often plucked from the ranks of the bureaucracy, which must reduce the risk of cross-purposes). Occasionally they come to grief: one brilliant stategist of French international economic policy in the 1960s was unwise enough to cross swords with M Giscard d'Estaing when Giscard was Finance Minister, and ended up in a siding. He was unlucky (and unwise).

The *esprit* of the American bureaucracy drifts in and out with the political tides. The French politicians 'parachute' their think-alikes into key positions in the ministries when the electorate changes its allegiance and their lot comes out on top: but their parachutists are already there, somewhere in the departmental woodwork. When American administrations change, the furniture vans are busy. Entire top tiers depart: back to their law firms and the boardrooms of big business if they are Republicans; back to their law firms and their universities if they are Democrats. Each new team consists of a cavalry-charge of bandwagons. In theory they are committed to a common electoral platform. In practice they are harnessed to particular stars – Cabinet Members or key figures in the White House entourage, any one of whom, in that land of opportunity, may one day turn out to be 'presidential timber'.

They amaze their British counterparts by their enthusiasm. Their British counterparts amaze *them* by their detachment. Probably it is because we have a uniquely 'adversarial' political tradition: we have to balance it with a sceptical bureaucracy. Apart from those members of the 'Old' Commonwealth which have copied our example, the geography of Westminster – the inescapable confrontation between the 'ins' and 'outs' across the gangway – is unmatched. The more conventional hemicycles, around which the spectrum of political opinion spreads imperceptibly, can afford the back-up of more starkly differentiated civil servants.

Our permanent divide cannot. Civil servants in retirement dream dreams of standing Royal Commissions to straddle the gangways of our two Chambers. They know better when they are on the job. So commitment to ideologies in conflict is not an option open to our mandarins, as it is to their counterparts in Washington or Paris. They must find their emotional fulfilment somewhere else.

They find it in their individual kraals – the departments. Just as the politicians at Westminster have long been convinced that the senior civil servants all wear bowler hats and old school ties or twinsets and pearls, and spend their Friday evenings at Tory party shin-digs in the suburbs, or else – according to Party standpoint – go in for beards, unisex jeans, and secret conclaves with militants from Islington, so the mandarins insist that for them the ideal minister is one who knows his mind and how to get his way in Cabinet even when they think he's wrong. Both groups delude themselves.

Like most of those who have visited the Whitehall village on ministerial assignment over the years, I would not like to wager on how the senior mandarins I had to deal with in the Treasury cast their votes on polling-day (or indeed whether they cast them at all). I can only recall offhand one civil servant (not in the Treasury) who made no secret of his – Tory – political allegiance, and it rang false. On the other hand, the picture of their ideal minister which the civil servants like to paint no more corresponds to their real preferences than they themselves, in their behaviour, correspond to the picture painted of them by the politicians.

Heclo and Wildavsky (*Private Government and Public Money*, op. cit.) sum up the civil servant *beau idéal* of a minister revealingly: 'Given a choice between someone who passively accepts their advice, and someone who can effectively protect and advance *the departmental interest*, officials in the Treasury and the spending departments would unanimously choose the stronger character' (my emphasis). Precisely.

They want a minister with 'bottom', and with clout. But they expect him to use those qualities in advance, or defence, as the case might be, of their chosen departmental priorities. It is important therefore to understand what those departmental priorties are. For they do not change much from one generation to another.

In some cases they reflect essentially the interests of their captive clients. The Ministry of Agriculture, Fisheries and Food, for example, has always treated those responsibilities in declining order of significance. The farmers are their prime concern, and the senior mandarins and their counterparts from the National Farmers' Union are never far from each others' doors and telephones. Fisheries are regarded as much more peripheral; significant only because the fishermen's influence as lobbyists is concentrated (and therefore maximised) in a handful of constituencies around the coasts. Food hardly gets a look in. In this as in many other ways, the consumer interest is too diffuse to make an impact on Whitehall.

Then there is Defence. This has been traditionally the battleground between three sparring services, each of which has gone public when it has lost an argument to an extent that mere civilians in Whitehall would never dare. In more recent times it is the relationship between the MoD and its shrinking band of home-grown armaments manufacturers (who recruit assiduously from its senior echelons) which has sometimes looked incestuous to outsiders.

Other departments are liable to go in for dislikes rather than likes. The DHSS, for example, has a perhaps inevitable distrust of private-sector health care in general, and a deep suspicion of the commercial hearing-aid dispensers in particular. This was illuminated startlingly when VAT was first introduced in the early 1970s. Opticians, albeit commercial, were given zero-rating. Not so the commercial hearing-aid dispensers. An amendment to the first VAT Budget, to zero-rate commercial hearing aids, was drafted with care and to the satisfaction of the Customs and Excise (the lead department with direct responsibility for VAT). The DHSS rejected it. Nothing would move them: the commercial hearing-aid dispensers were a bunch of rip-off merchants, and not to be encouraged in any way. It was only when it became apparent that there was sufficient cross-party Commons support for the amendment to make a Government defeat a probability that the DHSS was eventually induced to go quietly.

The Foreign Office is another department with strong inherited likes and dislikes. In ascending order of preference it approves, from one generation of diplomats to the next, of the Germans, the Americans, and the Arabs. In descending order of distaste it disapproves, from one generation to the next, of the Russians, the Jews, and – above all – the French. About the French it is paranoid (a paranoia which, it must be added in fairness, is handsomely reciprocated by the Quai d'Orsay).

The Treasury, like Nancy Mitford's Uncle Matthew, tends to distrust *all* foreigners, and hence the Foreign Office, as their advocates in Whitehall. But its particular suspicion is reserved for the Bank of England (a suspicion which is, once again, handsomely reciprocated).

The old Board of Trade was the last true bastion in Whitehall of Manchester free trade liberalism. The Department of Industry, by contrast, tends towards paternalism. It favours an interventionist approach to commerce, with an enthusiasm for regional policies and a propensity to promote 'Great Britain Limited' and the selection of commercial flagships and winners, modelling itself proudly on what it believes to be the example of Japan's MITI. Now that the two departments are amalgamated, the Department of Trade and Industry inevitably displays signs of schizophrenia.

Ministers, regardless of Party, are expected to absorb as rapidly as may be the ethos of the departments to which they happen to be assigned. Mandarins do so without hesitation. The Treasury regularly seeks to colonise the spending departments by contriving the promotion of its senior officials to top jobs elsewhere in Whitehall. It is as regularly disappointed: the emissaries promptly 'go native'. Thus Sir Richard (Otto) Clark, who had directed Treasury resistance to the Concorde project at the beginning of the 1960s, became a Concorde enthusiast as soon as he took charge of the Ministry of Aviation. No doubt their past experience makes them wary of pushing the Treasury beyond endurance; but any hope that they will carry with them a stern bias in favour of retrenchment is invariably misplaced.

Most politicians are as swiftly domesticated. Lord Thorneycroft resigned rather than countenance an increase of just £50m in the public spending estimates at the end of 1957: six years later he re-emerged as a most enthusiastic advocate of the spending progamme of the Ministry of Aviation (where he had joined forces with Sir Otto Clark). But then he had been put up to resignation from the Treasury by his more hawkish subordinates, Enoch Powell and Nigel Birch, respectively Economic and Financial Secretaries. Sir Geoffrey Howe supervised Ted Heath's prices and wage control from 1972–74, and, like the skilled barrister that he is, went on to advocate free market monetarism as Opposition spokesman under Mrs Thatcher, and then to apply it as Chancellor following the Tory Election victory in 1979. In this case, however, it was the political climate that changed rather than the departmental attitude, and Sir Geoffrey, like most shrewd politicians, changed with it. The way in which he moved from measured scepticism about British participation in the European exchange rate mechanism as Chancellor to enthusiastic advocacy as Foreign Secretary more nearly reflects adjustment to departmental attitudes.

A purer example of adaptation to departmental environment, however, concerned Geoffrey Howe's successor, Nigel Lawson. Between 1981 and 1983 Nigel Lawson served in his first Cabinet post, as Secretary of State for Energy. A long-standing bone of contention between Energy and the Treasury concerns the price of fuel. The Department of Energy likes it low, to promote sales of its captive corporations, Gas, Electricity and Coal (although not, of course, low enough to render retention of the Coal Board's least economic coalpits too ruinously expensive), and to divert flak from commercial customers prone to making invidious comparisons with the costs of energy to the continental competition. The Treasury, by contrast, always wants to get fuel prices up. This way, the producing corporation (even, conceivably, one day, the National Coal Board) make hefty profits, which can then be creamed off by the Treasury.

Over time some sort of compromise has been reached by which the fuel producers are supposed to go for prices designed to reflect the 'long-run marginal cost' of producing their supplies. In other words, the price of gas should reflect not just the cost of extracting and delivering existing (cheap) supplies of gas from the southern North Sea, but also the cost of developing (far more expensive) future gas supplies from the northern North Sea; while the price of electricity should reflect the cost of building the power stations of the future to replace those becoming out-dated and worn out.

Life being what it is, however, 'long-run marginal costing' is by no means a precise art. It depends, for example, on how demand for the product is to grow, and how technology evolves. At any rate, in the early spring of 1983 Nigel Lawson, Energy Secretary, commissioned a great report from accountants Coopers and Lybrand, which showed – to nobody's surprise – that the Treasury's estimates of the 'long-run marginal cost' of electricity supply were *far* too high. Five months later Nigel Lawson returned to the Treasury as Chancellor. He lost no time whatsoever in demonstrating, beyond a peradventure of a doubt, that Coopers and Lybrand were incapable of adding two to two correctly. It should perhaps be added, however, that in this instance personalities were involved.

For Nigel Lawson and his successor at Energy, Peter Walker, are never happier than when engaged in trying to gouge each other's eyes out. The desire to score points off the new Energy Secretary played at least as large a part in the Chancellor's remarkable conversion as did adaptation to his new environment.

The Foreign Office is perhaps the *locus classicus* for the domestication of the politicians. Here the contrast between the reputation within the Foreign Office of Lord George-Brown and Dr David Owen is particularly revealing. No Minister in modern times treated his senior civil servants more offensively than George Brown. He frequently berated them, and insulted their wives, on semi-public occasions; his indiscretions and insobriety caused them regular embarrassment. But when the chips were down, he did as he was told: he 'effectively protected and advanced the departmental interest'. His sins were forgiven.

By contrast no Foreign Secretary since Anthony Eden (with whom he shares many characteristics) was so cordially disliked by his department as Dr Owen. He was alleged to be arrogant and discourteous, although his arrogance and discourtesy could not have remotely matched the arrogance and discourtesy of George Brown. But he did not always do as he was told: over nuclear policy, over policy towards Europe and Southern Africa, he defied the wisdom of his mandarins. That was not forgiven.

The litmus test of good Ministerial behaviour from the angle of the Foreign Office relates to relations with the French. Throughout the 1960s the prime objective of our diplomats was to frustrate the ambition of General de Gaulle to build a 'third force' European strategy, midway between, and independent of, both the superpowers. Harold Macmillan correctly perceived that this opened up the possibility of a deal by which the General would allow us into the European Community in exchange for essential co-operation with the development of the French independent nuclear '*force de frappe*'. The Foreign Office was appalled, and, as Macmillan acknowledged in his memoirs, succesfully short-circuited him. The General predictably vetoed our Common Market application.

There followed a period of eight long years during which the Foreign Office induced successive Foreign Secretaries under Harold Wilson to renew our application for membership of the Community even though it was obvious that it stood no chance, and was also profoundly antipathetic to sentiment in the then ruling British political Party. Michael Stewart, one of the more amenable of Foreign Secretaries of the period, was persuaded at one point to circulate a memorandum to his colleagues exposing the double-dyed wickedness of General de Gaulle in seeking an accommodation with the Soviet Union and in blocking all progress towards a more genuinely integrated Community. Since both these *Gaulliste* strategies precisely corresponded with the instincts of the Labour Party at the time, Mr Stewart suffered a bloody nose.

Wiser Foreign Secretaries handle their departmental briefs with greater care. Lord Carrington, equipped with a cast-iron Foreign Office presentation in favour of immediate British accession to the European exchange rate mechanism, and knowing that his Prime Minister would not touch it with a bargepole, read it out with due solemnity, and concluded 'that, Prime Minister, is what I was told to say, and it seems to me a load of rubbish'. Similarly, when the Foreign Office had promoted what amounted to a sale-and-leaseback deal with the Argentines over the Falkland Islands (a deal which would have averted the Falklands War and all the expense which followed it), and it became apparent that there would be trouble in the House of Commons, Lord Carrington withdrew behind the parapet, leaving one of his subordinates to take the flak. Yet Lord Carrington, from the viewpoint of the Foreign Office, was 'sound'. He pursued the departmental line. That from time to time he left it in the lurch only enhanced respect for his political 'nose'.

The overriding duty of a departmental minister, in the eyes of his mandarins, however, is to defend, and where possible to advance, the territory of the kraal to which he happens to be assigned. For British civil servants are territorial animals, and nothing arouses such passions round the village as trespass. In the summer of 1984 Mr David Young was suddenly plucked by the Prime Minister from the relative obscurity of the Manpower Services Commission to a peerage, a seat in the Cabinet, and a roving, if somewhat ill-defined, brief to 'loosen up the labour markets'.

Seasoned observers shook their heads. The newly ennobled Lord Young, it was said, would soon discover that a Cabinet Minister without a powerful Whitehall department behind him was whistling in the dark. But Lord Young had a powerful card up his sleeve: he had the energetic backing of the Prime Minister ('others', she was reported to have commented, 'bring me their problems. David brings me solutions'). His small team soon produced a series of specific recommendations concerning ways in which the burdens of bureaucracy on enterprise could be lifted. But it became as swiftly known that the Department of Employment was fighting every inch of the way against what it saw as Lord Young's attempts to knuckle in upon its field of exclusive responsibility. Relations between Lord Young and the Employment Secretary, Tom King, were said to be strained almost to breaking-point. Since neither of the two (unlike several of their colleagues in that Cabinet) is much given to belligerence, Lord Young being one of nature's diplomats, and Tom King notably easy-going, these reports looked distinctly over-written. But they reflected the intensity of tensions between the officials of the Department of Employment and Lord Young's small band of freebooters accurately enough.

Fortunately, within a matter of weeks Tom King had been sent off to Northern Ireland, and Lord Young himself took charge at Employment. Even so the dust did not settle promptly, for Lord Young persuaded the Prime Minister to arrange for him to bring with him a package of responsibilities for 'enterprise promotion' which had hitherto belonged with the Department of Trade and Industry. Trade and Industry's nose was put out of joint (and in this instance, unusually, Employment was not altogether sure about its territorial acquisition, which was felt to sit uneasily beside the Department's traditional relationship with the Trades Unions).

Another recent instance of territorial aggression and defence has involved the Department of the Environment and the Ministry of Agriculture. At the Department of the Environment, Kenneth Baker as Minister of State and then as Secretary of State, and William Waldegrave as Parliamentary Secretary and then as Minister of State, were neither of them slouches at spotting bandwagons. Both saw mileage to be gleaned from the 'green', or 'environmental' ticket. Inevitably they trespassed on Agriculture's kraal.

The first bone of contention concerned an interesting aspect of Michael Heseltine's Wildlife and Countryside Act of 1981. This provided that owners of land designated as 'sites of special scientific interest' could be compensated for leaving well alone. How the Treasury ever let this one through was a mystery to me – fortunately it was before my time. For unsurprisingly landowners swiftly set to work. Lord Thurso announced plans to afforest a large area of bog in Caithness. Experts consulted averred that it was a wholly inappropriate site for afforestation. Lord Thurso was undeterred. The conservationists were appalled. Eventually he accepted £280,000 for abandoning his plans. Another extensive landowner, Lord Cranborne, proposed to commit a similar frightfulness in Dorset (the site chosen was said to be one of his better pheasant covers). He got £83,000 for abstaining.

Things soon got out of hand. The Min. of Ag. was caught in the crossfire. For while the cost of compensating farmers and landowners, for desisting from doing what – just maybe – it would not have occurred to them to do in the first place, had to be carried on the Department of Environment's budget, the subsidies available to them for going ahead were Agriculture's babies. 'Sources close to' the Department of the

Environment let it be known that the Min. of Ag. was behaving quite irresponsibly in giving grants for the destruction of the last known habitat of the peg-leg bumble bee. To which 'sources close to' the Min. of Ag. replied, 'read the statute book: we have no choice'. It was a saga which promised to run and run.

But there were limits. At the beginning of 1986 a joyous bout of public fisticuffs between the mandarins of Environment and the mandarins of Agriculture surfaced. William Waldegrave was invited to address the annual Oxford Farming Conference, British agriculture's equivalent of the annual gathering of the world's financial fat cats at the 'Fund and Bank' in Washington. Agriculture Minister Michael Jopling was not.

The Min. of Ag. was purple. 'Ministry sources', it was revealed, reckoned that Mr Jopling was 'privately very angry'. 'Waldegrave', they were quoted as opining, 'is a blue-eyed boy of the Tory Party and he gets a lot of press coverage. Jopling's speeches often tend to be a bit wishy-washy. But at the end of the day Waldegrave is speaking as an environmental minister – and a junior one to boot – at what is an agricultural conference'. Here was Whitehall nature rarely exposed, red in tooth and claw.

Michael Jopling, subsequently interviewed in person, did not sound all that angry – certainly not as angry as his mandarins evidently thought he should be. He could have been forgiven for feeling angry – with his mandarins. After all, if his speeches 'often tended to be a bit wishy-washy', who wrote them but those mandarins? But perhaps Jopling was the sort of Minister whom all Whitehall departments from time to time experience. For the good of their collective souls.

The subtle strategies of Whitehall territorialism can, on occasion, leave the Minister bemused. One former Education Secretary recalls how he was mystified to discover, from his briefs for Cabinet one morning, that he was advised to speak up in support of objections from the Energy Department to a pet scheme due to be promoted by the Minister of Agriculture. The relevance of this project, for good or ill, to the day-to-day concerns of Education escaped him. He asked his Permanent Secretary, and received a rambling answer. In the end he disentangled it. It was the season of the annual public expenditure reviews. By coming to the aid of the Energy Minister against their Agricultural colleague, his officials calculated, he might earn the aid of Energy in resisting the Treasury's designs upon some pet spending plans of Education.

But it is to the late Professor John Mackintosh that we must turn for perhaps the most revealing glimpse of Whitehall territorialism. In 1965, he reported (Mackintosh, *Government and Politics in Britain*) that Dick Crossman, as Minister of Housing and Local Government, found himself presented by his mandarins with a brief for Cabinet concerning the allocation of responsibility for an aspect of the national culture which it would not have occurred to previous Governments to meddle in: sport. From Professor Mackintosh's account it sounds suspiciously as if Mr Crossman had not read his brief before he got to Cabinet. But when he did, he read that sport was going into Housing and Local Government. He found this bizarre, and said so. Sport, he argued, belonged logically with Education. His Cabinet colleagues all agreed. And so it was decided.

However, as Crossman was himself to acknowledge (*Inside View*, op. cit.), Cabinet Ministers not infrequently find, when they come to study Cabinet minutes, that its decisions as recorded contrast strikingly with their own recollections. So it was on this occasion. The Cabinet, he read, had allocated sport to Housing and Local Government. Only on this occasion he exploded. Summoning his Permanent Under-Secretary, he insisted that that was not what the Cabinet had decided at all. The Permanent Under-Secretary smoothly explained that this *was* what the parallel committee of top mandarins had decided. They had indeed noted the course of the discussion in Cabinet thereafter; but they had naturally assumed that the Minister of Housing had not been serious in denying himself responsibility for sport, and surrendering it to Education. They had therefore ventured to set right his momentary aberration. Crossman got his way. Sport went to Education. But it is not to be surprised after that he was always regarded in Whitehall as basically too frivolous to make a 'rounded' Minister.

Sometimes, it is true, the villagers watch with some dismay as their temporary political *patron* goes, in their eyes, over the top. In the spring of 1984 the Civil Aviation Authority produced a report which called for a large-scale forced transfer of some of its most profitable routes from British Airways to the leading private-sector airline, British Caledonian. The Transport Secretary, Nicholas Ridley, welcomed the report unreservedly. But a ferocious public battle ensued, with the Department of Transport and British Caledonian ranged on one side, and British Airways on the other. Lord King, the British Airways Chairman, who was known to be highly regarded by the Prime Minister, let it be known that he and his board would defy orders to hand over the routes selected by the CAA, insisting that the Government would have to sack them first. The Transport Secretary was all for calling their bluff (if bluff it was). Indeed at one stage village gossip had it that if the Cabinet was not minded to back him in so doing, he was ready to resign.

Now the CAA's report reflected approved departmental policy; and Whitehall departments do not take kindly to nationalised industry chiefs practising defiance of their intentions. But Whitehall departments do not believe in their ministers behaving as kamikaze pilots either. The Ministry of Transport shrewdly reckoned that if Nicholas Ridley asked his colleagues to choose between Lord King and him, they would come down on the side of Lord King. They thought, in other words, that their Minister was painting himself into a corner. If he resigned, a successor would only be in a weaker position to bargain with Lord King. Worse still, he might in the end draw back from resignation, leaving himself and his ministerial clout (which might be needed for more important departmental battles in the future) permanently diminished.

In the end all was well. A compromise was arranged. Lord King surrendered his lucrative Gulf routes to British Caledonian, and agreed to open up a piggy-bank to help finance future fledgling private-sector competitors for his airlines; but took British Caledonian's currently less lucrative Latin American routes in part-exchange. Best of all – from the departmental viewpoint – it was widely felt (whether justifiably or not) that Nicholas Ridley's stand had eventually induced Lord King to go a good deal further than he had originally been prepared to do. So the Minister, and hence his department, emerged with its credit-rating unimpaired.

The epic – indeed unprecedented – battle between Michael Heseltine as Defence Secretary and Leon Brittan as Secretary for Trade and Industry over the future control of Westland Helicopters in the winter of 1985/6 was something else again. Undeniably there were elements of territorial protection involved: Westland looked to Industry as its sponsoring department, but to Defence for its essential orders. But in this instance departmental *amour propre* faded into insignificance by comparison with Ministerial order-pecking. Leon Brittan, as already mentioned, had suffered what Whitehall had perceived as a demotion when he had been moved from the Home Office to Trade and Industry in the autumn of 1985. He was determined to assert himself. Michael Heseltine was after altogether bigger game. He had for some time been impatient to move from Defence, which he perceived as a department lacking popular electoral appeal, to somewhere nearer the central levers of economic power. He had been left to stew. He saw his star, as a potential aspirant to the topmost post of all, waning as that of the only other prominent dissenter in the Cabinet, Peter Walker, seemed to wax. He seized on the Westland affair as an opportunity not just to humiliate the Industry Secretary (with whom he had some scores to settle) but to stare down the Prime Minister herself. On such occasions the villagers are prone to go into hiding. They know somebody is going to get hurt. They hope their man will win (although it has to be conceded that at the Ministry of Defence, at least, there were mixed feelings: Mr Heseltine was not universally beloved by his Generals and his Admirals). But as far as possible they would prefer not to get involved.

For while departments expect their ministers to fight the good fight for departmental interests and departmental territory, and to be seen off by a neighbouring predator is regarded as a badge of shame for which the minister will not be forgiven lightly by his mandarins, the whims of 10 Downing Street are accepted as the blows of fate. The mandarins much dislike recruitment by Prime Ministers of personal advisers to second-guess their collective wisdom: when Harold Wilson recruited Thomas (subsequently Lord) Balogh to second-guess the Treasury and the newly created Department of Economic Affairs in 1964, those two departments swiftly conspired with the regular civil staff at No 10 to shut him in an office ('with a blotter and a telephone', it was said with glee) and keep him out of mischief. Ted Heath's invention of the Central Policy Review Staff, or 'Think Tank', although it was partially staffed with career civil servants, and supposed to offer independent advice not just to the Prime Minister, but to the whole Cabinet, was never really accepted in Whitehall. It lingered on through the second Premiership of Harold Wilson, and the Callaghan régime, until it was finally extinguished by Mrs Thatcher, its effectiveness never recovering from the departure in 1974 of its founder. Yet Mrs Thatcher's decision in 1981 to add Professor Walters as her personal financial adviser to her Whitehall staff was viewed with even deeper suspicion by the Treasury; he revealed subsequently (*The Renaissance of Britain*, OUP, 1986) that he had shrewdly insisted on an office in 10 Downing Street, rather than in the Treasury or Cabinet Office, precisely in order to preserve his independence from those two departments. Mrs Thatcher's subsequent insistence upon the appointment of a personal diplomatic adviser outraged the Foreign Office, notwithstanding the fact that her choice fell on a former career diplomat in good standing with his profession. Yet in the end the collective honour and self-respect of a department are not felt to be besmirched by losing a tussle with Number 10, in the way that they are if the tussle lost is with another department.

So the mandarins pride themselves on their skills as Premier-watchers. The complaint is frequently voiced that Mrs Thatcher has broken with hallowed traditions of Whitehall impartiality by demanding an unquestioning, almost fawning, allegiance as the price of preferment to the topmost rungs of the civil service. This is almost entirely fiction. Prime Ministerial preferences inevitably influence selection for Whitehall's prizes: they always have, and they always will. It was Harold Macmillan, not Margaret

Thatcher, who defied the Whitehall *mores* and publicly humiliated the Treasury by imposing upon it, as Permanent Secretary, a career diplomat summoned home from Washington. The present Prime Minister, far from favouring toadies, likes to deal with those who know how to stand up to her. But the Permanent Secretary who failed to keep himself abreast of Prime Ministerial instincts with potential impact on his departmental strategies would be reckoned by his caste to be falling down on the job, under this or any other Administration.

No other Whitehall department, however, needs to watch the shifts of sentiment at Number 10 with greater care than the Treasury. For it is part of Whitehall folklore – and a generally reliable part at that – that the Treasury, sole protector of the public purse and advocate for the nation's taxpayers, can never hope to win its perpetual battles with the spending ministries unless it has the backing of the Prime Minister; but equally that *if* the Prime Minister and Chancellor are of one mind, then they outnumber all the rest.

Heclo and Wildavski (*op cit*) graphically describe the still-poignant memories (at the time they were writing, in the mid-sixties) in the Treasury of the dreadful days in the late 1950s when the sun of Prime Ministerial favour was withdrawn from them. Harold Macmillan is the only Prime Minister in modern times who came to office with a preconception which he never shed (and has not shed today, as his recent speeches in the House of Lords bear witness) that the Treasury was Up To No Good. He saw himself, as his memoirs tell us, as a lone Cassandra prophesying the new world slump the Treasury had in store for us. (Although a professional classicist, that lady's reputation for *accurate* predictions of disaster never appear to have struck him as constituting an inappropriate parallel to his own chosen role). The first four years of his rule are even now remembered in Great George Street as a time of exile.

Harold Wilson, a self-confessed plagiarist of the Macmillan style, also entered Downing Street in 1964 full of ideas for cutting the misers of the Treasury down to size. But it did not take the Treasury (or Whitehall in general, for that matter) very long to get the measure of Harold Wilson. They soon discovered that they were dealing with a timid soul to whom appearances were all, and substance scarcely interesting. He set up the Department of Economic Affairs ostensibly to divide and rule the Treasury (his critics saw it, perhaps more accurately, as no more than a device to get his mercurial erstwhile rival, George Brown, out of his hair). But within weeks the first sterling crisis which swiftly followed the 1964 Election brought him to the Treasury's heel; and thenceforth his characteristic obsession with the pound exchange rate – though not of the Treasury's choosing – tied him hand and foot to Great George Street.

Ted Heath soon proved determined to be his own Chancellor, at any rate from the untimely death of Iain Macleod within weeks of his election. This was not a relationship much to the Treasury's liking. Although its ingrained departmental neo-Keynesian upbringing found his incomes policy corporatism from 1971 much more *sympathique* than the free market 'Selsdon' period which had preceded it, it was profoundly sceptical about his simultaneous 'dash for growth'. But it took comfort from the provenance of his all-powerful *eminence grise*: Sir William Armstrong came from the Treasury stable. Maybe they would have preferred a more equal partnership with 10 Downing Street. But at least there was a partnership.

Harold Wilson's second Government offered no unexpected shocks: Whitehall knew their man. Bernard (now Lord Donoughue, whom Harold Wilson had recruited from *academe* to run a new 'political Think Tank' at No 10 following the first Election of 1974, recently described on television his dismay at the absence, as the summer of that year wore on, of any warnings from the Treasury about the imminent financial crisis which he felt looming. Finally he took a senior Treasury mandarin out to lunch to protest. The response was simple, and conclusive. 'It's no use', his guest replied. 'Of course you're right. But until the Government has fought – and won – another Election we might as well save our breath.' The Treasury knows its politicians. Jim Callaghan was the first Prime Minister since Macmillan to have done time in the Treasury, and unlike Macmillan he was rightly deemed to know which side his bread was buttered.

So for the Treasury – indeed for Whitehall as a whole – the next big shock to the system occurred in the autumn of 1980. Here there was no conflict with No 10's priorities: Mrs Thatcher's commitment to the Treasury's ambitions for constrained public expenditure and more nearly balanced public budgeting left that department breathless. As the Government headed for the annual Whitehall horse-deal over public spending programmes, the Prime Minister led, with the Chancellor clumping gamely in her wake. But contrary to all Whitehall conventions, they lost. They lost painfully in public: the Prime Minister's Cabinet dissenters saw to that. Now by village custom that should have been more or less the end of the Thatcher Government. It didn't work out that way. Come Budget time in 1981 the Prime Minister decided, her Chancellor anxiously acquiescing, that the nation should be made to pay – literally – for the *gourmandise* of her spending ministers. Contrary to all received opinion, taxes, in the depths of recession, did not go down; they went up. The Treasury, like the rest of Whitehall, was adapting itself to a most unusual Prime Minister.

Prime Ministers constitute, for the dwellers in the Whitehall village, one end of the spectrum of political authority which it is their task to steer. Junior ministers constitute the other end. Departments have to make the best of the Cabinet Minister they are stuck with. For better or worse he – or she – carries their flag in Cabinet, and his or her humours and fancies therefore have to be accommodated, at any rate so long as they do not conflict too directly with a departmental interest or shibboleth. If they do so conflict then departments can always play the waiting game. As Crossman put it perceptively (*Inside View*, op cit) 'If we think of the civil servants as marine animals and the politicians as fishermen operating on the surface, we will have some idea of relations between the two. The civil service takes a long view. It knows that the boatloads of politicians now anchored above them are certain to be changed within five years'.

The junior ministers – Ministers of State, and Parliamentary Under-Secretaries – are a different matter. Some Whitehall mandarins (although not, I should add, the ones I encountered in the Treasury) are inclined to think of them as little more than public relations officers for the department, reading out the departmental script in answer to late-night debates in the House of Commons, or to dinners of the department's satellite lobby-groups, topping and tailing departmental answers to MPs, and keeping their opinions to themselves. If they should get ideas above their station, then their chiefs – the departmental Cabinet ministers – can always be appealed to to overrule them. In the early months of the Heath Administration, one junior minister in the Department of Industry chaired a meeting with the management of British Steel. British Steel was seeking a 6 percent price increase. The minister enquired 'why six percent? Is that your assessment of what your market will take?' 'Well no', replied the steelmen, 'we reckon the market would take an increase of up to 12 percent'. 'In that case', asked the Minister, 'why not go for 12?' The senior civil servants were aghast. 'But Minister', they exclaimed in alarm, 'that would conflict with Government policy to hold nationalised industry prices down'. The Minister was unrepentant. It was British Steel's job, he insisted, to maximise its profitability. If it thought it could get away with 12 percent, then 12 percent was what they should be going for.

The civil servants promptly went in search of the Secretary of State, who rapidly agreed with them that six percent was more than enough. Within months the junior Minister had been despatched once more to the back benches. The Whitehall assessment that he was altogether too opinionated for his station, although not the only, or perhaps the major, reason for his eviction, was a contributory factor.

Yet Whitehall also rapidly adjusts when it is confronted with a reversal of the normal order of power and influence. Legend has it that all new appointees to junior office in the Treasury are told the cautionary tale of Winston Churchill's Financial Secretary during his tenure of the Exchequer in the 1920s. One evening when the Finance Bill was passing through the Commons, Winston had gone out to dinner, leaving the Financial Secretary in charge. The FST's brief for the debate on the particular amendment under discussion was marked 'resist'. Unfortunately some powerful Government backbenchers spoke up in favour of the amendment.

The Government Whip on duty warned the FST that he was going to have to concede. Eventually, he did. The next morning he was sacked. Here again, I have to add that nobody ever mentioned this piece of cautionary Whitehall folklore to me.

Some junior Ministers, at any rate, break the rules and get away with it. Harold Lever was a spectacular case in point in the first Wilson Administration. Members of the Parliamentary Committee to which, by that time, the Finance Bill had been consigned for detailed scrutiny, watched with fascination as the Financial Secretary faithfully read out his brief to resist a particular amendment, and then cheerfully conceded that it seemed a lousy case to him. He accepted the amendment. He survived.

Harold Lever was an exception to most rules. Apart from anything else, the Labour Government had soon discovered his usefulness as someone – perhaps the only politician in its ranks – who could plead Labour's cause with the sceptical financiers of the International Monetary Fund, and win them over. He was indispensable.

Another interesting exception when he held junior office was the present Chancellor. Following the formation of the Treasury team after the 1979 General Election, the Treasury mandarins soon realised that their new Financial Secretary was the man to watch. He espoused with crusading vigour the notion of a 'medium-term financial strategy': a four-year flow-chart for the management of the economy which would set out specific goals, for public borrowing, the money supply, and inflation – and be published. The mandarins saw this as a hostage to fortune. The Chief Secretary, John Biffen, a sceptic with low expectations of the ability of any Government to do much for good (or for that matter much for evil, but rather more), had no patience with such fancy scheming. The Bank of England saw nothing but trouble. Nevertheless the Financial Secretary's advocacy prevailed. The Prime Minister listened to him; the Chancellor found him too awkward to contravene; and he was not afraid of staring down the formidable Governor of the Bank of England. The mandarins took note: and adjusted accordingly.

5

The Guided Missile

It is time to return from the general to the particular. As I have already noted, my specific responsibilities as Minister of State and then as Economic Secretary at the Treasury concerned essentially two areas: monetary policy, and relations with the financial sector; and customs and excise.

Like the Inland Revenue, the Customs and Excise might be described as a 'Quago' – a Quasi-autonomous Governmental Institution. They have their own staff, and their own career structure, reporting to a Chairman who may – indeed usually does – emerge from the Treasury mandarinate, but who swiftly 'goes native'. Their task, until 1971, concerned essentially the collection of the so-called 'excise duties' – taxes on spirits, tobacco, and petrol, and the collection of duties on imported goods. They were also concerned with the supervision of export and import documentation, and the application of the related budgetary rules.

In 1971 they underwent a major transformation. They took on responsibility for VAT. Since this too was an expenditure tax (as opposed to the assorted taxes on incomes and on capital, where the Inland Revenue held sway), it was undoubtedly the logical place for VAT to rest. Nevertheless Whitehall legend has it that the Inland Revenue fiercely contested the allocation – territorial disputes can occur within individual Whitehall village kraals. But the Customs and Excise won. Their victory resulted in a substantial extension of Customs and Excise territory, personnel, and political exposure.

Value-added tax, introduced as one of the obligations we assumed following our accession to the European Community, has much to commend it by comparison with the tax which, for us, it replaced: purchase tax. For purchase tax applied to a relatively restricted range of consumer goods. As a result changes in the rate of purchase tax could have a dramatic impact on the industries to which it applied. From the sixties onwards to its demise, Governments had endowed themselves with powers to raise or cut the rate of purchase tax by ten per cent for purposes of general economic management. Because of its far wider spread, increases or reductions in VAT by a single percentage point could have the same impact on Government revenues.

Some continental Governments apply VAT to virtually all consumer purchases (albeit sometimes at varying rates). The pressure of influential lobbies had ensured that our VAT system was riddled with 'zero rates' – which meant that farmers, builders, and most nationalised industries could reclaim the VAT element in the purchases, without charging VAT on their sales – while others, less wholly fortunate, such as the small business sector, were made 'exempt' – which meant that they did not have to charge the tax to their customers, but could not recover it on their purchases either. The resulting tax 'frontiers' were frequently uneasily, if at all, reconcilable with logic. They caused me a lot of trouble.

However, my first major assignment with the Customs and Excise concerned our excise duties. In particular our excise duties on beer and wine. For some time the European Commission had been campaigning for the harmonisation of national duties on alcohol. There were many cross-currents of interest at stake. The French, and still more the Italians, had for long been accused by the Scotch whisky industry of practising discrimination against Scotch by rigging their duty structure in favour of home-produced brandy and grappa. The Germans were similarly charged with artificially sustaining their home wine production *vis-à-vis* imported wines from France and Italy; while the French had from time to time brazenly flouted Community rules to keep out Italian wine. We were in the dock for perpetuation of an excessive – by Community standards – disparity between duties on beer (low) and duties on wine (high).

In the second half of 1981 Britain held the chair in the Community (a position which rotates between the member-countries every six months). This meant that for major meetings of the Council of Ministers of the Community we had to field two Ministers: one to take the chair, and one to represent HMG. At lesser meetings one Minister was deemed to suffice, to take the chair: HMG was represented by a senior civil servant.

It thus came as a rude shock to me to find that almost my first assignment after entering the Treasury in the autumn of 1981 was to preside over a meeting of the Community's Customs Council consisting of the national Ministers responsible for Customs and Excise Duties, called in that most inaccessible of Europe's several headquarter-cities, Strasbourg, to consider the awkward topic of alcohol duty harmonisation.

First I had to be briefed by the Chairman of Customs and Excise, Sir Douglas Lovelock. Sir Douglas was – is – a gallant Christian gentleman to whom I fear I caused a certain amount of trouble and disappointment. My task in Strasbourg, Sir Douglas explained to me, was to preside over the meeting in such a manner as to ensure that it would fail.

I suppose I looked slightly fazed by this explanation. 'Yes, Minister', Sir Douglas assured me with a cheerful mixture of metaphors which seemed entirely appropriate, 'we're throwing you in at the deep end. From now on it'll be downhill all the way.' The point was that harmonisation of beer and wine duties would *not* suit HMG one little bit. It would involve either a large cut in our taxes on wines, which the Chancellor would not appreciate, or else a substantial increase in beer duties, which would bump up the retail price index and, even more serious, be highly politically contentious.

I mentioned frivolously that personally I never touched beer, and had a strong addiction to wine. Harmonisation sounded like a splendid wheeze to me. Sir Douglas patiently explained that, be that as it might, I would not win friends and influence people if I went down that road. I hastily conceded his point.

Fortunately, Sir Douglas added, nobody else really wanted harmonisation either. But there was a snag. The Commission was running out of patience with the Council of Ministers. A number of suits before the European Court were pending, against a number of member Governments, including HMG, on this particular issue, and it was therefore vital to 'keep the ball in play'. So long as the Council continued to pretend that it was vigorously pursuing harmonisation, the Commission, which was the plaintiff in the pending suits before the Court, would have to hold its hand.

So my task was to make sure that the Council failed to reach agreement; but to avoid an admission of failure; and – above all – to ensure that the blame for our failure to agree rested on the shoulders of some other participant, and not – repeat not – on the shoulders of HMG. 'You see, Minister, as President, you've got somehow to contrive to give the impression that you want us to reach an accord even though, as I say, you don't.'

Eager to enter into the spirit of these interesting diplomatic manoeuvres, I enquired who was to be the fall-guy. The French, I suggested, knowing the pleasure which our civil service takes in scoring off the wicked froggies? 'Well, no, Minister', the worldly-wise Sir Douglas advised, 'I don't think that would be a good idea on the whole. I think I'd go for the Greeks if you can. Nobody likes the Greeks'. Since the Greeks seemed to be a little peripheral to the argument I was worried about this. But I promised to do my best.

We set off for Strasbourg by air. Our party consisted of my Private Secretary, Sir Douglas, and a trio of his Customs henchmen. I apparently ranked a first-class seat on the aeroplane, and my Private Secretary took up station at my right hand. But not for long. First-class accommodation on the Strasbourg 'plane was limited, and Sir Douglas had 'matters to discuss'. So my Private Secretary was rapidly dislodged.

Needless to say we had copious dossiers for the meeting ahead of us. But fortunately we didn't seem to have all that much in the way of urgent business to discuss on the flight. So instead I told Sir Douglas about my only personal experience with his minions.

I had been a 'VAT trader' in my days of innocence as a backbencher, and had been notified one day that the VAT inspector wished to pay me a visit. I had protested that my VAT affairs were so basic that there was really nothing to inspect. 95 percent of all the VAT I collected from my customers passed straight on to the Customs and Excise (after a three months' delay which did my cash flow no harm at all: but that is the system).

The VAT-men had been obdurate: inspected I was going to be. In due course two of them, a lady and a gentleman, had descended on my doorstop. They had been civility itself (and I was to learn in the ensuing months that allegations of 'Gestapo tactics' on the part of the Customs and Excise invariably came from citizens who were happily engaged in trying to fiddle their books: and that my fellow-MPs were often too gullible by half in swallowing horrendous tales from crooks). But I had to tell Sir Douglas that the purpose of the VAT lady's presence had been obscure. She had never opened her mouth. 'I expect she was under instruction', he suggested. To which I felt bound to reply that, if so, she was starting late, being all of 55.

We had had, I recalled, some awkward moments. At one point the VAT-man with the speaking part had detected a shortfall of something like £1,000 in my returns for a single quarter. Since my VAT business was distinctly modest, I had been shaken. Fortunately, however, I had been able to point out that the VAT-man was working on the cumulative annual figure for my VAT business with the customer under scrutiny; and that since we were looking at the fourth quarter of the VAT year, this might, I hoped, explain the disparity.

Alas! It had done no such thing. The VAT-man, having hastily redone his sums, had announced that it now appeared that I had overpaid by some £600. That had seemed like good news, but still improbable to me. Eventually, I recalled, I had noticed that the VAT-man was consulting a computer printout relating to the fourth quarter of 1978, whereas the return we were agonising over related to the fourth quarter of 1979. After an hour and a half the VAT-man had finally informed me that he reckoned they owed me 6p, and would I be prepared to put that down to experience? I had replied that I'd happily pay him and his companion £100 to depart and allow me to get on with my work.

'And I suppose this will be taken down and used in

evidence against us', Sir Douglas commented ruefully. I conceded that it might be.

So we arrived in Strasbourg. The following morning my first appointment was with Sir Kenneth Christofas, a senior British diplomat on the staff of my erstwhile Westminster colleague, Christopher Tugendhat, who had been unexpectedly elevated to the position of second British Commissioner in Brussels by Jim Callaghan (legend had it that his most important qualification for the post had been an inability to speak French, since Callaghan's first Commissioner, Roy Jenkins, was not proficient in that language, and had not wished to be upstaged by his team mate). With innocent but misplaced frankness I told Sir Kenneth that, as I understood it, our purpose was to abort the meeting as swiftly as could decently be achieved. Sir Kenneth was aghast.

Naturally, he conceded, Her Majesty's Government might have views about the harmonisation of taxes on wine and beer about which he, as a servant of the Commission, could know nothing. But it was a matter of life and death, certainly for the good name of the Community, but also – he ventured to suggest – for the reputation of the British Government, that I, as President *ad interim* of that afternoon's Council, should be, and be seen to be, dedicated to the discovery of a generally acceptable compromise outcome. It would not be easy, that he acknowledged. But we must bust a gut if need be.

We proceeded to a gargantuan meal at one of Strasbourg's better restaurants (where the risk of busting guts appeared to me considerable), during which a fair amount of preliminary sparring was conducted. As President I found myself subjected to bizarre courtship rituals, being advised by Sir Kenneth Christofas, who had now emerged as my principal minder, entirely displacing Sir Douglas Lovelock, hovering anxiously in the background, to take pudding with the Italian Minister, and coffee with the French. Then there was a second round of coffee, *tête-à-tête* with Christopher Tugendhat, his mandarins, and the ubiquitous Sir Kenneth. I naïvely assumed that Christopher and I, as old backbench (and even before that *Financial Times*) contemporaries could dispense with the diplomatic niceties. There was, I pointed out, a 5 pm 'plane from Strasbourg back to London, and I was keen to catch it. Since it was obvious from our lunchtime conversations that nobody was remotely interested in a settlement, I suggested that we cut the cackle, agree to disagree, and disperse.

Once again, dismay. 'I think', Sir Kenneth hastily intervened, 'the Minister is understandably disappointed by the conversations over lunch. But I am sure, Commissioner, you would agree with me that appearances can be deceptive. The Minister will, I am sure, wish to impress upon his Ministerial colleagues the gravity of the situation which would arise in the absence of agreement this afternoon.' The Commissioner agreed emphatically.

OK, I said, so we'll give it a whirl. We would conduct the time-hallowed ritual known in Community circles as a '*tour de table*'. This is a stately minuet in which the Chairman invites each of the Ministers seated round the table to read out his brief. But if, as looked to be self-evident, these briefs displayed a gulf of conflict, then we would call it a day. That seemed to be acceptable. Or so I thought.

We all assembled. After a suitable and apparently indispensable exchange of *politesses*, we launched upon our *tour de table*. Sure enough this demonstrated that nobody agreed about anything. I told Christofas, seated at my left hand, that I proposed to recognise our incompatibilities, and call it a day. Once more, consternation. On the contrary, I was told, my only proper course was to call for an adjournment, during which I, as Chairman, would be available to receive suggestions for compromise solutions from my colleagues. I did as I was told.

I adjourned to the Presidential suite, where tea was served, and a stream of visitors was ushered in, led by Christopher Tugendhat who, far from being amenable to an acknowledgement of failure, now warned sternly that all sorts of Governments – and most certainly our own – would find themselves promptly in the dock if the Council dispersed without agreement.

Eventually we all reassembled. Taking a line which caused Sir Kenneth Christofas considerable distress, I said that we seemed to have come to an impasse, and suggested that we might as well call it a day. Immediately the French representative asked to be heard. He felt, he told us, that in fact some useful progress had been made, and he suggested that we should adjourn and agree to meet again in three weeks' time, at which point he was confident that compromise solutions would be found. This was a proposition which commanded general support (after all, the more the meetings, the more the allowances properly claimed by all and sundry). And thus it was resolved.

Three weeks later we duly met again. Apparently honour had been satisfied. Another Lucillan feast was digested, and then one and all rapidly acknowledged that there was no possibility of agreement about anything. The Commission would have to do its worst at the European Court. Everybody dispersed cheerfully for the Christmas holidays. At least the threat of an immediate obligation to harmonise our duties upon wine and beer had been averted, and to that extent I had presumably done my duty. But I was left with a suspicion that, as a Community diplomatist, I had left something to be desired.[1]

I was to attend one more Customs Council. The precise bone of contention on that occasion escapes me, since so did the actual meeting. It was in the middle of a period of exceptionally severe weather in December 1982. I was suddenly told on Saturday, when I was spending the weekend at my farmhouse in Cheshire, that my presence was required – in Brussels, on this occasion – on the Monday morning. So shortly before midnight on Sunday I set out to catch the overnight sleeper from Crewe. The car broke down, and I missed the train. Instead I had to catch the milk train, leaving

[1] There was an entertaining postscript to this affair. In due course the Commission had indeed gone on to take the British Government, amongst others, to Court. Introducing his first Budget, in the spring of 1984, Nigel Lawson conceded mournfully that he was obliged by the Community to harmonise our wine and beer taxes. This would, most regrettably, oblige us to thump up taxes on the people's beer. The Opposition howled in anticipation. Having got them salivating eagerly he finally announced that he was in fact going to go most of the way by cutting wine duties: the increase in the duty on beer would be (from the Opposition's point of view) a distinctly disappointing 1½p per pint. By skilful stage management he had persuaded the Labour Party to fall into a mantrap. His handling of this secondary issue contributed substantially to the presentational triumph of his Budget.

at 3.15 in the morning. It was unheated, and I arrived half frozen at Euston, whence I was whisked to a Heathrow deep in snow. No 'planes were taking off. So after a reviving breakfast I rang my office at the Treasury to say I couldn't get to Brussels, and was coming in. My private office, however, insisted that the honour of the British nation depended on my travelling to Brussels. Around 11 am we were invited to climb aboard the Brussels 'plane. That was as far as we got. After sitting on the ground for half an hour, we were bussed back to base. I rang the Treasury again; but still they begged me to hang on at all costs. Eventually we took off sometime after noon. I arrived to find the meeting finished, and my colleagues adjourning to a salubrious watering-hole, where we consumed a huge lunch, drank numerous toasts, wished each other compliments of the season, and departed to the airport for our various journeys home. It had, I reckoned, been quite an expensive luncheon for the British taxpayers.

I also attended one Budget Council of the Community. This was a more heavyweight affair: an annual exercise to determine (very approximately and most haphazardly) what the Community should spend in the year ahead. I owed my presence to the British 'presidency': my colleague the Financial Secretary, who would normally have represented the British Government, had to take the chair, and I his place as leader of the UK team.

We started at 10 in the morning, and worked at a fairly leisurely pace up to 1 pm, when there was the usual large and lengthy luncheon. We then resumed at about 3.30 pm, and struggled on through the evening. My role, as it was explained to me, was to keep a fairly low profile, offering occasional suggestions designed to help my colleague Nicholas Ridley in the chair, while at the same time protecting British interests (which, I was glad to find, were essentially concerned with keeping as tight a grip as might be on the purse-strings.

Progress appeared to be minimal. There were endless *tours de table*, interspersed with regular adjournments, during which (as I had done in Strasbourg), Nicholas Ridley held court. At about 8 in the evening an extremely modest pack meal was served to us at the conference table; at about 11 pm we were offered whisky. The night drew wearily on. The patience and good humour of my Treasury colleague astonished me – how different, I realised, from my own performance in the chair at Strasbourg.

Around 3 am the Irish Minister asked to speak. He had, he revealed, a compromise proposal to put forward. He did so. 'Well,' said the Financial Secretary, 'I am sure that we are all grateful to our Irish colleague for that suggestion. Only I confess I thought we had already tried that one about three hours ago, and it didn't seem to command much support. But if colleagues feel we should try it again, I'd be very happy to do so.' Nobody dissented, so he did.

Round the table we went. The Belgian voted in favour, the Frenchman against, the German abstained, the Irishman . . . voted against. Back to the drawing-board.

Finally, at 5.30 in the morning, agreement of sorts was reached. The Belgian, as the next name on the Presidential rota, proposed a lengthy and flowery (and also, it seemed to me, well-deserved) vote of thanks to M. le Président, which was carried *nem con*. Nicholas Ridley thanked the assembled company, and rose to his feet.

At this point so did the Greek delegate. 'I have to inform the Council, on behalf of my Government, that it is not prepared to accept the latest proposals before the Council.' Nicholas Ridley cheerfully thanked the Greek, and announced that the meeting was adjourned. Everybody, including the Greek, seemed happy.

Most of my business with the Customs, however, was domestic. A constant theme throughout my time at the Treasury was economy in manpower. The Prime Minister had decreed, shortly after taking office in 1979, a target for her first Parliament: to reduce the size of the civil service to its lowest level since the war. Considerable progress had already been made before I got to Great George Street: but inevitably the going was getting tougher all the time. Much could be achieved by something akin to sleight-of-hand: a public asset sold off to the private sector, or a service contracted out to private firms to provide, naturally took its manpower with it. There was, however, but limited scope for such easy ways out for the Treasury departments. Yet the Treasury, as the department once more responsible for the management of the civil service, had to set a good example.

This process soon produced a fine example of one of Whitehall's favourite ploys: the 'bleeding stump' syndrome. This involves the selection by the mandarins of a proposal for economy which they are quietly confident the politicians will not swallow. Sir Douglas Lovelock produced a wizard scheme to prevent traders whose annual turnover for VAT did not reach the threshhold at which VAT registration became compulsory from registering.[1]

It was an impeccably logical proposition. Manpower savings which would result from non-collection of VAT from small traders would handsomely surpass revenue thereby foregone (indeed there would be a net saving if the VAT threshold were lifted substantially higher – to £50,000 a year or thereabouts – but that would be against Community rules). But it was politically fraught.

Tens of thousands of small farmers – mostly residing in Tory-held constituencies – would be up in arms. For farmers, as already mentioned, are zero–rated. Unlike other small traders, they can reclaim the VAT on their purchases, without charging it on their sales. And then there were the barristers. Many beginners at the bar, it seems, like to register for VAT simply in order to impress solicitors who might employ their services, by creating the impression that they are already in a larger way of business than they really are. This gentle deception hardly seems a good and sufficient reason for not changing the law to ban small-trader registration (as the Customs fairly pointed out to us). But the Lord Chancellor, ever a vigilant defender of his profession, would have blown his top. We knew, and the Customs and Excise also knew, that however defensible the proposition might be in a logical world, we would not dare to try it on.

So less politically contentious alternatives had to be sought. Lord Rayner and his team of Whitehall sleuths,

[1] As already explained, small traders are VAT 'exempt'. Each year the VAT 'threshold' is adjusted upwards – it is currently approaching £20,000. Those whose annual turnover does not reach that figure do not have to register. This means that they do not have to charge VAT on their sales – but by the same token they cannot recover VAT on their purchases. But they are free to register if they wish to do so.

whose task it was to identify economies, had come up with some quite far-reaching proposals by which Customs coverage would be withdrawn from some of the less frequented ports and airports; and traders wishing to clear goods – and even passengers – arriving out of normal hours, or at weekends or holidays, would be charged a service charge to reflect the costs involved.

This, too, proved a little hot to handle. An interdepartmental committee (one of Whitehall's classic stalling ploys) had been set up to consider the implications. The Departments of Trade and Transport were furiously opposed. The argument was not resolved while I was at the Treasury. But in practice it was obvious that the Rayner team's suggestion would get nowhere.

It did, however, produce a side-effect. Word went out from Cabinet that, if the withdrawal of existing Customs cover was too much to ask for, at least the Customs would not be obliged to *extend* cover to small ports and airports not currently enjoying it where the likely scale of traffic would not justify it. This ruling proved scarcely less contentious.

I was soon receiving urgent letters and deputations from my Parliamentary colleagues, many of whom turned out to have local airports with limitless potential for development if only the Customs would help instead of hindering. I gritted my teeth. It seemed to me that I could not very well require the Customs to provide facilities for which they could convince me there was no prospective justification, and at the same time expect them to reduce their numbers.

In due course there was a hiccup. A Scottish independent airline operating out of Aberdeen, Air Ecosse, was seeking Customs coverage at Wick airport. This would enable them to operate a service between Iceland and Aberdeen and the Faroes. Unless they could discharge and pick up passengers at Wick, the service, it seemed, would not be viable. And since those passengers might be coming from, or going to, destinations outside the UK, customs clearance was essential.

It was a not unalluring proposition. Air Ecosse was a thrusting, free enterprise airline: just the sort of business the Government was out to help. Yet if we conceded Customs coverage at Wick, the Customs swiftly pointed out to me, the flood-gates would open. There were at least a dozen other airports around the country also seeking Customs coverage, with a larger turnover in prospect than Wick.

The civil service is often accused of obsession with the avoidance of dangerous precedent. In a perfect system – or the infinitely less politically sensitive system operated by, for example, the French – it would no doubt be possible for Ministers to exercise untrammelled discretion: to say that because Air Ecosse is our sort of business, we will give it privilege, and tell the rest to get lost. But those who criticise our civil servants' fear of precedent-creation are ignoring the brutal logic of our system. Precedent, in this country, is taken down and used in evidence. On this the civil service caution is eminently justified.

Nevertheless, over Wick the Scottish lobby got to work. In the end my erstwhile school contemporary, the Scottish Secretary, accepted the inescapable if awkward logic of the Cabinet decision. However the leader of the Scottish Nationalists, Donald Stewart, joined the fray. Exercising the privilege of a Privy Councillor, he wrote to the Prime Minister direct. A suitable reply was laboriously composed. But it was not sent. Eventually I was warned that the Prime Minister was not happy with it. I was summoned to the presence. As all who have dealings with our present Prime Minister rapidly discover, she is nothing if not fully briefed. No matter how minuscule the issue – and Wick airport was hardly in the mega category – she invariably knows the papers backward. Fortunately I managed to persuade her. It did occur to me to wonder whether this was the ideal use of a Prime Minister's crowded schedule. On the other hand it also occurred to me that a system of Government which persuades the Prime Minister to engage herself in such minutiae could hardly be accused of insensitivity (even if it was).

Once a year the Customs and Excise had a celebratory dinner. This was, for me, the equivalent of the Parliamentary three-line whip. Attendance was compulsory (even if – as happened two years running – I was escaping for a few days' fishing in Scotland the next morning, and hence had to set off from the dinner to drive through the night). The first year I was bidden not just to attend, but also to speak. Sir Douglas presented me with a suitable text, in which I was to express admiration verging on idolatry for the loyalty, devotion to duty, etc. etc. of all our brave excisemen, and also – or so it seemed to me – to sympathise with their plight in having to cope with a heartless and fundamentally hostile Administration. I slightly toned down the first part of these sentiments, and dropped the second.

But it was the problem of numbers which complicated my relations with the Customs and Excise throughout my stay at the Treasury. They argued that restrictions on recruitment and staff numbers were threatening, in particular, to turn VAT into a 'voluntary tax' – a tax which traders were in danger of coming to think they could evade with impunity. Already, I was told, it was proving only possible to inspect those traders who were deemed to be least at risk about once every eight years on average, and that was far too infrequent a visitation to enforce the law.

I was never convinced by these arguments. It seemed to me that the Customs and Excise's first duty was the maximisation of revenue rather than the pursuit of possible malingerers. I accepted that a point could theoretically arise at which traders would feel that they could default with impunity; but judging from my ministerial postbag we were light years from there. On the contrary, most small traders felt themselves to be pursued by the VAT-man in a way that they were not by the Inland Revenue. I continued to believe (I still do) that the Customs devoted excessive, and labour-intensive, resources to the supervision of relatively low-risk, low-return quarters of their parish. Certainly they could show that additional VAT inspectors employed in hot pursuit were cost-effective. They did not dispel my instinct to believe that far more restricted manpower resources devoted to the areas of highest potential return would be far *more* cost-effective.

I was invited to have a look at one of the Customs 'Collections', or area commands. Chester was chosen for the purpose, and I was given a comprehensive survey of the pursuit of pornography, drugs and smuggling in the estuary of the Mersey, as well as of the more humdrum business of VAT collection over a scattered area. Who, I asked, was their largest single VAT customer. GEC at Stafford was the reply. And did they pay their VAT bills on time? No, I was less than astonished to hear, they did not. And how much difference would it make to the Collection's cash flow, I wondered, if GEC at Stafford could somehow be persuaded to pay up one week earlier than they normally did. The answer, it transpired, was that the Collection's cash flow would be transformed. There seemed to be a moral here of sorts, I thought.

I cannot leave the Customs without mentioning the affair of the 'rum letter'. In the run-up to the 1982 Budget, the excisemen came to me with a proposal for the phasing-out of a special duty on immature spirits. This duty had, I was told, originally been introduced during the First World War to discourage munitions workers from drinking red biddy. It was relatively expensive to collect, and yielded almost nothing. Furthermore the Common Market did not like it. I was assured that 'the stocks were sold, the press was squared, the middle classes quite prepared' – in particular there was on the file a letter from the most important of the 'middle classes' in this context, the Scotch Whisky Association, saying that, while they were not keen on the idea, they were prepared to live with it providing the duty (which was a mild deterrent to some imported competitors for the domestic Scotch market) was phased out and not abolished overnight – a point which the Customs had conceded. So I gave the OK.

Two or three days after Budget Day there was a minor explosion. A letter, written on the very eve of the Budget, had been despatched from the Scotch Whisky Association not to the Treasury, but to their sponsoring Ministry, Agriculture, to protest that the phasing-out of the immature spirits duty would spell the end of the world as the Scotch whisky industry knew it. I was not particularly surprised. In days of yore, when I had myself represented a Scots constituency at Westminster, I had frequently witnessed the elephantine clumsiness with which this particular pressure group endeavoured to defend the interests of its clients.

The Customs told me that, in their judgment, if we did not move on the immature spirits duty we were quite likely to be taken to Court by the Brussels Commission; that if we were we would certainly lose; and that if we did lose there would be no question of phasing out the duty in a genteel manner: it would have to go in one fell swoop. Which, they reckoned, the Scotch whisky industry would find a lot more painful.

Nevertheless it hardly seemed worth a serious Parliamentary row, which the Scotch Whisky Association might easily provoke. So we had them in. I drew their attention to their earlier letters, and gently suggested that if they had had last-minute second thoughts they might at least have had the gumption to get in touch with the Treasury. I pointed out the European hazard. Now that we had announced our intention in the Budget, the Commission would be all the more likely to act against us if we reversed it.

They were duly contrite. Yes, they had had second thoughts. Yes, they should have told the Treasury. But it really was a matter of life and death. They would happily run the risk of a European prosecution. But would we please, please, withdraw the relevant clause.

So I said, 'On your head be it. If the Brussels Commission puts us in the dock, don't come to us for sympathy.' But rather than simply withdrawing the offending clause, we could at least win brownie points on the Tory back benches by allowing one of our Scots MPs to put down an amendment to scrap it, and then yielding gracefully to his persuasive oratory.

Which is what we did. It all went swimmingly. Our Scots colleague got glowing press notices for sticking up for Scottish interests, and the Treasury basked in a warm glow of back bench approval. But not for very long.

Some weeks later I discovered, nestling coyly in my overnight red box, an interesting exchange of correspondence with the Rum Importers' Association. First there was a furious letter from the Association, which pointed out that when Customs had first canvassed the idea of abolishing the immature spirits duty round the spirit trade the previous autumn they had responded – copy enclosed – to the effect that, for them, abolition was essential, and could not come too soon. Consequently they had been delighted by the appearance of the promised clause in the Budget – and outraged by its subsequent withdrawal. They had been even more outraged, on perusing Hansard, to discover that I had not even shown a trace of awareness that they had an interest in the matter – even that they existed.

Appended to this letter was a draft reply for me to sign. This had me say that I was saddened to see that they were in such a pet. But of course I had known all about their interest in the matter: it was just one of those occasions when somebody has to be sacrificed for the greater good of the nation as a whole.

I declined to sign. When, I asked, had I been alerted to the interest of the Rum Importers' Association in the matter? So far as I could recollect the Association was absolutely right: I had indeed been unaware of their existence.

My Private Secretary swiftly passed this bad news back to the Customs. He subsequently informed me that they were sure that I had been alerted somewhere, somewhen. Ten days later I found a new draft reply to the Rum Importers' Association sitting in my box. The references to my awareness of their feelings about the immature spirits duty had disappeared. Otherwise the original letter was unchanged.

Once again I declined to sign. I said I assumed that in fact Customs had been quite unable to produce any evidence of my previous awareness of the rum importers' anxieties; and that before any letter went out the whole affair would have to be discussed.

In the end it fortunately transpired that it would be possible to devise a special phasing-out of the duty on rum, and on rum alone. Customs were by no means happy with this: they argued that the rum importers had lived with the duty since time immemorial, and another year or two would not hurt them. Which was indeed perfectly logical. But by now my dander was up, and I was determined that the rum importers should be the beneficiaries of a miscalculation for which I had been expected to carry the can.

6

Expertise vs Loyalty

Hugh Gaitskell is supposed to have complained when he was Chancellor of the Exchequer that the Treasury displayed loyalty without expertise, the Bank of England expertise without loyalty.

Relations between Central Banks and Ministries of Finance around the globe are liable to be fraught. Some Central Banks are highly autonomous. The most obvious examples are the US Federal Reserve, and the German Bundesbank. The 'Fed' owes its autonomy to the security of tenure of its members. They are appointed by the President for a term of 14 years; and, once appointed, are virtually immovable. This means that each successive President has to live with a majority of nominees chosen by his predecessor for at least his first term in office: nor is there any guarantee that his own nominees, once appointed, will prove amenable to the White House. Much depends on the personality of the Chairman. When the Chairman, as is the case with the present incumbent, Paul Volcker, has earned the reputation of being perhaps the outstanding central banker of our generation, his authority is immense, and his control of US monetary policy more or less impervious to pressures from the White House or Congress.

The autonomy of the Bundesbank has a different explanation. As part of the federal structure imposed by the victorious allies on the West German Republic after the war, the central bank was made answerable to the *Länder*. Happily for it the *Länder* have more interesting things to do than to agonise about monetary conditions. So the Bundesbank is arguably the perfect example of the free-wheeler Central Bank.

At the other end of the spectrum of autonomy among central banks come those like the Banque de France, effectively a creature of the Finance Ministry, and the Central Bank of China. I once had an official visit from the deputy Governor of the Bank of China when I was in the Treasury. Over copious cups of Treasury tea, and much nibbling of stale Treasury biscuits, we exchanged notes (through elaborate interpretation) about the relative autonomy of our respective central banks. I had a feeling that the Bank of England man who was bear-leading our eminent visitor around was unsure about one or two of my comments. But the way the autonomy of the Chinese Central Bank came through in interpretation sounded wildly improbable to me, and I am confident that my indiscretions, filtered through, sounded equally improbable in Chinese.

The Bank of England fits somewhere in between. In 1947 the post-war Labour Government, in a gesture of machismo, 'nationalised' the Bank of England. It didn't make much difference. The only Governor of the Bank in its history to be sacked by HMG was Lord Cunliffe, by Lloyd George in 1917. It is at least arguable that nationalisation in practice made the Bank more autonomous, not less. You can always sack your jobbing gardener. Sacking your finance director can prove more adventurous.

Be that as it may, since 1947 the Bank has been, constitutionally, the creature of the Treasury. The Treasury can, in theory, direct the Bank to slash or bump up the exchange rate or interest rates, to sell the sterling reserves or to accumulate them, to abolish exchange controls or to reintroduce them, to sell gilts or to desist from selling them. The only thing it cannot do – in theory – is to sack or appoint the Governor or Deputy Governor, since those posts rest within the patronage of the Prime Minister.

The reality is rather different. Labour Governments, since nationalisation, have proved invariably dependent on the Bank to defend or rescue their credit-worthiness from the scepticism of overseas commercial creditors and the brokers' men of the International Monetary Fund. Tory Governments enjoy a higher international credit-rating. Yet they too soon discover that the Bank cannot necessarily deliver the interest or exchange rates they would like to have, and that they may be no more capable of enforcing monetary policies which the

Bank dislikes than a Labour Government would be (indeed arguably less able).

The Bank has always laid a discreet emphasis on its practical autonomy, whatever the 1947 Act may say. In recent years its Quarterly Bulletin has been used regularly to mark a certain coded distance from Treasury strategies, and some Governors have gone rather further. Lord Cromer in the 1960s repeatedly infuriated Harold Wilson and his Chancellor, Jim Callaghan, with a good deal less than coded public comments on the profligacy of their public spending programmes. He was in an exceptionally strong position, with great personal wealth and a family bank (Baring's) always available to retire to, not to mention the Government's dependence on his support to drum up the international loans it was constantly in need of. Admittedly when his contract expired in 1966 it was not renewed; but it is doubtful whether he was any keener to renew it than the Prime Minister was.

There is also a striking contrast in life-styles between the Bank and Treasury. If the Treasury prides itself on high thinking and plain living, the Bank exudes grandeur. Its corridors are wallpapered with rows of footmen in pink tailcoats. Its Court of Governors dines in a splendour unknown to Whitehall or to Downing Street. Its executive salaries and top-hat pension schemes make the mouths of mandarins salivate with envy.

So there is always tension. It would be unnatural were it otherwise. Treasury men resent the Bank's airs and graces, and are loath to miss a chance to remind it of its subordinate constitutional position. The great men of the Bank, in their turn, are riled by the Treasury's reminders of subordination, and tend to see themselves as men of the world obliged to humour a bunch of theoreticians and hobbledehoys at the other end of town.

To these traditional strains was added, in the early 1980s, something of a conflict of personalities between an exceptionally determined Prime Minister and an exceptionally formidable Governor. Gordon Richardson, a barrister by training who had subsequently run Schroder's merchant bank, had been a surprise choice of Ted Heath's for the Bank of England in the early 1970s. At first he had been almost reclusive – City wags christened the Bank 'the tomb of the unknown Governor'. But he acted with speed, decisiveness and skill when the so-called 'secondary banking crisis' hit the City of London at the end of 1974, and emerged from the affair with considerable prestige. By the time Mrs Thatcher reached Downing Street, Richardson, reappointed to a second five-year term by Jim Callaghan, was widely perceived to be the most dominant central bank Governor London had known since the fabled Monty Norman in the 1930s.

What ensued was not so much a clash of attitudes as a clash of temperaments. Unlike his immediate predecessor, Sir Leslie (subsequently Lord) O'Brien, Gordon Richardson had no instinctive difficulties with 'monetarism'. If he was – like the Bank in general (and much of the Treasury, for that matter) – inclined to be sceptical about the attachment of magic properties to particular monetary targets, he entirely shared the incoming Government's commitment to monetary restraint as an essential precondition for squeezing out inflation. Unfortunately, however, as an unnamed but perceptive source (either Denis Healey or Harold Lever, for sure) remarked to *Daily Telegraph* journalist Grahame Turner at the end of 1981, 'of course Gordon and Maggie don't get on. For she is canine, and he is feline'.

Although I had visited the Bank on several occasions both as a journalist and as a back-bench member of successive Parliamentary Expenditure and Treasury Select Committees, and knew the Governor, his Deputy, Christopher (Kit) McMahon, and several of his senior henchmen quite well, my first encounter with Threadneedle Street as a Minister came as something of a shock.

Within a week of my arrival I was bidden to luncheon with the Governor. On arrival I was ushered up to Kit McMahon who, after a brief exchange about the weather, took me on to the Governor's sanctum. Once again, a brief word of welcome, and then in we passed to a substantial dining-room. Gathered there were about 16 assorted Bank top brass awaiting our arrival. In silence. A glass of sherry was proferred, and then the Govenor took me round the circle of introductions. No-one else spoke. We sat down, myself on the Governor's right hand, Lord Croham (formerly head of the Treasury, and a director of the Bank) on his left, Kit McMahon opposite. Apart from these three, and a rare intervention from the head of the Bank's market operations, Eddie George, no-one round the table used his mouth for any other purpose than to swallow food throughout the entire meal. One and all stared, as if mesmerised, at my host. I emerged to my waiting car sweating.

In private Governor Richardson was – is – a charming and most civilised companion of tremendous courtesy. But there is no doubt that within the Bank, and on official occasions outside it, 'formidable' was the adjective that came to mind. One clearing bank chairman once described a regular meeting of the clearers' club with the Governor at which his colleagues, before getting down to business, had all congratulated the Governor on his handling of the 'Royal Bank affair' (see below). Greatly daring, when his turn came he had followed his congratulations with the comment 'of course the Bank has not always been right'. The Governor's pale blue eyes turned coldly upon him. He persevered unabashed. 'No, Governor, you may recall that one of your predecessors, Monty Norman, took such exception to my bank's decision to set up an international subsidiary that he effectively sent the new subsidiary to Coventry for years. Well, he was wrong about that'. 'That', replied the Governor icily, 'remains to be seen'.

The 'Royal Bank affair' had in fact been one of the more controversial episodes in Gordon Richardson's tenure of the Governorship. In the summer of 1981, before I joined the Treasury, Standard and Chartered had made a bid for the Royal Bank of Scotland, having first obtained the blessing of the Bank of England. The Royal Bank accepted with alacrity: only to be confronted with a rival (and higher) bid from the Hong Kong and Shanghai Bank – which, by all accounts, had neither sought nor received the Bank of England's blessing. An epic battle ensued.

Both suitors upped their bids. City opinion was virtually unanimous that, if matters were left to run their course, Hong Kong and Shanghai would eventually emerge victorious. But it soon became clear that matters were most unlikely to be left to run their course. Rival camps were swiftly formed in Scotland, supporting one or other suitor, or clamouring for the preservation of the Royal Bank's independence. More surprisingly, the Governor went out of his way, when giving evidence to the Commons Treasury Committee in public in the summer, to endorse the acceptability of the Standard and Chartered bid, and to express strong reservations about the suitability of Hong Kong and Shanghai and in particular of the Hong Kong banking regulatory system to which that bank was answerable.

In due course both bids were packed off to the Monopolies and Mergers Commission to be chewed over. Whitehall and the City was, when I reached the Treasury that autumn, awaiting the adjudication of the Commission with bated breath. For if the Commission came down in favour of Standard and Chartered, the colony of Hong Kong, supported by the Foreign Office, would be hopping mad; while were it to give a wave to both the rival bids then, under the rules, the Government would be debarred from intervening (it can clear a bid turned down by the Commission but not – bizarrely – stop a bid which has been cleared) and Hong Kong and Shanghai would presumably win. And what would the Governor do then?

The Treasury, in particular, was on tenterhooks. We were enjoined to a collective vow of silence. A vow which, it would seem, I did not find it altogether easy to observe. Just before Christmas I found myself sitting, at a large City luncheon, next to a distinguished banker who turned out to be both a director of the Royal Bank and helping to mastermind Standard's bid for it – who said the City isn't used to 'Chinese walls'? – and most anxious to talk about both. I kept my responses as monosyllabic as courtesy permitted. However, by sheer chance, I found I had a long-standing engagement to dine with the self-same banker that very evening. When I arrived at his home, who should turn out to be my fellow-guest but Lord Barber, Chairman of Standard. As we 'joined the ladies' after dinner, my wife heard our host addressing Tony Barber. 'I'm afraid', he confided, 'he's not sound.'

Rumours proliferated. It was said that the Monopolies Commission was going to say, like Chairman Mao, 'let a thousand flowers bloom'. The Governor came up with a wizard scheme to pre-empt the Commission with a lightning bill to ban *all* foreign bids for faithful British banks. This did not meet with much favour. It would, we felt, look a little odd abroad, where our faithful British banks had been busy buying up such prizes as the Crocker Bank of California. Besides, it would be against the rules of the European Community.

Happily the Commission did its duty. Neither suitor, it decided, should be allowed to win the hand of Royal Bank. Its report was widely (and perhaps justifiably) criticised as a piece of special pleading for the so-called 'tartan mafia' – the Edinburgh establishment. That's as may be. In Whitehall there were sighs of relief all round. No need for a blazing row with the Foreign Office, or alternatively, to find another Governor. So the Royal Bank lived on to fight another day. As no doubt it will.

The most enduring bone of contention between Treasury, 10 Downing Street and Bank, however, both before and during my turn of ministerial duty, was so-called 'indexed funding'. As inflation had accelerated in the 1970s, independent commentators had increasingly criticised the Treasury for its reliance on fixed-rate funding. It was argued that those who lent their money to the Government were being taken for a ride as the rate of interest on their capital ceased to compensate for the erosion of its value. Furthermore as the lending public got wise to this process, borrowing by the Government became ever more expensive, so that if inflation ever were to ebb the Treasury would one day face horrendous bills. Successive Chancellors were urged to consider that if instead the public were offered gilts whose value at maturity (when their loan was repaid, in other words) was indexed to the domestic inflation rate over the intervening period, then not only would this constitute 'honesty in borrowing': it would also enable the Chancellor to borrow much more cheaply. Not only that: the Treasury was likely to find (it was told) that 'indexed' gilts would be saleable when nobody would touch the traditional sort with a bargepole because of expectations of accelerating inflation.

The Treasury was sceptical: the Bank, under the lead of the Governor, profoundly hostile. Soon after the Tories took office in 1979, however, a change of tone began to be perceptible, in the Treasury at least. It was said that the new Financial Secretary, Nigel Lawson, was an enthusiastic advocate of index-linked gilts. Professor Alan Walters, who joined the staff of 10 Downing Street at the beginning of 1981, was positively messianic on the subject. He it was who soon secured an essential, conclusive recruit: the Prime Minister herself. To the Prime Minister the key attraction to indexed funding proved to be the very calculation that gave others pause: the fact that repayment on maturity of indexed gilts would poleaxe any future Government which let inflation rip again. She saw this as an admirable hostage for future good behaviour (on the part of her own colleagues, as well as her opponents). The possibility that future Governments which had not contrived to behave themselves in the matter of inflation might simply renege on their obligations cut no ice with her.

A running battle thereupon ensued with the Bank of England. To the Governor in particular, indexed funding smacked of banana-republic economics. He fought it tooth and nail. Nevertheless a restricted pilot scheme *was* introduced: indexed gilts were offered exclusively to UK life funds. This was seen by the Bank as the thin end of the wedge: and rightly so. By the time I joined the Treasury the artificiality of the life funds' privilege was looking increasingly indefensible. Moreover as sterling weakened in the autumn of 1981, and interest rates had to be pushed up twice, the force of the argument that indexed gilts would be saleable when others weren't – as was currently the case – increasingly impressed the Treasury.

The Bank's resistance was unflagging. At one meeting between the two, the Chancellor described the Treasury's attitude towards opening up indexed funding to all would-be investors as open-minded – to which one of the senior mandarins added the cheerful gloss that it might be more accurately described as definitely positive. The Governor explained that at the Bank the general view, he thought, was that it was a bad idea: whereas he thought it was not only bad, but also mad. But he invited his colleagues to comment. They entirely agreed with him.

As it became ever more apparent that the Bank was poised to lose the argument, horrendous prospects were placed before our shuddering gaze. Access to an index-linked gilt (something which only banana republics had offered hitherto) issued by a prime borrower such as Britain would, we were warned, prove irrestible to the sheikhs of Araby. Money would come pouring into sterling. The exchange rate would once more shoot up to the giddy heights of 1980.

It was no good. Chancellor and Governor were confronted with the Prime Minister. Both pleaded for more time for reflection: the Governor in the hope that the wretched things would somehow go away; the Chancellor to avoid a wrathful Governor. To no avail. The Prime Minister's mind was made up. Index gilts for one and all would be put on sale.

Now if there is one golden rule for Whitehall watchers, it is that stable doors are never closed until the horse has bolted. Whitehall's strategies are always framed with the previous war in mind. So it was on this occasion. The coming of comprehensive index-linked funding was the surest indication that the high inflation to which indexed funding is supposed to be the logical response was, for the time at least, behind us.

Needless to say the sheikhs of Araby did not come pouring in. Nor did anyone else. Indexed gilts duly proved a modestly useful adjunct to the Chancellor's armoury of funding instruments. But with inflation sinking swiftly down to five per cent or less, traditional gilts on much higher coupons seemed generally more appetising.

Although it absorbed a lot of time, energy and not a few tears, the great indexed-funding battle was in reality almost peripheral to the main issues of funding policy. At this point I fear that a brief technical digression is necessary. As Lady Bracknell advised her niece Gwendoline, about the chapter on the fall of the rupee, sensitive readers may prefer to omit this passage as 'somewhat too sensational'.

The basic purpose of so-called 'funding policy' is perfectly straightfoward. It is to borrow sufficient money to cover the gap between what the Government (and local authorities) propose to spend and what it grits its teeth to raise from taxation. But not to borrow from anybody: in particular, not to borrow from the banking system. For if Government borrows from the banks, then that borrowing expands the asset base of the banks, and hence their capacity to lend to their customers. Which is precisely what they do. That way lies inflation: it is what is meant by 'printing money'. No, borrowing has to be from the 'non-bank public' to be respectable and non-inflationary.

Essentially the Government has two routes of access to the nation's savings: gilt-edged sales through the City of London, and national savings issues through the Department of National Savings. Up to 1980 the DNS lay gently languishing. It was looked upon as a means to tap the 'great unbanked' – the substantial proportion of the population without bank accounts – and critics were inclined to argue that they were treated also as a bunch of suckers, to be fobbed off with rates of interest which City institutions would not look at. In 1980 Nigel Lawson awoke the DNS from its long sleep. Equipped with smart new savings instruments offering competitive terms (including 'granny bonds', inflation-proofed certificates which were the true precursors of indexed funding), it was set a far more ambitious target, running into billions of pounds instead of hundreds, of money to raise. The DNS rose bravely to the challenge.

This was one Treasury initiative for which the Bank of England had nothing but praise. For it took some of the load off the gilt-edged market. Later on the Government came increasingly to look to the privatisation programme of asset sales to share that load (although the manner in which Treasury book-keeping treats asset sales as reductions in the Budget deficit, rather than as another way of funding it, remains highly controversial). But this was still largely in the future: the early candidates for privatisation, Amersham, Cable and Wireless and the like, were comparatively modest offerings. So the bulk of the Budget deficit still had to be covered with gilt-edged sales.

Monetary targeting added a fresh complication. For if the chosen lodestar of the early 1980s, sterling M3 (£M3) proved to be growing faster than the Chancellor had decreed it should, then this might be because the Government's own deficit was turning out to be larger than planned, or it might be because commercial bank lending was roaring ahead. In the second case it was not enough to 'fund the deficit': the Government, to bring £M3 back on course, had to 'overfund' – i.e. to sell *more* gilts than it needed to sell to bridge the deficit. And in this instance there was an additional restriction to the category of acceptable lenders. Not only were the commercial banks inadmissible: so were foreigners. For gilts sales overseas did not affect £M3.

This led to a further complication. Private investors – and that means principally the investment institutions of the City – buy gilts either because they reckon the rate of interest offered competes favourably with that available to them from alternative claimants for their cash flow, or because they reckon interest rates are liable to move down, pushing up the price of the gilts which they have purchased, and leaving them with an acceptable capital gain. Inevitably the more the Government issues gilts, the more sated the institutions become, and the more their appetites need whetting with ever juicier interest rates. Yet when they think that the next move in interest rates is likely to be upwards – leaving them with a capital loss on their hands – they are liable not to be seen for dust.

So if Government sees £M3 behaving wildly, and therefore faces the need to 'overfund' aggressively, it may well find that short-term interest rates need to go through the roof before the investing institutions will be prepared to nibble. In the period 1979–81 Paul Volcker of the US Fed allowed precisely this to happen. US interest rates shot up into the twenties, and in due course US money growth came back the way he wanted it. Sir Geoffrey Howe went some of the way down this path in 1979, allowing our interest rates to soar to the high teens. But this had been followed by sterling rushing up to $2.40 (whether that was caused in whole, or even in major part, by high interest rates is a matter of debate), and by 1981 this was deemed in the Treasury to have been a definite mistake, contributing unnecessarily to the severity of the recession. Moreover high interest rates mean high mortgage rates, which are politically most unpopular – particularly with Tory voters. So there was great reluctance to see our interest rates shoot away again.

Yet 'over-funding', other things being equal, was calculated to have them doing precisely that. Happily – if inelegantly – there was one way out. If the Bank stuffed gilts down the throats of the institutions as if they were so many Strasbourg geese, and then pumped the money it had thus collected back into the short-term money markets, the circle could be just about squared. £M3 would behave. So would short-term interest rates. With luck the watching world – and the watching citizenry – would not lose sleep about the circularity of the proceedings.

Now in all this the Treasury is (theoretically, at least) the bridge, and the Bank the engine-room. Monetary and interest-rate policy is determined by the Chancellor (with more than a passing concern displayed by the occupant of No 10). Then it is up to the Bank to go down into the market-place, using the services of the Government Broker, as a sort of inverted Mr Bumble, doling out the gruel and begging the institutional Olivers to come back for more. In practice the relationship between Great George Street and Threadneedle Street is necessarily a two-way traffic. My task, as Economic Secretary to the Treasury, was to act as a sort of traffic policeman.

Once a month I found it was my duty to preside over a so-called 'funding meeting' at the Treasury. The Bank was represented by Eddie George and a phalanx of supporters; the Treasury by Peter (later Sir Peter) Middleton and another phalanx; the Department of National Savings by its Director and a smaller team; and then there was the Government Broker.

Each month we reviewed the latest signals from the money dials, studied the flow-chart for our funding, and considered how much we should aim to raise in the ensuing two/three months. What about a smart new issue from the DNS, with some fancy trimmings? An indexed gilt? A string of 'taplets' (with subtle little *noisettes* of gilt-edged stock of varying maturities, calculated to tempt the market's appetite when it was feeling jaded). The Treasury team would usually start, followed by the Bank, after which I would be looked to to sum up. These were emphatically not the sort of meetings to go to unprepared.

At some point I would ask the Government Broker for his comments. My first Government Broker, David (Lord) Cromwell, a popular and much-respected contemporary from university days, knew his place. He invariably assured me that he agreed with the Bank in all particulars.

Tragically, within months of my arrival, David Cromwell was killed in a riding accident. Some weeks later Peter Middleton accosted me in the corridor. 'I believe you know our new Government Broker, Nigel Althaus.'

I did indeed. He was – is – one of my oldest cronies, from Oxford days. He is an immensely experienced and shrewd gilt-edged broker whom I knew I could trust implicitly. So when I first joined the Treasury I persuaded him on several occasions to steal into my office about the time my boxes were being bundled up to pick his brains about the fairly hairy complexities of my new responsibilities. His help and advice had been invaluable. On top of that he had been for some time one of the informal panel of City and academic sages whom the Chancellor regularly consulted around the turn of the year about the shape of the Budget to come. I had not been remotely surprised to discover that his comments on these occasions were invariably robust and wise, and not infrequently witty as well. I couldn't believe my luck. I looked forward to his contributions to our funding meetings.

It soon transpired, however, that the Bank of England had not fully briefed itself on the exent of our acquaintance. At David Cromwell's memorial service I found myself seated next to Eddie George. 'I believe you know the new Broker,' he murmured enquiringly. I agreed that I did. 'Indeed is it true,' he followed up, 'that he is godfather to one of your children?' 'No', I was able to reassure him, 'I am godfather to one of his sons'.

The Bank was plainly not best pleased. The Broker is Bank property (indeed since those days he has moved right inside the Bank). He has no business, in the Bank's eyes, to be too pally with a Treasury Minister. Least of all with the temporary tenant of responsibility for funding policy.

When the first 'funding meeting' following Nigel Althaus's

appointment loomed up, my Private Secretary appeared. The Bank, he informed me, had rung to say that they saw no need for the Broker to attend the Funding Meeting. I told him to inform them that I issued the invitations to the Funding Meeting, and Mr Althaus was on the list.

Not long before, I had added another name to the list of Funding Meeting participants I had inherited. Professor Walters was a long-standing friend from the early 1970s, when we had swapped notes about the fate which we both saw awaiting the monetary policy of those days. During my first week in the Treasury, I had invited him round for a drink. I was astonished to receive the impression that although he had been in Number 10 for nine months already, this had been just about his first visit to Great George Street. I soon became aware of the deep suspicion with which his role in the Prime Minister's entourage was viewed in the Treasury.

This seemed silly to me. For like it or no, his access to and influence with the Prime Minister were obviously considerable. Besides, it seemed to me that he could well prove a useful ally. As it happened, our respective attitudes towards monetary policy had diverged since the early 1970s. Alan Walters had returned from the United States convinced that £M3 was no longer an appropriate star to steer by. He reckoned that watching it had led to excessive tightness in monetary conditions. He argued fervently for 'monetary base control' along the lines practised by Paul Volcker and the US Fed. I was doubly sceptical. For one thing I was convinced that neither Whitehall nor the Bank would stand for the volatility of short-term interest rates which reliance on monetary base control implies. For another, I harboured a suspicion that £M3 was denigrated not so much because it was misleading as because the message that it gave was unwelcome.

Yet while the Treasury shared my scepticism about the practicality of reliance on monetary base control, it was coming increasingly to share Professor Walters' scepticism about the reliability of £M3. Be that as it may, I was convinced that the Professor and the Treasury needed to get closer together.

So in due course we recruited him to join the Funding Meetings, at which he swiftly proved himself a valuable contributor. Indeed it was not long before the Treasury discovered in him a useful ally not only in its dealings with 10 Downing Street but also in its regular hassles with the Bank.

It would be wrong to give the impression that funding policy was settled, month by month, at the Funding Meetings. Inevitably, it was a continuous process. The Funding Meetings simply applied what Whitehall likes to call an 'overview'. The actual course of funding, and the choice of instruments appropriate for the purpose, were the subject of continuous converse beween Treasury and Bank. At regular intervals, depending on the conditions of the markets, I would find grinning at me from my nightly box a weighty dossier calling for a new piece of funding.

There would be a submission from the Treasury, and a submission from the Bank. Usually they reached the same conclusion, the product of long hours of skilled negotiation between officials of the two institutions. If so, the course was clear. Once or twice, greatly daring, I ventured to suggest we might do something else – or, indeed, desist from funding at that precise moment.

I was spitting in the wind. But occasionally life became more interesting. The officials had failed to reach agreement. Then my dossier would faithfully report what the Bank had in mind, and why, and the different ambition of the Treasury, with supporting arguments.

My duty was clear. It was to back the Treasury. On rare occasions I dared to do the opposite. This was received with dismay. The officials would go back into another huddle, and usually contrive to come up with a mutually acceptable solution – which I would reject at my peril.

Once affairs went more seriously awry. The Treasury had come to me with a suggestion for a particularly succulent new morsel from the Department of National Savings. I was unconvinced. For the trouble with succulent new morsels from the DNS was that, while they might enable us to raise a lot of cash without putting pressure on the gilt-edged market, they were liable to invite competition from the Building

Societies. The Building Societies saw the DNS as direct competitors, forever seeking to seduce their depositors. It seemed to me that what was proposed might induce the Building Societies to thump up mortgage rates, which would not win brownie points for the Treasury.

We had a lengthy meeting in my office. Eventually my mandarins convinced me that, while there could be no guarantee that the Building Societies would not react aggressively, there were good grounds for hoping that they wouldn't: and furthermore that the alternatives, involving gilt sales to a sticky market, could be more painful.

Nevertheless, the risks were there. So I thought it judicious to forewarn the Chancellor of what I planned to do, pointing out the hazards, and the reasons, on balance, for accepting the proposal. The Chancellor agreed.

So we met with the Bank of England to finalise the details. The Bank was collectively enchanted – for the reasons already explained, they always liked funding by the DNS. Suddenly I found that the official Treasury had changed its mind. On reflection it had come to the conclusion, I was told, that the proposition was altogether too hazardous.

The Bank was adamant. The message was conveyed discreetly that if the proposition did *not* go through, the Governor was liable to demand his officials' guts for garters. The Treasury was equally adamant.

The moment came for me to adjudicate. I said that I had listened carefully to the arguments, and I understood the Treasury's anxieties. Indeed I had shared them. But they had convinced me that the risks involved represented, on balance, the less bad alternative. And I remained convinced. The Bank departed, purring. The Treasury departed with the blood rising around its collective hairline. 'I think', I said to my Private Secretary as my visitors departed, 'we shall have a call to see the Chancellor.'

Sure enough we did. At crack of dawn. This time there was no Bank of England. The Treasury officials ventured to suggest that what I proposed to do was too hazardous by half. I pointed out that that, indeed, had been my original response to their original suggestion. But they had convinced me otherwise: and I had explained my intentions to the

Chancellor, who had gone along with them. My view was unchanged.

I did not say – though I thought it – that I had been left with the impression that the Treasury's *volte face* might have had less to do with the merits of the issue (which were, by any standards, finely balanced), than with the discovery that the Bank of England was so hell-bent on a particular proposition that the official Treasury owed it to its *amour propre* to frustrate it.

The Chancellor thought, all things considered, and due weight given, etc., etc., that maybe the official Treasury had a point.

Later he was kind enough to express the hope that I had not taken his adjudication hardly. I told him that I put it down to experience: but that the motivation, as I perceived it, for the Treasury's *volte face* still seemed to me absurd.

The moral of the tale is that a junior minister's lot is, like the policeman's, not a happy one.

So the Bank, for all my treacherous endeavours on its behalf, lost this encounter. Another one it won on points.

One morning on arrival at the Treasury I was confronted by a grim-faced group of mandarins to inform me that an important file of Treasury documents had gone walk-about. A senior official had been reading them when he had called in at a coffee-shop on his way to work that morning, and when he reached his office he discovered he had left them behind. Since they had originated from the Bank of England they were all stamped 'Secret';[1] since they were addressed to me they thought I ought to know.

I was filled with sympathy for the luckless official. I recalled how, 30 years before, when I was working as a very junior pen-pusher in the Foreign Office, I had been directed to represent that department at one of Whitehall's inter-departmental committees one afternoon. Over lunch I had

[1] I was delighted to find, on joining the Treasury, that apart from Budget papers (marked 'Budget Secret') almost nothing ranks a security classification of more than 'Confidential', and not much ranks even that. This seems to me a mark of sanity. Highfalutin' security classifications do not enhance security. They enhance the value of absconding documents. That is not the opinion of the Bank of England.

planned to visit a friend laid up in hospital with cartilage trouble. But it was a time of my life when I was much upon the tiles. Having taken the underground towards my friend's hospital, my briefcase tucked beside me containing all the precious papers for the afternoon's meeting, I had swiftly succumbed to sleep. I woke somewhere in North London, switched platforms, and headed back, briefcase faithfully in tow. Alas! I passed out again. This time I awoke to find the train standing in the station adjacent to the hospital. I leapt out. The doors closed. Only then I remembered the wretched briefcase.

The top paper in the briefcase – it is burnt into my memory – was a letter headed SECRET, and addressed to 'Dear Anthony' (Anthony Eden) and signed 'Bobbity' (the soubriquet amongst his intimates of the locum Foreign Secretary of the moment, Lord Salisbury). The subject I do not recall, but I have a nasty suspicion that it was nuclear.

I thought my short career was at an end. I did not dare await the arrival of the lift. I ran all the way up the stairs – all 180 of them – to the station master's office. He cheerfully assured me that my briefcase would be handed out somewhere. But I needed it immediately. I finally persuaded him to ring to the next station down the line, and sure enough, there it was.

So I arrived, *sans* lunch and *sans* hospital visitation, only five minutes late for my meeting, briefcase intact. My Treasury friend had been less fortunate. He had returned to his café, to find the missing package vanished.

Twenty-four hours later the same grim-faced group returned. The Bank of England had been on the line. The City Editor of one of the national newspapers had rung them to enquire about an interesting package of papers, apparently relating to future funding policy, all emanating from the Bank of England, which had come through the post to him in a plain envelope that morning. After informing the City Editor that one thing was certain, and that was that his sheaf of papers had not, repeat not, escaped from the Bank of England, they were inviting comments.

There was a happy ending. The City Editor refrained – as others might not have done, though their readers would have been not a whit the wiser – from reproducing awkward photostats. He did, however, write an article.

To us it reeked of inside knowledge. Somebody, surely, in Westminster or Fleet Street, was going to ask 'what is this?' They never did.

Months later I was spending a weekend with my friend the future Government Broker. 'Oh by the way', he mentioned *à propos* of nothing, as we sipped our sherry, 'did you see a funny article the other day in the *Daily Grind*?' What article, I asked, all innocence, did he have in mind? 'You must have noticed it', he insisted, 'it looked strangely well informed to me.' So far as I am aware, he was the only person to have noticed it.

The world continued on its even course. But there was one aspect which continues to perplex me. The package of papers was marked 'secret', and for that reason alone might have seemed alluring to a passing acquisitionist. For that reason alone it might have been perceived to have a market value in Fleet Street. But no value was demanded. On the other hand the contents would have been the purest gibberish to all save three citizens in a hundred thousand. Yet someone reckoned it would be interesting reading for a City Editor.

Who? A mandarin from another Whitehall department with a score to settle with the Treasury? I have no idea. But I wonder.

As the 1979 Parliament approached its term, so did the contract of Governor Richardson. Several names – some of them exotic – had been mentioned as potential successors, ranging from David Scholey of Warburg's to Sir Phillip Haddon-Cave, the Financial Secretary of Hong Kong (an appointment which would have constituted a remarkable riposte to the out-going Governor's comments on that colony's banking regulations). Governor Richardson himself was said to have originally advanced the claims of his Deputy, Kit McMahon, and then, more recently, as enthusiasm for that choice had faded, of Sir Jeremy Morse, a former director of the Bank of England and currently chairman of Lloyds Bank. But those with any awareness of the fierce resistance put up by Sir Jeremy to the levy which the

Treasury had imposed – Financial Secretary Nigel Lawson leading – on the clearing banks in the 1981 Budget knew that his prospects of getting past a Prime Ministerial veto were virtually non-existent. So the impression was that Governor Richardson was minded to stay on for a third three-year term, to see the Bank past the next Election, after which – who could be sure? – there might always be a different incumbent in Downing Street more receptive to Sir Jeremy's qualifications.

Nevertheless, in the dying months of 1982 it became apparent that the Prime Minister felt it was time for a change. The name which finally emerged, that of Robin Leigh-Pemberton, Chairman of National Westminster, had been on no-one's short list. A considerable landowner and former Tory chairman of Kent County Council who had trained as a barrister, Mr Leigh-Pemberton had come late to banking. Labour spokesmen promptly denounced him as a Prime Ministerial poodle. A good many in the City thought he would be at sea in the environment of international central banking.

His early comments – to the press about the 'sovereign debt crisis', and then to the Commons Treasury Select Committee about foreign bids for British banks – gave some support to the sceptics. Yet it was at least arguable that he was what the Bank was needing at that juncture. Lord Richardson had been a remarkable Governor; but his had been the sort of shadow under which it was not always easy for the second echelon to grow and flourish. Robin Leigh-Pemberton had a deserved reputation as a 'team player'. Admittedly the Governor of the Bank has traditionally been the Chief Executive; but perhaps it might do no harm for it to experience operating under a more 'hands off' chairman.

In any case it swiftly became clear that however willing Lord Richardson might have been to carry on for another term, he was to have no reason to regret denial of the opportunity. For his relations with Nigel Lawson had been tempestuous enough when Mr Lawson had been a mere Financial Secretary. Imagination boggles at the thought of what the climate between Bank and Treasury would have been like had Governor Richardson been reinstalled for a third term when Nigel Lawson returned as Chancellor in the summer of 1983.

Not that the climate which did materialise turned out to be set fair. Far from it. The Bank's standing in the City had already slipped a bit in the closing years of Lord Richardson's tenure. The City felt that the Bank had fallen down in not aborting the 1981 Bank Levy – although what the Bank was supposed to have done in the face of an utterly determined Financial Secretary was by no means clear. But much worse was to follow Mr Leigh-Pemberton's arrival. In his first full Budget, in the spring of 1984, Chancellor Lawson announced the phasing-out, over a three-year period, of initial tax allowances on capital investment, together with a phased reduction in Corporation Tax.

These changes were justified on grounds of 'tax neutrality': the Chancellor argued effectively that at a time of high unemployment it made little sense to encourage firms to displace men with machines for no better reason than to reduce 'tax exposure'. The City, however, was convinced – perhaps with some justice – that his real target lay elsewhere: that it was, once more, the clearing banks. For the clearing banks had shown those many companies whose profits were too low to enable them to recover tax on capital investment (or which had no tax at all to recover, since they were making losses), that they could borrow – or more precisely lease – equipment instead of buying it, with the banks putting up the finance and collecting the initial allowances themselves. This had made the banks remarkably 'tax efficient' – far too tax efficient for the liking of the Inland Revenue. Scrapping initial allowances put paid to this. Once again, it was by no means clear how the Bank could have made the Treasury think again. Yet, once again, it was blamed.

As already illustrated, relations between the Bank and Treasury, always uncertain, had not improved in the early 1980s. But Nigel Lawson is an unusual Chancellor. Ever since his years in Fleet Street – as a 'Lex' columnist on the *Financial Times*, and subsequently as City Editor of the *Sunday Telegraph* – his admiration for the City and its ways has stopped well this side of idolatry. A politician of exceptional determination, he would have been a cross for any Governor to bear. There must be days when Mr Leigh-Pemberton wishes he had never taken on the job in the first place.

There then ensued the Johnson Matthey Bank affair. Very few people outside the City of London (very few people in the City, for that matter) had ever heard of this modest institution before they woke up one weekend in the autumn of 1984 to discover that the Bank of England was working round the clock to save it from collapse.

Only weeks before, Governor Leigh-Pemberton had uttered a stern public warning against the notion that the Bank was a 'lender of last resort', ever ready to rescue businesses from the consequences of their own incompetence or wickedness. There were those who saw Johnson Matthey Bankers as a prime chance for the Bank to demonstrate that it meant what he had said. But there were 'special factors'. For Johnson Matthey Bankers was one of only five participants in the London gold market, and it was feared that if they bit the dust the whole market might collapse. More to the point, perhaps, another player in the gold market was a subsidiary of the Midland Bank. Now the Midland Bank was currently facing horrendous losses from its unhappy purchase of the Crocker Bank in California. The Bank of England was said to be scared that if it had not devised a rescue package for Johnson Matthey Bankers before the markets opened on the Monday morning, there might have been a run on Midland.

Be that as it may, the Bank itself finally agreed to take Johnson Matthey Bankers into its own capacious bosom shortly before dawn on the Monday morning. But not before the Chancellor had rung the Governor to demand – and to receive – an assurance (which was to be made public) that the Bank was only putting up its own cash to rescue JMB, and that no public funds would be involved.

This assurance he subsequently repeated to the House of Commons. Unfortunately, no sooner had he done so than it transpired that this was, arguably at least, not strictly correct. For the Bank had – without telling the Treasury – put up a £100m guarantee for JMB, and this ranked as public funds. Since JMB was by this time a Bank of England subsidiary, its liability to JMB creditors was in fact automatic anyway. But nobody was left in any doubt that the Chancellor was vastly unamused.

Furthermore it was by then becoming clear that the Bank had had good reason for alarm about JMB's lending practices many months before the crisis burst, and had not contrived to do anything very practical about it. It faced stern criticism on every side. Previous Chancellors, whatever they might have said to the Bank in private, would have thought it politic to defend it in public. Chancellor Lawson, ostentatiously, declined to do so.

Soon after the Johnson Matthey Bank collapse, Deputy Governor Kit McMahon's contract was coming up for renewal. It had been he, rather than the Governor, who had master-minded the actual rescue operation. Rumours began to circulate that he was to be scalped. In the end he was reappointed (the reappointment resting, as already noted, with the Prime Minister and not the Chancellor); and the Treasury denied responsibility for the circulation of the stories of his imminent dismissal. It cannot be said that its denials convinced the Bank.

Another report was not denied. In the autumn of 1985 the *Daily Telegraph* gossip column, *Peterborough*, carried a story that at a recent meeting of the National Economic Development Council, presided over by the Chancellor, and attended by the top brass of the CBI and TUC as well as the Governor, the Governor had sought to make an intervention. He had not gained a hearing. Eventually, *Peterborough* reported, he had held his hand up to indicate his desire to speak. The Chancellor had stared at him, stared through him – and called someone else.

The condition of Bank–Treasury relations was, if possible, even more publicly aired in a somewhat ungainly sequel to the 1986 Budget. To compensate for a cut in stamp duty on share transactions, the Chancellor announced in his Budget speech that he was introducing what he subsequently described as a 'season ticket' for dealers in American Depository Receipts, the increasingly popular warrants through which shares in UK companies are traded on Wall Street: a five per cent tax.

Uproar followed. The correspondence columns of *The Times* were filled with howls of protest from the captains of industry, who denounced the tax as protectionist, likely to invite retaliation by the American authorities, grossly damaging to capital-raising by UK multinationals – and certain to produce no revenue for good measure. The Governor of the Bank, cross-questioned by the Commons Select Committee on the Treasury, having defended the principle of the tax with notably small enthusiasm, went on to acknowledge that the rate selected did seem somewhat 'punitive'.

Eventually the Chancellor was obliged to cut the rate to 1½ per cent. The sniggers from the Bank were audible. So the Treasury struck back. *The Guardian* reported 'Treasury dissatisfaction with the quality of advice it has received from the Bank . . . over . . . the decision in the Budget . . . [regarding] American Depository Receipts'. It had concluded that 'the Bank does not have experience in dealings in international equity markets.' Consequently the Treasury was 'considering setting up a financial markets unit to advise the Chancellor on policy towards the markets'.

The Bank replied in kind. It described as 'inaccurate and misleading' reports that it had told the Treasury that the 5 per cent duty rate would be acceptable to the markets. Precisely where such reports had come from it did not elaborate. It did not need to.

What seems to have happened is this. The Treasury did invite the Bank's reactions to the concept of a tax on ADRs, albeit at a fairly late stage. The Bank was unenthusiastic, but thought he might get away with a tax at 2½ per cent if he felt he had to. It asked permission to take soundings. Not only was such permission instantly refused: the Bank was told that even discussion within the Bank of this proposal must be restricted to the doggy, doggy few at the very apex of its structure. The first they knew of a 5 per cent rate was when they heard the Budget speech. They made it very clear to all complainants following the Budget that in selecting that rate the Chancellor had been on his own.

The obsession with 'Budget secrecy' has not infrequently led to troubles in the past. What was unprecedented about this incident was the extent to which the Bank and Treasury went public in attributing ignorance, incompetence and folly to each other.

In the early summer of 1984 I was enjoying a brief holiday in the company of, amongst others, one of the City's most eminent merchant bankers. He expressed considerable concern about the position of the Governor. His was widely seen, he argued, as a political appointment. The worry was that if ever Labour came to power they would invoke this precedent to displace Mr Leigh-Pemberton with a Socialist, with disastrous consequences for the City of London.

I disagreed. I suggested that any incoming Labour Government would have its work cut out to prove its international credit-worthiness without lumbering itself with a suspect central banker. The real danger, I argued, was much nearer to home. With every day that passed, it seemed to me, the authority and independence of the Bank of England was being undermined. We were heading for a Bank of England like the Banque de France: a poodle of the Treasury. That, I thought, not just the City, but all of us (including the Treasury) might live to regret. I still do.

7

Working the System

Michael Heseltine, it is said, hopes to win a small niche in history as the architect of a landscape garden at his home in Oxfordshire. Most politicians who contrive to reach the Whitehall village hope to leave their stamp upon the Statute Book. Few British statesmen of the post-war era held more senior offices, without ever achieving the topmost post of all, than R. A. Butler. But it was as a wartime Education Minister that he achieved what many considered his outstanding monument: the 1944 Education Act.

The Treasury offers limited opportunities for legislative initiative, apart from the annual Finance Act, which is more of an evolving saga, and only rarely secures a place in history for its architects. Fortunately I have always belonged to the minority political faction which doubts whether new laws add to the sum of human happiness. In fact I can only think of one, possibly enduring, monument which I left behind me in the Treasury, and this was more of a pebble than a tombstone.

The first thing I noticed about the official Treasury documents which greeted me on the day of my arrival was that they were headed by an impressive list of addresses, usually starting with 'Chancellor', and working down through 'Chief Secretary' and 'Financial Secretary' to the most senior officials. This, or so it seemed at once to me, was of somewhat restricted value, since if your name was not in the list you would not receive the document, and if you received it you were assuredly upon the list.

What they did not tell you was who had written it, or when. For that information you had to travel through the file.

If you turned to the end to extract it before you started reading, you were liable to find that the file ended with an appendix, which meant that you had to burrow back again to the middle to find what you were seeking. Yet it seemed to me that author and date were useful introductory information. Why could it not be conveyed upon the top sheet of the file?

Breaking all the rules of Whitehall confidentiality I confided to my wife, with whom I lunched on my first day at work (they had not contrived to 'block in' my diary at this early stage) my concern on this score. 'Why don't you do something about it, then?' was her stern rejoinder. I thought I might. After lunch I had a meeting with the Chancellor . . . I told him of my anxiety. 'D'you know,' he informed me, 'I made exactly the same point when I got here.' I was encouraged. But that, I ventured to point out, had been all of two years before: and evidently nothing had happened. He agreed.

So I set to work. Greatly daring, I drafted a brief memorandum suggesting that it would arguably be conducive to the general well-being if we could be told, at the head of every file, who wrote it, and when. I was informed that when George Brown had run the Foreign Office he had insisted on having a single sheet précis of the contents of every file attached to its front. I detected an implication that my proposition reflected similarly lazy thinking. Nevertheless I persevered.

Nothing happened. After some weeks I asked my Private Office if there was any news. It appeared that there was not. There were, it seemed, major hurdles to overcome. Eventually I tackled the mandarin in charge of internal administration. Oh yes, he assured me, they were working on the problem: 'but I must tell you, Minister, that at least one senior official has warned that such an innovation would be introduced over his dead body'. I suggested that this was a little drastic: after all, when he drafted a file, he signed and dated it anyway. We were simply considering whether he should sign and date it on page 12, or on page 1.

Then, one morning, I received a file which was attributed to its author, and dated, on page 1. From then on, all were. Nothing was ever said. Are they still? I wonder.

Other adjustments were more easily achieved. I have an obsessive loathing for split infinitives. I rapidly discovered that, in the Treasury, it was not universally shared. Several letters and memoranda presented for my signature contained the offending grammatical construction. I signed them off, but said I would sign no more containing it. They still came, and I didn't sign them. They swiftly vanished.

Ministerial visitors to the Whitehall village soon learn that their speeches are no more their own. Whitehall has three categories of Ministerial speech. First there is the speech made in an official capacity on an official occasion: in the House of Commons; at an official function outside the House of Commons; or to a gathering to be addressed by the Minister on his department's behalf. Second there is the speech made – usually outside the House of Commons – by the Minister as a Party politican. And third there is the speech made by the Minister, albeit to a Party function, but advancing departmental policy.

The first will be drafted by the Department, and form the subject (if the occasion or the contents are deemed worthy of such treatment) of an official departmental handout to the press. The second will emphatically *not* be drafted by the Department, and will equally emphatically not be the subject of a departmental handout. The third can cause much *angst*. The fact that the Minister is addressing the West Barsetshire Women's Conservative Advisory Committee militates against an official handout. On the other hand the fact that the (unlikely) subject of the ministerial address is 'the management of £M3', and that the Minister's purpose is to correct some wicked aspersions about the handling of these mysteries from an Opposition spokesman, may justify the departmental imprimatur. Much seems to hinge on tone: if the speech 'corrects some recent misapprehensions', it may be deemed worthy of endorsement. If on the other hand it suggests that the Opposition spokesman who perpetrated the offending aspersions is neither numerate nor patriotic, the official imprimatur is likely to be withdrawn. Thus are the niceties of civil service political neutrality preserved.

Regardless of the imprimatur, though, the machine is anxious to vet the contents. Soon after John Biffen moved into the Treasury as Chief Secretary in 1979, his Private Office learned that he was planning to address the Young Farmers of Llangollen, or some such, the following weekend. His Private Secretary wondered politely if he had a text for the villagers to glance through. John Biffen explained that he didn't normally speak from a prepared text. The Private Secretary retired baffled. Twenty-four hours later he returned. Had the Chief Secretary some notes, by any chance, that he planned to use? Eventually John Biffen surrendered a rather scruffy envelope with some hieroglyphics on the back. The Private Secretary retired, bearing his trophy before him.

The next morning he was back. Officials, he told his 'master', were immensely grateful to have had a chance to glance through these notes. There was just one point though. The Chief Secretary appeared to be planning to refer to a peak 32 per cent inflation rate experienced under Labour. This was thought to be unwise: for the highest rate of inflation of Labour had never exceeded 27 per cent.

John Biffen hastened to reassure his Private Secretary. The 32 per cent referred, not to the inflation rate under Labour, but to the proportion of the electorate voting 'yes' in the 1975 European referendum. Officialdom departed, scratching its head.

Yet Ministers who express their thoughts in public without first submitting them to Whitehall scrutiny can find themselves in trouble. In the summer of 1981, Keith Speed, then a junior Minister in the Ministry of Defence with responsibility for the Navy, took time out one evening to warn that current Government policy was in danger of causing mutiny at Spithead (or wherever the Royal Navy mutinies nowadays). Nobody doubted that his maritime advisers would have cheered him to the echo. Still, his views did fit rather oddly with the concept of ministerial solidarity. The then Secretary for Defence, John (subsequently Sir John) Nott happened to be visiting my constituency in Cheshire when the offending speech was made. When he came down to breakfast the following morning, I laid the morning newspapers before him. 'It appears', I said, 'you have a mutiny on your quarter-deck.' John Nott read the headlines, and then said 'can I borrow your telephone?' I agreed that perhaps he had better.

Twenty-four hours later, Keith Speed was called to 10 Downing Street and given his discharge. As he contemplated the public exchange of ruderies between Cabinet colleagues over Westland helicopters four years later, he must have concluded that there was one law for the Cabinet, and another for the lesser mortals. But then, indeed, there is.

The commonest hazard, in my experience, arose over getting clearance for any sort of speech at all. As each Friday night approached, there was a wine-and-cheese in Hale, or a barbecue at Over Peover to satisfy. Of course one could address the future of the Knutsford Memorial Hospital and forego the national press, and the Treasury would look the other way with equanimity. But if one wanted – as one usually did – to use the occasion to send a message to constituents through the national press (or vice versa), then only a comment on current events of wider significance was liable to serve. To trespass on the territory of other Whitehall departments – a feat which could be performed with impunity from the back benches – was likely to be hazardous. A 'message from the Treasury' often therefore seemed to be appropriate. Much agonising ensued.

The Treasury, like all Whitehall departments, is a vigilant warden of its jargon. The Public Sector Borrowing Requirement is, well, the Public Sector Borrowing Requirement. From my training as a journalist I shied away from inflicting such mouthfuls on a public audience. I preferred the cruder 'deficit'. The Treasury did not. In any case each word and phrase had to be checked for compatibility with the departmental stance, and by the time that exercise had been completed the press deadline was liable to be past.

Sometimes it almost seemed as though the Trappist vow to silence would have been preferred. Once I was called upon to address the annual conference of the Building Societies of the North-West. This was a Treasury occasion, no bones about it. An official handout, on Treasury notepaper, was going to be in order. In due course a suitable text appeared in my nightly box. It was full of appropriate sentiments, the results of long hours of cross-drafting between the Treasury and the Registrar of Building Societies. But it was, unfortunately, in the literal sense of the word, unspeakable. I redrafted it in terms which I reckoned I could get my tongue round, and sent it back. The next day it emerged again. Someone in the Treasury press office had got hold of my text and reworked it. The result was a vast improvement. The order had been rejigged, the wording tightened up. I was delighted. I said 'snap' at once. My Private Secretary looked dubious.

Three hours later someone from the engine-room was ushered in. 'Minister', he told me, 'there were just one or two aspects of the latest draft of your speech for Friday which we were not entirely happy with. So I've ventured to suggest a few amendments.' He laid his handiwork before me. I read it through. 'Well,' I said, 'that's fine. Only whereas the previous draft might, I think, have earned a place in Fleet Street – might even conceivably have won a headline – this will sink without trace.' 'But Minister', came the pained response, 'we don't want *headlines*, do we?'

Just occasionally there are more profound tensions between the whims of the political travellers and the ethos of the village. The 1979 Tory Government came to office with a predisposition to review the case for a switch from student grants to student loans. With the arrival of Keith Joseph at the Department of Education in the same reshuffle that had carried me into the Treasury, this predisposition began to take shape. Superficially it was no business of the Treasury. In practice the Treasury had a double interest.

For the scheme which eventually emerged from the Department of Education involved borrowing by students from the clearing banks. Since the banks would not come forward with student loans without security which the students would not, presumably, be in a position to offer, Treasury guarantees were going to be required. Such guarantees would have potential implications for public borrowing. Furthermore there was a dark suspicion – as there always is in the Treasury – that the Department of Education, instead of cutting back its budget to reflect the end of student grants, was out to try and hang on to the resultant savings.

So the Treasury had a view to give, and I found myself entrusted with the drafting of it. A lengthly official submission arrived, and became the subject of an equally lengthy conference in my office. I said that while I entirely accepted that the Treasury had its interests to protect, it did not seem to me to be the business of the Treasury to rubbish the whole concept of student loans, which was what, I felt, the submission did. The officials present proved splendidly robust. Student loans, they told me, had been tried and found wanting right around the globe. The feckless and the negligent defaulted; for the scrupulous, the repayment of the loan became a crippling burden. One had been at an American university, and had watched his American contemporaries ruining their health or their academic prospects 'working their way through college'.

I was wholly unimpressed. I assured them I was prepared to argue the merits of loans versus grants in principle some other time. That was not the Treasury's business. We must start from the premise that the Government, in its wisdom or its folly, was determined to give them a whirl. Our task was to ensure that the proposition eventually put before the Cabinet was compatible with the Treasury's responsibilities for monetary control and public spending. That, and that alone.

The draft was taken back. But it took a second meeting, and a third draft, before I was finally satisfied that the philosophical bias of the villagers against the concept of the student loan had finally been squeezed out.

Happily the villagers won the battle in the end. A submission duly went forward to the Cabinet, finely honed by all the Whitehall inputs. Only to encounter the unyielding opposition of the Lord Chancellor. He was not open to negotiation or persuasion. Up with student loans he would not put. Not for the first time, or the last, his stance proved decisive. So the large majority of our fellow-citizens continue to foot the bills for the minority of (predominantly middle-class) young men and women who qualify for further education to enjoy that privilege and the access to a higher earning power which must be presumed to flow therefrom. What would the middle classes do without Lord Hailsham – and the civil service?

Another area of potential tension between villagers and visitors concerns the delicate subject of gifts. The code of Ministerial conduct is very stern about gifts. As already explained, Ministers, unlike backbenchers, cannot receive payment for broadcasts or newspaper articles; moreover gifts of any value presented to them in the course of their official duties have to be surrendered.

These rules are strictly enforced by the Whitehall village. And assuredly it is in the Ministers' interest that they should be. Whitehall has not forgotten the embarrassment of the late Tony Crosland when, amongst the papers of bankrupt architect John Poulson, charged with corruption, was discovered a fulsome note of thanks from the former President of the Board of Trade for a silver teapot which he had evidently been given by Poulson. Happily, in this case, the offending teapot turned out to be plate and virtually worthless. Still, it was a cautionary tale.

Fans of 'Yes, Minister' may recall the episode in which the luckless James Hacker returned from an official trip to the Gulf with a ceramic pot which his wife was far too keen on to allow him to surrender, and the press got wind of its retention. Hacker contrived to get it certified as a fake, which only got him into awful trouble with his erstwhile Arab hosts. In real life, I fear, even a fake pot would have been impounded.

Early in 1983 I visited Hamburg on official duty. Before I came home I was presented with a coffee-table book, half in German, half in English, about the port of Hamburg. My Assistant Private Secretary, who accompanied me, received a fetching silk scarf.

When I got home my daughter, who was preparing for an interview in German, pounced upon my book. Could she have it to help brush up her German? I was only too delighted to be shot of it.

A couple of days later my Principal Private Secretary came in. 'I gather', he began, 'that you received a book in Hamburg, Minister'. I pleaded guilty. 'Unfortunately', he went on, 'it is reckoned to be worth more than £25, and so if you want to keep it I'm afraid you'll have to pay £25 for it'. How it came to be valued at £25, or anything like it, was a mystery to me. But I hastened to assure my Private Secretary that nothing would induce me to pay £25, or even £5 for that matter, for the privilege of keeping such a piece of flotsam. They could have it back, and welcome (I just hoped my daughter hadn't thrown it away). But what, I couldn't help wondering, would become of it? 'Oh it'll be used as a prize at the Treasury sports day ' was the comforting reply. Runners-up, I imagined, got two such books.

'What, then', I enquired, 'about Theresa's scarf?' 'Oh yes', I was told, 'she'll have to pay for that too I'm afraid, if she wants to keep it'. I put my foot down. 'She will do nothing of the kind. And if anyone tries to insist, then send them to me.' So far as I am aware they did not insist.

Gifts are one potential source of Ministerial embarrassment. Security is another – a much more complex one. Ministers, unlike their mandarins, cannot be 'positively vetted'. For 'positive vetting' arises normally when an appointment is under contemplation; furthermore the appointee who fails the test must – presumably – be shipped elsewhere. Politicians cannot very well be notified that the Prime Minister is contemplating their preferment; nor could they very well be shipped elsewhere when the Prime Minister had appointed them. Rumour has it – one hopes correctly – that the Security Services have ways of forewarning the Party Whips' offices when they have good grounds for believing that a back-bencher's private proclivities or connections would make him or her unsuited to promotion (and the Whips themselves are supposed to keep their eyes and ears wide open). What the Security Services would do were a Party with hopes of office to choose as its leader a 'security risk' is the stuff of which political thrillers are made. But it was said – whether accurately or not – that sensitive papers were regularly withheld from a junior Minister in the Labour Government of 1974–79 whose outside contacts were not all that they should be.

Be that as it may, an early appointment for the newly elevated Minister is with a gentleman from the Security Services, for a lecture on the Official Secrets Act and the awful perils to which Ministers can be exposed. In practice, the commonest hazard is the difficulty of recalling the source of information: did you read it in the *Daily Telegraph*, or in a minute from the Cabinet Office? The only safe course is, obviously, 'when in doubt, stay silent'.

Inevitably my bicycle was a cause of continuing preoccupation. For when I had but a single file to carry to a meeting outside the Treasury, the obligatory box or briefcase seemed an unnecessary encumbrance. I believe it is still part of Treasury folklore that on one occasion I contrived to scatter 'Budget Secret' papers across Birdcage Walk. Quite untrue. The wind did pluck some from the folder: but all were rescued before they even hit the ground.

Then there was the trousers incident. I had travelled overnight by train from Crewe in the next-door sleeper to my colleague Peter Morrison, then a junior Minister in the Department of Employment. When I was dressing in the morning, he burst in to report that his trousers had been pinched.

Fortunately the trousers were soon recovered from the loo, minus all his cash. Understandably he saw it as an entertaining incident, and word of his escapade soon reached the press. Later in the week one of the Treasury Press Officers came to see me. 'Minister', he said, 'the press seem to have got hold of a story about you'. 'Oh, God', I replied, 'what have I done now?' 'It's about your trousers, Minister . . .' I interrupted. 'No, no, it was Mr Morrison who lost his trousers.' 'Oh yes, Minister, we know all about Mr Morrison's trousers. But the press seem to think you lost yours too.' I thought I might be in luck. 'Is there', I asked, 'supposed by any chance to be a sexual angle to this story?' 'Certainly *not*, Minister' was the shocked reply. 'Pity', I said, 'I'd hoped there might be a nice juicy libel action in it'. The press officer was not amused. Had he but known! Some weeks later it was the Chancellor's turn, when making the same journey, to be parted from his nether garments. And he did not get them back.

But it is the 'leak' which holds the limelight nowadays. 'Leaks' come in many shapes and forms. At their most dramatic they can cost a Ministerial career. In the 1930s, Jimmy Thomas, a member of the National Government, departed in disgrace having revealed some of the Chancellor's intentions at a private-dinner party just before the Budget. That was clear-cut enough: those present were obviously in a position to exploit their inside information for financial gain. Hugh Dalton's dismissal from the Treasury under Attlee for talking out of turn to a lobby journalist on his way into the Commons to present his Budget was much more marginal. It was difficult to believe that the Prime Minister did not have more substantial reasons for accepting his proferred resignation.

Careless talk is not the commonest form of Ministerial 'leak', and never has been. The usual Ministerial 'leak' is perfectly intentional. The unique system of the Parliamentary 'lobby', that secret society of political journalists who are bound never to quote or reveal their sources without the specific permission of the sources in question, enable Ministers to secure publicity, when it suits them, for their legislative and policy plans, for their stance in Cabinet (or even the stance that they – or their officials – think in retrospect they should have taken, though they didn't), for their victories over Ministerial colleagues or even the Prime Minister, for the heroic resistance they put up (or, again, would like it to be thought they put up) to the vicious assaults of Treasury or Number 10 upon their departmental plans for the nation's welfare – and all this without a hint of personal responsibility for the appearance of the stories of their prowess. Insiders and outsiders may have their shrewd suspicions: but there is no proof. Technically they have breached the Official Secrets Act on each occasion. In practice no Government would dream of functioning without such breaches.

Mandarins also leak, and this is where the plot inevitably thickens. For mandarins may leak to the greater glory of their 'masters' – or very much to the contrary. They may get the departmental policy, or their campaigns to spike the guns of departmental enemies, subliminally across to the press, just as the ministers do. Or occasionally they may pass on information which the ministers are dead keen to keep well out of sight. Which is when the sparks fly.

There is nothing new to this. Before the First World War, the admirals fed official information to J. L. Garvin, legendary Editor of *The Observer*, to advance their campaign for naval rearmament against Germany. In the 1930s Winston Churchill's similar assault upon the Baldwin Government's failure to rearm was fuelled by invaluable 'leaks' from within the Air Ministry in particular.

What has added a new dimension to this ancient sport is the photocopier. Garvin, or Winston Churchill, could – and did – produce embarrassing statistics which could only have come from official sources. They could not produce photostated documents, as their modern counterparts are able to do. And there is something undeniably alluring about a photocopy of the original document, with the heading 'Secret', or better still 'Top Secret', for all the world to see.

Every time I passed the photocopier in my Private Office in the Treasury it gave me the shivers. There it stood, solitary and vulnerable, winking evilly, in an office of its own, midway between the office of the private secretaries, and the office of the typist, archivist and registrar. The door to the passage was permanently closed: it could only be approached from the private secretaries' room, or that of the typist, registrar and archivist. Yet I knew all the time that it was the work of but a moment to snatch an extra copy, for onward passage to a receptive Fleet Street newsroom.

This had its effect, inevitably. Certain subjects – a wider spread for VAT, for example, or the reintroduction of exchange controls – were regarded as too 'sensitive' to be put on paper at all. Yet Whitehall lives, and is bound to live, by paper. Matters that cannot be debated in memoranda and in minutes are liable, in practice, not to be debated at all.

During my time in the Treasury we were lucky. There were no official 'leaks' (the escape of documents referred to in Chapter 6 came into a slighly different category). Nevertheless in the run-up to the Budget the Chancellor became mildly paranoic. Mandarins were liable to be required to log the slightest chance encounter with a journalist. Ministers were liable to find theirs at least discouraged. Following the revelation of Nigel Lawson's plans to lay the axe to single-premium life insurance policies in the 1984 Budget some weeks before Budget Day in *The Guardian*, in an article which reeked of mandarin briefing, it was reported that in the run-up to the 1985 Budget the mandarins were required to log their visits to the loo.

Soon after Geoffrey Howe migrated to the Foreign Office in 1983 he suffered a more serious inconvenience. It transpired that a young lady in his Private Office, Miss Sarah Tisdall, had succumbed to the temptation of that winking photocopier, made a copy of a document relating to the arrival of Cruise missiles in this country and passed it on to Fleet Street. She was sent to prison for her pains. Soon afterwards a second, rather more senior, official at the Ministry of Defence was similarly arraigned, for passing on documentation which called into question at least the precision of Ministerial Parliamentary answers about the sinking of the Argentinian battleship *HMS Belgrano* during the Falklands War. Mr Ponting was more fortunate than Miss Tisdall. The jury acquitted him.

This has led, inevitably, to furious heart-searching. Why is it acceptable that Ministers and their mandarins should be free to surrender information to the press – including, on occasion, the photostats of documents – which happens to suit their purposes, although it transparently transgresses the Official Secrets Act, and yet feel able to prosecute those self-same mandarins, and even send them off to prison, when they do likewise in a manner which happens not to suit the Ministerial convenience? Nobody disputes that there is a category of material, relating to national defence security or lending scope for private gain, the divulgence of which to unauthorised persons deserves immediate incarceration. The protection of Ministerial convenience, or, worse still, of documents calculated to show that Ministers have been less than wholly frank with Parliament, is something else again.

So there is a vigorous campaign for a Freedom of Information Act, which would switch the onus of proof and make the assumption that Whitehall documents would be generally available to public scrutiny unless it could be shown that national security, or essential commercial confidentiality, were at risk. It is far too early to judge the repercussions of the Westland Helicopters affair upon the rules of security. But one's instinct is that 'Freedom of Information' remains a cause much favoured by politicians in opposition, and civil servants in retirement, rather than one to be espoused by the current villagers, or their transient landlords, of whatever political persuasion those landlords may be.

8

Working with Westminster

Mandarins pride themselves on their understanding of the ways of their weird and uncouth neighbours, the denizens of Westminster. At the beginning of the 1960s I heard the then Chairman of the Board of Inland Revenue stating categorically that there could be no question of a tax on capital gains, since the then ruling Tory Party would not wear it. Within months, the Tory Chancellor, Selwyn Lloyd, had imposed a tax on short-term capital gains, and the Tory Party had worn it like so many lambs. Not long after the Party's defeat in the 1964 Election, Reggie Maudling, Chancellor of the Exchequer under Harold Macmillan and Alec Douglas-Home, confided to me – and no doubt to others – that, had he been a free agent, he would have floated the pound in 1963 or thereabouts. 'But the Party simply wouldn't stand for it in a hundred years.' The Party stood for it, without turning a hair, eight years later, next time it was in Government. But Reggie Maudling's wistful judgment reflected the collective wisdom of the Whitehall village. For at that time the Bank and Treasury were unusually unanimous in the view that sterling, unpinned from the Bretton Woods system of 'fixed but adjustable' exchange rates, would not float: it would sink. Furthermore the international trading community would not tolerate Britain trying to steal a competitive advantage by allowing its currency to shrink. The fact that the two propositions were not remotely compatible was neither here nor there. But confronted with a Chancellor prone to indulge in such heretical fantasies the safest line of counter-attack for the 'authorities' was the stern warning that the Government's backbenchers would go berserk.

The political visitors to the Whitehall village are supposed to know about Westminster and grassroots political opinion. They have few other qualifications. They have rarely achieved a track record outside politics; their skills in the arts of administration are, at best, unproven; their in-depth knowledge of the Health Service, the workings of the United Nations, or the arcane mysteries of public funding, as the case may be, is a matter of chance, since it will not be a decisive factor in selection for the job. But in most cases they know the House of Commons and its whims, and they have cultivated grassroots over many years. Yet when the mandarins murmur 'there'd be trouble with your colleagues, Minister, if we went down that route,' they often nod their heads.

It must be said that departments display differing skills and sensitivity in handling Westminster which cannot easily be attributed to their political tenants at any particular time. There was, for example, some astonishment at the apparent carelessness with which Geoffrey Howe ran headlong into a major Parliamentary storm over the banning of Trades Unions at the Government Communications Centre at Cheltenham in early 1984. It was widely felt that this reflected the Foreign Office's relative inexperience in handling Parliament. For the most part the Foreign Office has to cope nowadays with little more than the occasional set-piece 'foreign affairs' debate, when the Foreign Secretary tours the world horizon, and asserts the Government's abiding dedication to good, and antipathy to evil, and the backbenchers air their concerns about far off lands to which they have paid a recent 'freebie' visit. It is not often that our diplomats confront the sort of politically charged dramas which are the common currency of less exalted Whitehall kraals. So we shook our heads and agreed that, had Geoffrey Howe still been at the Treasury, the mandarins would at least have warned him that the move against the Cheltenham Trades Unions was liable to prove 'courageous' (one of the many other Whitehall euphemisms for 'don't').

Regardless of their departmental location, politicians raised to office soon learn, if they are going to survive, to treat Parliament with care. Those who are parachuted in from outside have a wretched time. For the House of

Commons displays many of the behavioural characteristics of the rougher sort of school. Implants are resisted, as Frank Cousins, recruited by Harold Wilson from the Transport Workers to the Ministry of Technology to placate the Unions, and John Davies, recruited by Ted Heath from the CBI to the Department of Industry to impress the bosses, were each in turn to discover. As back bench newcomers, their propensity to call their colleagues 'you' (which, in Parliamentary language, means the Speaker) and the Speaker 'Mr Chairman' would have been overlooked with tolerance. As front-bench newcomers they found that such harmless solecisms led to barracking.

That is the price exacted for the absense of apprenticeship. But for the Minister who has served his apprenticeship, as most have done, the front bench can still be full of pitfalls. Although I had sat in the Commons for 12 years before my elevation, I was caught out on the first occasion I performed at Question Time. When it is the turn of the department to which the Minister is attached to head the list for questions, he and his colleagues line up along the front bench awaiting their turn. The Chancellor sits behind the Despatch Box, with the Chief Secretary on his left, and the other departmental Ministers spreading out beyond him. In due course my turn came to answer my first question. Rather than disturbing all my colleagues seated to my right to reach the Despatch Box on which to place my precious folder of suitable responses, I answered from the table, in front of where I sat. As soon as my first trial by jury was completed, that stern defender of Parliamentary rules and niceties, Enoch Powell, rose on a point of order. Was it in order, he asked, for a Minister to address the House, or to answer a Question, when situated otherwise than at the Despatch Box? The Speaker gravely agreed that it was not. In my 12 years' apprenticeship I had never noticed this item of indispenssble *placement*. I did not forget it.

Even without such lapses, Question Time is the new Minister's first major Parliamentary ordeal. It is, perhaps, a little like one of those ritual canings by headmasters which used to be a hazard of public-school life, in that the experience is a great deal less alarming than the preparations.

Each of the Departments of State nowadays runs the gauntlet once a month for either 45 minutes or the last part of an hour. The length of time depends on whether it is slotted in on Mondays or Wednesdays, when only a handful of questions to one of the more esoteric segments of Whitehall – the Attorney-General, or the Church Commissioners, for example – may, or may not, take up a slice of the available Question hour, or on Tuesdays or Thursdays, when questions to the Prime Minister invariably occupy the last 15 minutes and take all the limelight. Owing to the prolixity of both questions and answers tolerated nowadays, it is unusual for more than twenty questions on the order paper to be answered in a 45 minute stint, or 30 in the full hour.

Sometimes, admittedly, the unexpected happens. MPs must be in their place to raise the questions they have tabled. If they are absent, their questions are demoted to receive a formal written answer, even when – as sometimes happens – their colleagues are eager to exploit an exposed flank in the Government's defences which their questions have opened up. When there are no major votes scheduled on the Parliamentary timetable for later in the day to draw MPs to Westminster, there may turn out to be a lot of absentees. I once had the experience, as a backbencher, of discovering that I had a late question on the Order Paper which in normal circumstances would never have been reached at all for oral answer. But there were an awful lot of absentees. So much so that I suddenly realised, before I rose to put my question, that it was the last question on the Paper for which the questioner was present: and that Question Time still had 15 minutes to run. Furthermore it happened to concern a highly topical issue about which the then Labour Government was dangerously exposed. The junior Minister called upon to answer could reasonably have hoped that my question would never be reached. But if it was reached he could at least have felt confident that after a possibly painful three minutes the next question would be called, and he would be released. Not so on that occasion. The supplementary questions from my colleagues could – and did – prolong his agony for what, I have no doubt, was one of the longer quarters of an hour in his life. He emerged sweating. Fortunately that was a rare experience, and not one that I had to face when I was in the hot spot.

In theory, questions for oral answer on the floor of the House of Commons can be tabled up to a few days before the moment for their answer. In practice, because of the restricted number of questions which time will permit, Whitehall departments can make their dispositions a long way in advance. MPs can start to notify their questions three weeks ahead of the date on which the target department will be required to produce its answer, and usually, unless they do so then, their questions will be relegated to written response.

This constitutes relegation, since the oral and the written question serve, essentially, different purposes. If an MP genuinely seeks information on the record, then a written answer will suffice. If he wants to know how many people are currently detained on remand, let us say, a written question will produce the answer. But if he wants to make the point that the conditions under which prisoners are detained on remand are a scandal, or that hundreds are locked in on remand although subsequently found not guilty of the crimes with which they have been charged, he will need an oral question and the supplementary questions (from him and his colleagues) to make his point. Written Questions, in short, should seek information. Oral Questions are, paradoxically, best framed in a form calculated to produce an answer which the questioner knows in advance. If you want to denounce remand conditions it would be – to put it mildly – disconcerting to be told that there were currently no prisoners held on remand.

So the Whitehall village has the charge-sheet laid before it three weeks in advance. It sets to work upon it with a will. In due course it presents the Ministers with a provisional allocation of the answers. The Treasury is one of the departments which shares its slot with the Prime Minister. So 45 minutes is the limit. There may be 60 questions to the Treasury on the Order Paper. But only the first 20 are likely to be reached, with perhaps back-up cover for the next 20 just in case. The last 20 will be treated like any other written questions.

Questions (in the first 40) will be provisionally allocated to the individual Ministers. If they relate to the general management of the economy, or if they are judged particularly delicate, they will probably be allocated to the Chancellor. If they concern public expenditure, then the Chief Secretary will be pencilled in. Other questions, about the Inland Revenue, or VAT, or capital taxation, or funding policy, will be parcelled out according to the demarcation lines within the Treasury between the other Ministers.

The Ministers themselves then join the haggle, passing responsibility between each other at the margin. It may be accepted that although questions four to eight inclusive on the order paper all relate to the Financial Secretary's patch, he will need a breather. So one of his colleagues will take on number six.

Following allocation comes the preparation of the dossier. The Question asks 'whether the Chancellor is satisfied with the impact of the current level of interest rates on industry.' The formal answer, which the Minister will read out from his dossier, says something like 'Her Majesty's Government is, and remains, concerned to lower the cost of raising capital for British industry whenever this is consistent with the achievement of our counter-inflationary objectives'. But this exchange is but the formal introduction. What matters is the follow-up.

For this the Ministers are nothing if not well prepared. The villagers will have done their homework on the questioner. He speaks for the motor industry? They will have devised the appropriate answer to a supplementary question about the ruinous impact of high interest rates on the car-makers: that their exports went up by 2 percent in the latest six months, or that they have benefited from the recent Budget relaxation of hire-purchase controls, or whatever.

But there will clearly be several further supplementary questions, from unpredictable backbenchers, and maybe an intervention by the leading Opposition spokesman on the subject. Whitehall prides itself on foreseeing all eventualities. There is an answer for every supplementary question – if only you can find it in the folder which you carry nervously before you at the start of Questions.

The composition of these folders is the subject of additional debate between the Ministers and their civil servants. This culminates in a final session on the morning of the day the Questions fall for answer, at which last-minute up-dates can be inserted, or extra briefing material called for.

Even so, things can and do go wrong. There was a celebrated occasion, while Roy Jenkins was Chancellor at the end of the 1960s, when it dawned upon us sitting on the Opposition benches that the entire file of answers to one of the Questions had gone walk-about. The question was put, and the Chancellor and his colleagues on the Government front bench stared at each other in agonised confusion. We shouted 'answer, answer' gleefully. Eventually Harold Lever, braver than the rest, rose to his feet – and dealt impromptu with both the original question and the supplementaries with considerable aplomb. The truth is that a ready grasp of a handful of statistics designed to show how splendidly the Government is doing, and how wretchedly the Opposition did when they were running things, will usually see you through a good deal more effectively than all the laboriously prepared answers to all eventualities in the folders, since the right one can all too easily be overlooked in the heat of the moment.

Good hearing comes in useful, though. The combination of selective microphones designed to amplify the voice of the MP on his feet, (and his alone), and loudspeakers in the backs of the Parliamentary benches, ought to mean that supplementary questions are audible to the Minister who has to answer them, however loud the surrounding din may be. But odd words can be lost, as I discovered to my cost.

The application of VAT to sanitary towels is a long-standing grievance of the women's organisations. Sure enough, when I was answerable for Customs, it duly appeared upon the Order Paper. The Customs and Excise provided me with a long list of toilet requisites – razors and shaving-soap, toothpaste and toothbrushes and soap and much else beside – all of which incurred VAT. To zero-rate the lot would be vastly expensive for the Revenue, and besides would land us in trouble with Brussels; while to make an exception for just one item – sanitary towels – would be indefensible. Nevertheless I knew the going would be rough, with the complaints by no means necessarily confined to the other side of the Chamber.

So when I heard the second supplementary, from an elderly Labour backbencher, I could not believe my luck. Could I, I heard myself being asked, point to any item on my list that was used by women? I was up in a flash. 'A number of ladies of my acquaintance', I answered cheerfully, 'use soap'.

Uproar. The Government Whip on duty sidled along the bench towards me. 'You're going to have to apologise', he murmured. What had I done wrong? All was rapidly revealed. I had missed a vital word in the supplementary: the word 'exclusively'. I had really been asked whether there was any other item on my list used by the ladies *and by them alone*. Which, of course, there was not.

Elspeth Howe – a dedicated enthusiast for feminist causes herself – came up as soon as Question Time was over. 'Jock', she said, 'you must go and see my man in Harley Street. He'll fit you up with just what you need behind your ear in no time'. I couldn't resist replying, 'Harley Street on my pay? You can't be serious.'

There was an endearing sequel to this pratfall. Some days later I was presented by my Private Office with a letter from a lady down in deepest Kent. 'I see,' she wrote, 'that you think that if we don't like paying VAT on our STs we should use soap instead. I tried it once, but my husband objected to the bubbles.' That, I said, deserves a superlative reply. It never got one. In fact so far as I'm aware it never got a reply at all. I think my Private Office was shocked by frivolity on such a serious subject.

Question Time is one regular fixture in the Whitehall calendar. Another, for the Treasury, is the Finance Bill. By tradition the Chancellor presents his Budget, and then leaves his companions to take it into law, with the Chief Secretary in charge.

The clauses are distributed between the three, four or five participating Ministers according to the subject. Since the first 15 or 20 invariably relate to Customs and Excise duties, I always had a busy start; whereas my colleague the Financial Secretary would come in around Clause 20 when we got to the Inland Revenue, with one or other of the Ministers of State picking up the baton when we reached the sections dealing with capital taxation, or North Sea revenues. From time to time each of us would take on a clause outside our normal remit, to give our colleague a breather when he would otherwise have had an indigestible sequence of clauses to carry on the trot.

Occasionally the Treasury would have some other legislation to pilot through, ranging from a mammoth Bill to redesign the ground rules for the Building Society to some tiny technical morsel to bring us into line with a Directive from the European Community.

The procedure is much the same. The Minister is once again equipped with 'speaking notes' – which, if he is wise, he will rewrite himself to render them appropriate and speakable before a Parliamentary audience – together with voluminous background briefing. But life is less hectic than it is at Question Time: if a backbencher bowls a bouncer there is usually time to obtain a hastily scribbled answer of sorts from the bench of watching mandarins in the corner before you have to play it. But a lot of the legislation for which the Treasury is responsible is technical, uncontroversial, and seen as boring by the mass of back bench members. So proceedings are usually quite relaxed, and about the biggest hazard for the Minister is making sure he turns up on time. For when his Clause or Bill is reached he had better be ready on parade on the front bench – or he will have a most uncomfortable meeting thereafter with his Party's Chief Whip.

One hazard which the Minister has to learn to cope with is speaking to a wholly unpredictable time-check. Since the Whips know full well that they cannot keep their flock in place around the clock, they like to be able to let it be known that the next vote will be at, say, 5 pm. And that means that the Minister replying to the debate preceding the vote must fill the space till 5 pm, whether it be long or short. I had an early experience of this. As I was waiting on the front bench for my moment to arise and answer the debate on my very first amendment, the Whip on duty murmured to me 'can you keep this going until six o'clock?' Since it was not then 5.15, and the amendment under discussion raised a point that was as simple as it was narrow, I replied 'not a hope'. To which the unfeeling response was 'Well, you bloody well try!'

So I did. I spoke very slowly. I complimented everyone who had spoken in the short debate on their constructive thinking, and I did so at inordinate length. As soon as any of my colleagues, on either side of the House, showed signs of rising to their feet, I sat down promptly to give way to them before they'd have a chance for second thoughts. After seven minutes I reckoned I was doing rather well. I hadn't even begun the guff supplied to me by the Treasury to justify its actions.

Alas! While I was speaking, there had been a change of plan. Suddenly, shuffled onto the Despatch Box, was a note from the Chief Whip, who had just come in. 'Sit down in three minutes' was all it said. And I had page after page as yet untouched, which the Treasury had solemnly assured me must be put upon the record or the Third World War would break out. From pottering along as if I found it difficult to get the words out, I switched within a sentence to a high-pitched, unintelligible gabble.

Sheer obscurity is always one of Whitehall's secret weapons, though. One morning, when the Finance Bill was wending its leisurely way through the House of Commons, I was suddenly informed that there was a spot of bother. I referred in Chapter 6 to the arcane affair of 'over-funding'. Now one of the consequences of this recondite procedure was that, for reasons that I cannot recall, it resulted in the Government's in-house buffer stock, the Public Works Loans Board, collecting massive balances. The mandarins, I was informed, had concluded that this might very well be Against the Law. The PWLB was allowed to hold a 'working balance': but the sums that were now accumulating could not, it was felt, be described as 'working' by any stretch of the imagination.

I demurred. I had visions of a very awkward amendment, which I knew that I would have to move on the floor of the House of Commons, which would cast an altogether lurid light on the remarkable circularity of our efforts to make our chosen yardstick of credit conditions, sterling M3, behave itself. Surely, I said, the definition of a 'working balance' is a matter of opinion.

The mandarins were unyielding. I was informed in tones of awe that the Permanent Under-Secretary, in his role as Departmental Accounting Officer[1], had decided that he could not accept responsibility for what was going on unless the law was changed. Against that verdict there was no appeal. So amendment it had got to be.

For once my luck was in. I knew quite well that there were only two MPs who understood what was going on: Enoch Powell, and Terence Higgins on the Tory back benches. Terence might be openly sceptical, but he would at least be kind, out of comradely fellow-feeling. Enoch, I feared might not be.

But when my day of trial arrived, Enoch was not in his place. He was detained across the water, on Northern Ireland business. Furthermore Peter Shore, who was leading for the Opposition, quite understandably got the wrong end of the stick, and I was able to put him straight. I still had to run the gauntlet of Terence Higgins, and although he was generously restrained, I did not enjoy it. When the debate was over I emerged sweating. 'You were on thin ice, you know', Terence Higgins told me afterwards. Oh yes, I knew.

In recent years an extra dimension has been added to the traditional relationships between the Westminster and Whitehall villages: the Select Committees. The grand-daddy of them all, the Public Accounts Committee, dates back to Gladstone. But it was Dick Crossman who gave them their modern shape in the late 1960s when, partly out of a genuine commitment to Parliamentary accountability, and partly to keep the Labour Government's restive backbenchers out of mischief, he set up a series of 'subject' Select Committees,

[1] Notwithstanding the general rule that Ministers are responsible for the actions of their departments, it is the Permanent Secretaries, who are statutorily answerable to Parliament for the disbursement of funds voted to their respective departments.

covering nationalised industries, science and technology, Scotland, and so on, to function alongside the PAC and the much larger Estimates Committee.

This structure was then substantially revised by Norman St John-Stevas, when he was Leader of the Commons in the first Thatcher Administration. He replaced the 'subject' Committees with a series of departmental watchdogs, one for each of the major departments of state. Each Committee, serviced by a small staff (apart from the PAC, which has the Comptroller and Auditor-General's Office to service it) conducts both long-term studies – into 'defence procurement', or 'monetary policy' – and more immediate ad hoc investigations, such as those established early in 1986 by the Defence and Trade and Industry Committees respectively, to review the Westland affair from the angles of those two interested departments, and the regular reviews conducted by the Treasury and Civil Service Committee into Public Expenditure White Papers and the Chancellor's Autumn Statements.

They take up a lot of civil service time, and they are also demanding in their calls on Cabinet Ministers. On the whole they do not take kindly to being fobbed off with junior Ministers (although I did appear before the Treasury Committee to be grilled on funding policy). They also take evidence from the heads of nationalised industries and the Bank of England, as well as outside witnesses who volunteer their services. And they are great travellers, visiting Japan to investigate industrial training methods, or Southern Italy to look at regional policies.

Both the Crossman Committees and those of St-John Stevas attracted considerable press attention when they were first established. But the novelty on each occasion soon wore off, and unless they are investigating a juicy scandal, or there is a row over – for example – their demand for the release of documents which Government is not inclined to let them see, their worthy deliberations pass for the most part unnoticed. They produce a constant flow of reports which are rarely discussed in Parliament, and seldom make much stir.

They take up the time of senior Ministers and mandarins, but rarely, in practice, do they make much impact on departmental policies. (There are, naturally, exceptions: the

Treasury Committee for example – then called the Expenditure Committee – played a powerful role in persuading the Labour Government to introduce cash controls on public spending programmes in the middle 1970s). Too often their questioning of witnesses is disorganised and repetitive; the members do not always do their (admittedly heavy load of) homework; and although they are supposed to eschew Party political divisions as far as possible, they often make things easy for Ministerial witnesses by preferring abuse and slogans to genuine inquisition. Furthermore their reports are too often written for them by their expert advisers, whose individual King Charles's heads are easily discernible.

The exception remains the Public Accounts Committee. This is the one Select Committee that the Whitehall villagers must take seriously. It does not take evidence from Ministers, but cross-questions mandarins about the apparent scandals dug out for it by the Comptroller and Auditor-General: cases where there appears to be prima facie evidence of maladministration and money-wasting. Their reports can be damning, and they have, over the years, given generations of Permanent Under-Secretaries some most uncomfortable experiences.

Their strictures undoubtedly affect life in the Whitehall village: and not always for the better. There was a typical instance at the end of the 1970s. The PAC discovered that the Department of Energy had been paying grants to North Sea operators and equipment suppliers to compensate them for high interest rates, when the firms' grant applications had been submitted out of time. There was no doubt about the entitlement of the recipients to the grants that they were paid belatedly: the letter of the rules had been breached, not their spirit. Moreover it is hard to believe that Scots Labour MPs, who were prominent in the pursuit of the Department's peccadilloes, would not have been indignant had the beneficiary firms, most of them operating from bases in Scotland, been refused their grants. Nevertheless there was a great fuss (it was even claimed – erroneously, as it turned out – that one of the senior officials responsible had been sacked). And the result was that thereafter Whitehall's preparedness to interpret the ground-rules covering grant applications with common sense ceased. The authority of the PAC was vindicated, and industry and commerce were the victims. The answerability of the Whitehall mandarins to the PAC is not, however, all gall and wormwood for the mandarins. It allows them, on occasion, to mark their distance from their temporary political *patrons*. The Permanent Under-Secretary can inform his Minister that the Minister is asking him to do something which, in the mandarin's judgment, would constitute improper use of public funds. If the Minister wishes to insist, then he must give the mandarin a specific directive in writing, which can, if need be, be waved before the PAC as a *laisser-passer* for the mandarin. Anthony Wedgwood Benn was particularly prone to incurring these dockets as Industry Secretary in the second Wilson Government: and not just incurring them, but seeing them mysteriously made public. They were, no doubt, some modest consolation for the unaccustomed strains he placed upon the traditions and the patience of the villagers.

Questions and debates constitute the public face of Whitehall's work with Westminster. But the MP who knows his way about has learned that when it comes to constituency casework, either is very much a longstop (and usually an ineffective longstop too). Challenged in the open forum, Whitehall owes it to its self-respect to resist. A letter to the Minister stands a better chance of securing a re-think to a constituent's benefit.

A substantial – and growing – proportion of the mail received in Whitehall from Westminster displays the member going through the motions. The National Association of Holeborers has mounted a campaign against VAT on holes. Their members up and down the country are instructed to write to their MPs, and supplied with a pro forma letter for the purpose. The MPs, in their turn, attach a printed slip demanding the Minister's response, pass it on, and forget about it (see Chapter 10).

MPs believe – no doubt correctly – that most of their constituents will be suitably impressed by the Ministerial signature at the bottom of Whitehall's reply, and will badger them no more. I often used to agonise about some of the replies I found laid out for me to 'top and tail' in my nightly boxes. Surely, I said to myself, the MP isn't going to swallow this lame defence? I rapidly discovered that they almost always did. Sometimes I would refuse to sign, and have the officials in to go over a particular case. In the end, after much heart-searching, I might be driven to accept that, however threadbare our case might look, it was the best that we could do. So I duly topped and tailed: and waited for an indignant rejoinder from the MP concerned. It hardly ever materialised.

There was not only the substance of the letter to watch, however, there was also the form. MPs, like lesser human beings, often lend their names to dubious cases. Whitehall's response is liable to be tart. There is no harm in that if the MP is a notorious barrack-room lawyer on the Opposition benches. A tart response to a senior Tory Privy Councillor, even if he is a barrack-room lawyer (and such do exist) is asking for trouble. Whitehall does not find it easy to make the distinction.

Not that Ministers themselves are always guiltless. Before I joined the Whitehall village I had received representations from a local solicitor about some legislation concerned with Court procedure which was making its way through Parliament. This was a closed book to me; but I duly passed on my constituent's letter to the Lord Chancellor, asking for his comments for my correspondent's benefit. In due course I received the Lord Chancellor's reply. He advised me to point out to my constituent that those far more learned in the law than any small town solicitor had deliberated on these matters long and earnestly, and that it was not for the likes of him to dispute their wisdom. I felt obliged to write back to the Lord Chancellor to remind him that MPs liked to have a letter from a Minister which they could pass on to their voters. I had, of course, no means of knowing whether Mr Smith was otherwise inclined to vote for me or not. But I had no doubt at all that if I passed on to him the Lord Chancellor's opinion of his wisdom he would not be so inclined in future.

Given the somewhat stylised nature of most exchanges between MPs and Whitehall it is scarcely to be wondered at that backbenchers – or frontbenchers, for that matter – are widely held to be powerless to secure fair treatment for their voters from the Whitehall machine. That was never my impression. On the rare occasions when I reckoned that a constituent had a genuine grievance I invariably found that Whitehall did its best to put it right. It did require persistence, though. Once – again as a backbencher – I was approached by a constituent who ran a road haulage business. He had obtained planning permission for a new lorry park from the local authority, on condition that he first demolished a derelict mill which overlooked the site. In due course his contractors embarked on the demolition. Twenty-four hours later he was confronted with a preservation order from the Department of the Environment.

So I wrote to the appropriate Parliamentary Under-Secretary, arguing that the left hand did not seem to know what the right hand was up to. He replied that this was life: the Historic Buildings Council had decided that the mill should be listed. There was nothing he could do about it. I replied that this was not acceptable. My constituent was only fulfilling his contract with the local authority; moreover the mill was falling down and dangerous, and he had undertaken to preserve the one feature that had justified the listing. I warned that unless there was a change of heart I would have to raise the matter on the floor of the House of Commons. The Minister looked again – and withdrew the listing.

For private members, as for Ministers, persistence is time-consuming, and time is short. Hence the Ombudsman, or Parliamentary Commissioner for Administration, set up in the mid-1960s by Harold Wilson when he was looking for a weekend headline. The private citizen who finds himself unable to obtain fair treatment from Whitehall asks his MP to pass his grievance to the Ombudsman.

This is often a convenient way out for the MP. Some constituents will not take 'no' for an answer. Particularly when their complaint is clearly based upon illusion, the Ombudsman constitutes an invaluable trashcan. There is not much point is asking the DHSS to look into a claim that a constituent has been subjected to black magic by the medical profession. He really needs a psychiatrist. But he has a vote, and would be unlikely to take kindly to such a suggestion.

Once passed to – and rejected by – the Ombudsman, he may with luck accept that the MP has done all he can.

When it comes to genuine grievances, however, the Ombudsman has always seemed to me something of an irrelevance. The MP should himself be able to obtain redress. The Ombudsman, by contrast, often seems hidebound by Whitehall's own rules. If they have been observed, he is satisfied, even if the rules make no obvious sense. If they have been flouted, the Whitehall department will receive a drubbing – even when common sense suggests that the citizen has been fairly treated.

So much for the House of Commons. There is also, though, the House of Lords. To the mandarins 'Westminster' means the Lower House. The House of Lords is *terra incognita*. I was once told that a Labour front-bench spokesman in the Upper House, Lord Bruce of Donington, was unhappy, and threatening trouble, over some modest little Bill which I had peacefully piloted through the Commons to tidy up the currency, or something of that nature. Would I please have words with him?

Now had he been a Labour spokesman in the Commons I would naturally have known him, and had ideas of my own about how to handle him. I would also have had a copious brief from the Treasury, describing his interest in the subject, and his known view upon it. For Lord Bruce there was nothing. Who, pray, I asked, *was* Lord Bruce? No-one seemed to know. So we looked him up in *Who's Who*, and in he came. I soothed down his ruffled feathers, and my hapless colleague in the House of Lords who had to cope with him was all gratitude. Nevertheless it was a revealing little incident.

Such insouciance towards the Upper House is entirely understandable. Through successive generations it has 'done nothing in particular, and done it very well'. It has occasionally bared its gums at Labour Governments, but usually it has soon discovered that discretion is the better part of valour.

Now, suddenly, everything is changed. Their Lordships, contemplating a virtually impregnable Government majority in the Lower House, have got uppity. Week by week throughout the summer months of 1984, and still more those of 1985, Government legislation was savaged and the Government embarrassingly defeated. The appetite has grown with eating. And then, to make matters worse, in the spring of 1985 their Lordships decided to put themselves on television. Attendance inevitably increased, and, equally inevitably, defeats for the Government commanded air time. Eventually, in the summer of 1985, one Government Bill – a highly contentious measure to replace elected metropolitan councils with nominated bodies for the last year of their life – was thrown out altogether.

All this is doubly embarrassing for a Tory Government. A Labour Government can always dismiss the Lords as a crowd of unelected backwoodsmen, and has no qualms about calling on the Commons to reverse any defeats it may have suffered at their hands. But the Tory Party traditionally upholds the rights and duties of the Upper House, and it is bound to be far more squeamish.

Yet Whitehall remains ill-equipped to handle the House of Peers. Few of its Ministers know anything about it; and, not least because junior Ministers in the Lords are even more miserably remunerated than their counterparts in the Commons, it is not easy to find volunteers to take on the jobs required. Those that do volunteer discover that they are maids of all work. Each department nowadays has a team of Ministers to cover for it in the Commons, whereas in the Lords one junior Minister will regularly be called upon to answer for departments quite other than the one he is officially attached to. As a result he has to handle – sometimes at a moment's notice – material with which he is wholly unfamiliar.

Fortunately their Lordships are nothing if not tolerant. The Minister who puts his head down and reads out a brief which is largely irrelevant to the issues raised in a debate in the House of Commons will swiftly find himself in trouble. In the House of Lords he will be listened to respectfully without a murmur of complaint. But there are limits. When every speaker in a debate – from the Labour benches, those of the Liberals, the SDP and the Tories, and from the cross-benches – attacks a Government proposal, and the Minister reads out his brief as though no doubts had been expressed, then their Lordships are inevitably encouraged to take the bit between their teeth and vote the Government down. For this is the paradox: the Minister in the Commons who is inadequately briefed or incompetent may well provoke a row, but at least he knows that when the vote is called his side will win it. His counterpart in the Lords will have a much easier ride, since their Lordships do not go in for rows: but when the vote comes neither he nor the Whips who sit beside him have any means of knowing who will win it. Yet one thing is certain. If he loses it the Prime Minister will not be amused. The miracle is not that the Government front bench in the House of Lords has from time to time to carry passengers who would not last a week in the 'other place', but that it contrives to attract the service of any occupants of calibre at all.

9

Traders Bearing Beads

Lobbying may not be the oldest profession. But it is an ancient trade. Whitehall would be lost without it. As the pretensions of Government have grown in modern times, the complexities and sophistication of the arts of bringing influence to bear have struggled to keep pace. In the United States the influence groups are so well organised that the would-be Senator or Congressman no longer seeks to put together, as he used to do, the backing of ward and county party power-brokers, and a cross-section of key ethnic groups and industrial interests in his prospective district or state, since they will not suffice. Broader national causes – feminism or anti-abortionists, 'born-again' Christians or gun-ownership – have proved their ability to line up their membership and dictate their voting behaviour to such effect that the tribunes of the people arrive on Capitol Hill committed to support a range of special interests as the price of their election. We have not got there yet. But perhaps we are heading in the same direction.

On this side of the Atlantic the top tier of the pyramid of interest groups is the property of a handful of what General de Gaulle called the *interlocuteurs valables*: in our case the CBI, the TUC, and the National Farmers Union. In the late sixties and early seventies, before 'incomes policy' fell into disrepute, there were times when Whitehall had virtually put Government into commission with the CBI and, in particular, the TUC. In the vain hope that he could thus secure the co-operation of the Unions with his legal constraints on wage bargains Mr Heath offered to discuss aspects of his legislative plans with the TUC, although he always insisted that Parliament's prerogatives be respected. Harold Wilson was less squeamish. One of his senior ministers, Joel Barnett, Chief Secretary to the Treasury from 1974–79, recalled in his memoirs how that Government's relations with the TUC were supposed to be marked by 'give and take'; but that in practice 'the Government gave, and the Unions took'.

The Thatcher Administration was elected on a strong tide of revulsion against the pretensions of the TUC. The age of 'beer and sandwiches', when successive Prime Ministers had sought to buy quiescence from the mighty barons of the TUC in late-night horse-trading at No 10 (the refreshment offered was usually a good deal less plebeian than the catchphrase coined in the days of Harold Wilson implied), was over. The door to No 10 remained wide open. But the Union leaders were shocked to discover that when they visited they were more often lectured at than lecturing. They also soon discovered that, for the first time since the 1950s, they were confronted by a Government which declined to intervene in major industrial disputes, except to the extent of holding the ring to ensure that individual Trades Unionists would be free to choose where their interests lay. The Union leaders had to revert to direct negotiation with those who employed their members. This was a bitter blow to their self-esteem.

The other side of industry fared little better. The CBI also found, to their dismay, that they were confronted by the unfamiliar phenomenon of a Government which declined to assume that the interests of the minority of producers and the totality of consumers, were necessarily synonymous. The National Economic Development Council, whose establishment at the beginning of the 1960s had marked the dawn of the corporatist 1960s and 1970s, embracing as it did CBI, TUC, Whitehall and the Bank of England, survived. Its effective influence did not.

The third traditional producer lobby, the National Farmers Union, alone retained its clout pretty well intact. The agricultural interest has always had its tabs on the Tory Party, as the survival of the Corn Laws through the first Industrial Revolution bore witness. Its colonisation of the post-war Labour Government under Attlee was a more improbable achievement. Perhaps the fact that the NFU calls itself a Union, albeit a Union of capitalists whose members vote overwhelmingly Tory, helped. At any rate large-scale subvention for farm output, however incongruous it may be for a country where the farming vote can carry but a handful of Parliamentary seats, is common cause between the Parties. Mrs Thatcher, a quintessential urban politician, representing one of the rare Tory seats, in North London, where even NFU propagandists would have been hard put to claim a decisive farming vote, might have proved a tougher touch. Fortunately for the NFU, by the time she took office subventions for the farmers were largely in the hands of a producer-managed European Community régime.

The eclipse of the traditional producer lobbies with a claim to lay down objectives for the nation removed a – broadly unwelcome – intrusion into the lifestyle of the Whitehall village. Lobbying of the kind to which the villagers have always been accustomed continues unabated. Like most of us, civil servants find it cosier to bargain with denizens of a similar culture. When a departmental purpose, or the whim of politicians, decrees that 'something must be done' about tobacco advertising, the Whitehall mandarin does not – as his counterparts in France, for example, would be liable to – summon the nearest and most influential tobacco baron and tell him to put a stop to it. (In France he might well obtain a *dossier* from the police about the unusual night-time interests of the baron, just in case it were needed for additional persuasion). He goes into a huddle with his opposite numbers, the tobacco industry's own officialdom. He breaks the news to them that 'my masters have decided' to ban all tobacco advertising. The 'masters' may be blissfully unaware of any such commitment: if things go wrong they will discover it soon enough. The tobacco industry's own civil service will reveal in response that they could rouse every corner-street tobacconist, and half the ruling party in the House of Commons, to defy the Government were it to dare to behave in such a manner. Then the horse-trading begins. The usual result – desired by both sides – is a compromise which gives Whitehall just enough of what it's seeking, and the lobby something which it reckons it can sell to its employers. Whitehall promises to deliver the acquiescence of its Ministers; the lobby civil servants to deliver the acquiescence of their corporate constituents.

It does not always work out. The civil service of our lobbies tend to reflect disproportionately the views and interests of the medium fry. Most trade associations operate on a basis of weighted voting which gives to ICI a much bigger vote than it gives to Caithness Chemicals. But the differentiation is a long way short of reflecting the real distinction between the two concerns. So the big boys, who usually know their way around Westminster and Whitehall without any need for guidance, are often inclined to bypass the bureaucracy of their lobby, and campaign on their own behalf. The mandarins are dismayed to find that, having struck their deal with the tobacco industry *apparatchiks*, their politicians have been nobbled by one of the fat cats. No wonder that Whitehall solemnly discourages out-of-hours conversations between a Minister and the Chairman of one of the dominant companies in an industry with which they have to deal.

Nevertheless the safest solution for the corporate lobbyist is first to fix his trade association, and then to watch his trade association fix the civil service. For once the deal is done, the honour of the civil service is engaged. If it then fails to deliver its Ministers bound hand and foot, it hangs its head in shame. Whereas the lobby which converts the politicians is inevitably confronted by the resistance of the civil service. Their collective departmental machismo is at stake.

Yet the best of causes (in the eyes of its promoters) does not always win the Whitehall battle. So the more hazardous second-line assault must be prepared. There may always be a susceptible Ministerial flank to turn. I was presented, as a Minister, with a scheme of wondrous complexity to enable horse-traders to escape VAT. I detected a considerable lack of enthusiasm in the Customs and Excise. Not being a horse-fancier by upbringing, I dismissed the whole proposal out of hand. I was swiftly warned that my predecessor, a devotee of the race-track and the hunting-field, had given the scheme his blessing. I was vastly unimpressed, until I was accosted by one of my senior Tory colleagues in the corridors of Westminster. 'I hear', he told me in a voice full of menace, 'that you're being bloody-minded about our horse-trading scheme. Well forget it. It was all fixed up with your predecessor, and I can assure you that if you muck it around we'll make your life a misery.' I had second thoughts.

Nobbling Ministers does not always work so smoothly. My predecessor may have been a horse-fancier by predilic-tion: by training and profession he was a tax barrister. He had set his heart on a scheme to amalgamate the appeal procedure for Inland Revenue and VAT cases. For all I know he may have been absolutely right; but his plan was bitterly opposed by sections of his own profession, and would have had to be forced upon them. This was not my scene, and not a battle which I was inclined to fight. The scheme was dropped. Apart from my predecessor there was none around at Westminster to lynch me on its behalf.

A fascinating example of the desirability of striking when the Minister is sympathetic is provided by the long campaign waged by the recording studios to impose a levy on blank video tapes. In 1985 Norman Tebbit's support was secured, and the levy plan went into a pending White Paper on copy-right law. Then Norman Tebbit made way for Leon Brittan, who had the scheme struck out. Happily for the recording studios, Leon Brittan gave way to Paul Channon in time. At the moment of writing the levy plan is reinstated.

The lobby that has lost the argument with Whitehall, and failed to find a sympathetic Minister, must needs turn to Westminster. In theory it might as well save its time and money. It is confronted with a Government backed by a solid Parliamentary majority, like the present one, which can afford to ignore a real or potential rebellion by 20, 30, 60 or even 90 of its own backbenchers, convinced by the persuasive arguments of the lobbyists, with impunity. Or it is confronted by a Government poised upon a knife-edge, liable to defeat by the desertion of handful of supporters: and for that very reason they do not dare rebel.

The practicalities are vastly different. No matter how seemingly impregnable a Government's majority, it always *feels* itself to be vulnerable to back-bench pressures. Only the lobbyists need to be subtle and selective, and all too frequently they are neither.

Every Government majority contains a quota of the disaffected, ever eager to rebel. They are fodder for the lobbyists, but all too often counter-productive. The most valuable recruit to the trader's cause is the influential loyalist.

Money is increasingly perceived as the key to Parliamentary influence. Copying the pattern that prevails on Capitol Hill, a new breed of influence-brokers is developing at Westminster. They recruit MPs as paid 'consultants' or 'advisers'. This causes much alarm. That the individual MP thus recruited may confront a conflict between his obligations as a 'tribune of the people' and his obligations to private paymasters is indisputable; but that the paymasters can thus dictate, or even substantially influence, the choices of the Government is much more doubtful.

For the opinions of the purchased advocate are accordingly discounted by his colleagues. High-pressure salesmanship can be self-defeating. When British Airways was faced with the unwelcome prospect, in early 1986, of deferment of its flotation as a private-sector company, it gathered 140 Tory backbenchers, or almost one in two, to a sumptuous luncheon at which they were harangued by BA's chairman, Lord King, about the folly of delay. Some, no doubt, were converted. At least as many, both of those who came and of those who did not, were alienated by what they perceived as crude pressure tactics.

Far more effective for the lobbyists, if more expensive and time-consuming, is pressure through the grassroots. For no MP can safely ignore representations from his voters, however those voters may have been motivated. Nor can the opinions of an MP be discounted when they reflect views pressed upon him by his voters.

The lobbyist must achieve evidence of personal commitment to carry weight. 10,000 or 100,000 signatures on a petition sound impressive: Westminster is rightly cynical about the willingness of citizens to sign almost anything to get the petition-carrier away (moreover, mass petitions are often said to contain, on close inspection, the signatures of such unexpected backers as Queen Victoria and Lord Nelson). Nor does the pre-printed form, requiring nothing but a signature, particularly impress.

In the summer of 1980 MPs were besieged with letters from Catholic constituents protesting at the threat allegedly posed to Catholic schools by a proposal that Local Education Authorities should be permitted to charge for school transport. On closer inspection most of these communications had fairly obviously been signed, not by Catholic voters at all, but by their children scribbling under the vigilant eye of their local parish priests. Similarly when I was Economic Secretary the single issue which provoked far more letters from my Westminster colleagues than any other was an imagined threat of higher tax on one-armed bandits. I must have heard from something like two-thirds of the House of Commons, spurred on by lobbying from the licensed victuallers. But in almost every case the MP had simply signed a pro forma covering letter enclosing a printed representation from the publicans. There were, in fact, no plans to raise the tax on fruit machines in the Budget then preparing. But if there had been, I doubt if we would have been deterred by this campaign, since it was obvious that MPs were only going through the motions.

At the other end of the scale of effectiveness ranks a lobby from the fag-end of the Heath Administration. In the summer of 1973 the Home Office, under pressure from the police, unveiled plans for stringent new rules governing the ownership of shotguns. The shot-gun lobby got to work. Tory MPs were soon receiving a modest stream of letters objecting to the proposal. It was by no means a cascade: but what it lacked in quantity it made up amply in quality. For most of the letters were not pre-printed forms that had been topped and tailed. They were hand-written, and by senior officials of our constituency associations – the chairmen of the local village branches. In next to no time a steady stream of backbenchers (and not only backbenchers) was calling on the Whips' Office to serve notice that the Home Office had better think again. It did.

A more recent example of effective lobbying occurred during the run-up to the Budget of 1985. Word got round that Chancellor Lawson had two targets in his sights. One was the zero-rating for VAT of books and newspapers. The other was the tax privilege of pension funds. Both targets swiftly took evasive action. Booksellers and newspaper publishers made common cause in denunciation of a 'tax on knowledge', led by Lord Macmillan, whose family firm had devised the 'net book agreement' to ensure (and which still ensures) that booksellers must observe the recommended retail prices set by publishers. The campaign in defence of the tax exemption enjoyed by the pension funds was even more high profile, and comprehensive. Tory MPs were snowed under with complaints about both subjects; and the CBI did its best to ensure that no politician could visit a boardroom without being deafened by denunciations of the Chancellor's evil intentions towards the senior citizens. At a luncheon with some of the senior directors of ICI a month before the Budget, I was finally obliged to remind them that I was no longer a Treasury Minister, or privy to the Chancellor's intentions. But well before Budget Day it was becoming apparent that the Chancellor was going to be forced to abandon both his rumoured ambitions. At his traditional pre-Budget meeting with the Government backbenchers, at which the Treasury team listens impassively to their last-minute messages, requests from some of those present to the Chancellor that he should 'for God's sake scotch these idiotic stories about VAT on books and taxes on the pension funds before we all collapse with writers' cramp from trying to answer all the protest letters' were cheered to the echo.

Sure enough, he got the message. On Budget Day he made a virtue of necessity, pooh-poohing all the silly stories about assaults upon the pension funds, and even paying tribute to the tax exemption enjoyed by 'golden handshakes' on retirement as a 'much-loved anomaly'. As to broadening the scope of VAT, he even went to the extraordinary – almost unprecedented – lengths of abjuring any such intention for the remainder of the Parliament.

The lessons for the lobbyists are clear enough. First, win the argument behind the scenes in Whitehall if you can. Second, if you cannot, then try to identify a Minister who, by background or temperament, is liable to be well-disposed towards your interest (and, bearing in mind that he is always liable to be reshuffled, having identified such a prize, waste no time in laying hold of him). Only if both of these approaches have been tried and failed does it become desirable to go public.

From then on it is all too easy to squander cash to minimal effect. PR agencies may earn their fees by assembling squads of backbenchers to be wined and dined; but, while there may be no such thing as a free lunch, MPs cannot be relied upon to repay the hospitality they have enjoyed. Even if they do, their usefulness depends on quality and not on quantity. The support of the Chairman of a back-bench policy committee, or of a Parliamentary Select Committee, is worth that of a dozen 'rent-a-quote' backbenchers, whose colourful phraseology on every subject known to man is woefully familiar to – and discounted by – press and colleagues equally. It is a similar story when it comes to mustering the general public. Petitions may appear impressive, but do not butter many parsnips. If the matchsticks industry can motivate the High Street tobacconists in every constituency in the land – or at least the ones in Government hands – to demand a meeting with their local member to put the fear of God in him or her, then it is likely to be getting somewhere.

The example of the National Farmers Union is often cited, and with reason. No doubt the farmers have much to thank the strength of the farming vote in other Community countries for the scale of the support they uniquely enjoy for producing unsaleable surpluses. But their readiness, over many years, to take time out to confront their local MPs several times a year has also paid handsome dividends. The mystery is that other industries have been so slow to learn the lesson.

There is, however, another dimension to lobbying in Whitehall which is by now a well-established annual ritual. The *interlocuteurs valables* come round to the Treasury with the regularity and predictability of snowdrops. The bookies, the car makers, the tobacco firms, the drink producers, the publicans, the caterers for gamblers, the Jockey Club, the Country Landowners: these are the Treasury's old faithfuls, each of them seeking to forestall an impost, or to promote a favour, in the forthcoming Budget. They are shared out between the Chancellor and the junior Treasury Minister responsible for the Customs and the Excise (since, apart sometimes from the Country Landowners, their concern is with changes in duties rather than in taxes). The precise allocation of responsibility for their reception depends on the whim of the Chancellor. There was one year, I recall, when the Jockey Club had not one but two sessions with Geoffrey Howe: but they are very grand. At the other end of the scale, the bookies and publicans never got further than me.

The ritual hardly varies. The visitors arrive, sometimes supported by a back-bench MP on their payroll, and almost invariably by at least one General (I sometimes used to speculate what would happen to our brass-hats if the lobbies were not around to sustain them in retirement). The bookies even boasted a Field Marshal: his familiarity with the niceties of betting tax was not, perhaps, his outstanding qualification for attendance. The receiving Minister is supported by a couple of desk men from the Customs (who have been engaged for weeks before in the receipt of special pleading from the officials of the lobbies, and know it all by heart).

Introductions are effected; tea and aged Treasury biscuits are produced (the Jockey Club, I think, once ranked whisky: but as I say they are a case apart); and play commences. The supporting MP, if there is one, or failing him the General, reminds the receiving Minister of the vital role 'the industry' – they are all 'industries' for the purpose of this exercise – plays in the nation's lifestyle, invisible exports, tourism and welfare; and then invites one of the real-life practitioners to display their wares.

These, too, follow a familiar pattern. The 'industry' is on its knees owing to the Chancellor's rapacity in previous years, and any addition to its burden of taxation will either 'kill the goose that lays the golden eggs' or succumb to 'the law of diminishing returns'. One or other of these two clichés is *de rigueur*. So, alas!, is the table thoughtfully provided for the Minister, which shows that notwithstanding the repetition of this dreadful warning every year, more tax invariably does produce more revenue.

The Private Secretary writes it all down in long-hand; and when each of the visiting deputation has had his (or, very rarely, her) appointed say, the Minister responds that he entirely understands their concerns, and will faithfully report each word of them to the Chancellor. But they will understand that, with the Budget only weeks away, he can make no promises, nor even venture comment. They entirely understand; express the deepest gratitude for the Minister's time; and cheerfully depart. Awaiting them on the doorstep of the Treasury is the photographer from their trade press, which duly displays them to advantage over a story reporting that they have 'made the strongest representations' and 'received a sympathetic hearing'. I occasionally wondered whether this was not the whole object of the exercise. Indeed it occurred to me that, for all the difference it could make to actual Budget choices, they would save themselves and Whitehall a lot of wasted time if they dispensed with the confrontation, and settled for the photo-call.

It would be wrong to give the impression, though, that Budget Day marks the end of lobbying. On the contrary: in a sense the real horse-trading only then begins. For months previously the tax lawyers and accountants will have been haggling with the Inland Revenue (and, to a lesser extent, the Customs) over which tax loopholes should be closed, and which opportunities for enterprise should be opened. Towards the end they will have a session with Ministers to try and press at least some of the points to which the Inland Revenue had proved resistant. With the publication of the Finance Bill, some three weeks after Budget Day, the real donkey-work begins. The cast of 35 MPs appointed to the Finance Bill Committee which will scan it line by line (after the floor of the Commons has had a couple of days of knock-about over a few of what are perceived to be the more politically worthwhile clauses) will be bowed down with lengthy submissions and suggested amendments from these selfsame lawyers and accountants, who will be simultaneously pursuing behind-the-scenes negotiations with the Ministers and civil servants.

They do not need a tax accountant or barrister to advance their case in Committee, although obviously it helps. It is by no means unknown for backbenchers – or even Opposition frontbenchers – to read a brief in support of an amendment which they plainly do not understand. (There was an occasion in the winter of 1985 in the House of Lords when Lord Teviot, acting as the spokesman for 'bus interests on the Bill to return the 'buses to the private sector, mislaid his brief and was lost for words to explain his own amendment. Their Lorships understood). Fortunately the Minister who has to reply will have a copy of the selfsame brief, and the Whitehall answer – which the lobbyists will very likely have gone over with the Inland Revenue beforehand.

Inevitably this form of lobbying tends to concentrate upon the Tory benches, whatever Government may be in power, since Tory MPs, with City knowledge and connections, are likely to be both more sympathetic and more interested. Yet wise lobbyists do not neglect selected Labour MPs. I remember that when the Heath Government removed the bias against company profit distributions inherited from Labour, the Unquoted Companies Group, an exclusive club of the largest family companies (which, by their nature, are low distributors, and therefore stood to suffer) lobbied one or two of Labour's accountants so successfully that the Opposition was persuaded to back Tory back-bench amendments in support of such inherently improbable victims – improbable, that is, for the Labour Party – and the Government faced defeat. In the end the Tory backbenchers were persuaded by vague promises of future reconsideration to withdraw.

That incident highlights the weakness of this form of lobbying. All too often, when it comes to the crunch, the Government's supporters will be talked into docility. So even at this late stage of a Bill's passage to the Statute Book, delicate backroom talks with the civil servants and their Ministers are liable to prove more productive.

On one occasion when we were busy processing the Finance Bill through Parliament I was confronted by some special pleading by the racecourse lobby. It transpired that many of the smaller racecourses depend for their prize money on the propensity of racehorse owners to enter horses for all sorts of races from most of which they will be scratched before the race begins. Wetherby, the hereditary agents of the Jockey Club, keep the stake money. But the racecourses were required to change and surrender VAT on it and resented it. The Customs and Excise had proved unsympathetic. Not being a racing man, I found it difficult to perceive the racing fraternity as specimens of the deserving poor, and agreed with the Customs. The Chancellor, however, was less hard-hearted. So in came the bloodstock boys, and we went carefully over the ground. The visitors swiftly played a joker. If a business booked hotel rooms, and then did not take them up and forfeited its deposit, they asserted, no VAT was payable. What was the difference? I looked to my Customs side. Not so, he assured us. Unfortunately he turned out to be wrong. So the bloodstock boys won their case. Which only goes to show how wise the civil service is to warn their Ministers against the hazards of creating precedents. They will assuredly be pressed into use by those for whom they were not intended.

10

When the Treasury Went Wet

In current political jargon, and under all political dispensations, the Treasury is inevitably the 'driest' of Whitehall departments. For 'dampness' is nowadays defined by reference to a scale of relative enthusiasm for state expenditure, and regardless of the labels of the politicians, whether they be Socialists, Social Democrats or Tories, the Treasury will always be against it, since it has to raise the cash to meet the bills. But for the same reason there is one cause which is normally espoused by those politicians identified with 'dryness' which has few friends in the Treasury: defence. For the Treasury (like other Finance Ministries around the globe) long ago discovered that if defence spending is given free rein then other fields of spending with more obvious sex appeal to the electorate – health, welfare, education, roads – become far more resistant to restraint.

Thus arguably one of the Treasury's greatest victories in modern times was the decision which Winston Churchill (of all people) persuaded his colleagues to approve when he was Chancellor in the 1920s: the so-called 'ten year rule'. This was a working assumption, to be reviewed each year, that the defence budget could safely be drafted on the basis that there would be no European war for ten years ahead.

No such comforting presumption was available to help the Treasury in the early 1980s. On the contrary. The Government had, in 1979, publicly endorsed a call from NATO for member countries to increase their spending on defence by three per cent per annum over and above the going rate of inflation, and was determined to set a good example.

Furthermore when the network of 'comparability' Commissions and review bodies for public-sector pay was dismantled in 1980, a special exception was made for the armed forces (and the police). As a result, by early 1982 defence spending had grown by more than two-thirds in three years: significantly faster than the overall rate of growth of public expenditure. The Treasury was not remotely reconciled to this rake's progress (as they saw it); at each annual public spending exercise successive Chief Secretaries were put up to try and get the 'three per cent real growth' commitment expunged from the record. But until the second Election victory had been safely gathered in 1983, all their powers of advocacy failed to shift the Prime Minister.

Against this background, the Argentinian invasion of the Falklands at the end of March 1982 hit the mandarins of Great George Street as a particularly vicious stroke of fate. They knew, by bitter experience, that when war breaks out their normal criteria of good housekeeping go to the wall for the duration. War, like high heaven, 'rejects the law of nicely calculated less or more'. Furthermore they had every reason to recall that the nearest modern precedent for the Falklands expedition, the Suez crisis in 1956, had provoked a run on sterling which had led the then Chancellor, Harold Macmillan, who had been one of the most vociferous advocates of military action, to advise his colleagues to call it a day.

So there was an atmosphere of foreboding at the Treasury Chambers. Among the Ministers there were additional reasons for dismay. By the early spring of 1982 there were the first faint signs that the painful medicines applied in 1979–81 were beginning to show results. Inflation was falling steeply; the explosive earlier growth of the monetary aggregates was abating; the CBI's regular quarterly survey of commercial sentiment had begun to suggest that the worst of the deep recession of 1980–81 was behind us; while unemployment continued to rise steeply, the pace of increase was slowing; and the opinion polls, in which the Government had been trailing far behind the other two main political groups in the autumn of 1981, were suggesting a modest recovery in its electoral fortunes. The Treasury, having borne the brunt of the opprobrium for the stern financial policies applied hitherto, was looking forward to reaping some reward. And now – as we saw it – all our hopes were put in jeopardy by a wild adventure in the southern seas.

We also had a special reason for feeling that it could have been avoided. For our colleague, the Financial Secretary Nicholas Ridley, in his previous incarnation as Minister of State at the Foreign Office, had secured the acquiescence of both the Argentinians and the Falkland Islanders to a deal whereby formal sovereignty over the islands was to be conceded to the Argentinians, while British rule would be maintained in practice on a 'lease-back' basis. This compromise had then provoked a noisy, if quite unrepresentative, explosion on the back benches in the Commons, and the Government had lost its nerve. Inevitably we felt that this had been a golden opportunity wilfully squandered.

The popular, although scarcely comforting, analogy at the time was with Suez. I could not get out of my mind what seemed to me a far closer historical parallel: a much more painful one. Eighty years before, another seaborne expedition had been despatched around the globe to recover stolen territory: the Russian expedition to Port Arthur. When it arrived at its destination it had been blown out of the water by the occupying power, Japan. If that were to be the fate of the Falklands expedition, it would assuredly be the end of the Thatcher Government.

For at a time such as this the unease of the denizens of Whitehall was reinforced for the Ministers by weekend experience in the constituencies. Undoubtedly the immediate reaction in the grassroots to the Falklands expedition was one of pride and relief – the 'walking tall' syndrome. But it was fragile. It was easy to detect the unease just below the surface. An almost bloodless victory would indeed be marvellous. But were there to be substantial loss of British lives it was all too clear that the game would be perceived as not worth the candle.

So on the Falklands the Treasury, so long the Praetorian Guard of the Thatcher Administration, was perceived to have gone 'wet'. At one of the Prime Minister's briefings for Ministers outside the Cabinet (to which reference has already been made) one of my colleagues asked her about hazards to the pound. On the contrary, she replied, the pound was holding up most resiliently. At this point I found my eye caught. 'Isn't it, Jock?' I gulped. 'So far, Prime Minister'. There was a predictable explosion. " '*So far*'? What d'you mean, 'so far'? What's the matter with the Treasury?".

Happily, within weeks the expedition force was safely landed, and our spineless fears proved groundless. They cost me dear. Ministers regularly leak and are regularly leaked against. The latter was my fate.

One afternoon towards the end of May 1982, free of an official lunchtime date in my diary, I had escaped by bike to that gregarious watering-place the Garrick Club. While I was having a pre-lunch drink at the bar, my erstwhile Fleet Street colleague Peregrine Worsthorne of the *Sunday Telegraph* came up to me. 'Splendid letter of yours in the *New Statesman*', he said. 'I very much agree with you'. 'Oh, good', I replied. And then did a double-take. I rushed after him. 'What letter? What the hell are you talking about?' He produced a copy of the left-wing weekly, hot off the news-stands, drawing my attention to an item prominently displayed on an inside page.

'No biffing cause' was the headline. Beneath was an extensive quotation from a letter. 'I think I'd dispute your claim that you've got to have a very good cause to go to war. I don't think the cause matters a tuppeny damn. All that matters is the stomach for the fight. The Kaiser in 1914 had given us far less cause to go to war than Hitler in 1939. Yet I suspect we marched into battle with twice the zest in 1914.

'The problem, I suspect, on this occasion, is that the travellers on the Clapham omnibus do not have the stomach for the fight. So biffing the Argies is fine. Being biffed by the Argies is a mug's game. But it's got nothing to do with causes or morality. I don't think it ever really has.'

I recognised the letter at once. Six weeks earlier, after emerging from hospital and a minor operation, I had been entertained to dinner by Samuel Brittan, the Economics Editor of the *Financial Times* and a very old friend. On the morning, a couple of days subsequently, when I came to pen a thank-you letter for my dinner, Sam happened to have published in the *Financial Times* a heated denunciation of the

Falklands expedition from an essentially pacifist viewpoint. So I had added a postscript to my bread-and-butter letter commenting on his article. This was it.

It was a Thursday. My first thought was that the Prime Minister would be facing Questions in the Commons that afternoon. If Peregrine Worsthorne had read the *New Statesman*, then so might others. I dashed to the telephone and called my Private Office. They had better get on to 10 Downing Street immediately, advising them to acquire a copy of the *New Statesman*. Yes, alas! The letter was genuine. How it had got to the *New Statesman* I had no idea – except that it had presumably been stolen.

For a few brief hours I clung to the hope that that might be the end of the matter. The circulation of the *New Statesman* is, after all, derisory: and Prime Minister's Questions had come and gone without a mention of it. My hope was quickly dashed. As the evening wore on my telephone began to ring and ring. The national press and TV were on to a story. It was at that point that a fresh, and even more horrendous, thought occurred to me.

Six weeks before, following the reoccupation by British personnel of the base-camp in Antarctic South Georgia which had first been seized by Argentina, I had been asked for my comments by my local weekly newspaper in Knutsford (whose editor, for reasons best known to himself, never missed a chance to cross swords with me). Clearly it was no time for half-measures, and I had produced a 'land of hope and glory' article which would have done Horatio Bottomley proud. The contrast between it and my private letter to Sam Brittan (written almost simultaneously) could not have been more flagrant. I thought it was high time for me to ring my constituency agent, and warn her what lay in store.

The following day was, I suppose, among the more unpleasant of my life. It started early. The door-bell rang at 7 am. My wife opened the door to be confronted with a reporter and a photographer from the *Daily Mail*. I decided to play possum as long as I could. A quick perusal of the morning papers offerred no relief. I was headline news in most of them, with ample references to the doubtful joys of 'biffing Argies'. Then when, at 8.40, my official car arrived to collect me, the *Daily Mail* was still in attendance. Bulbs flashed. The engaging young reporter told me that his Editor had instructed him to offer me a full page in the next day's *Mail* to present my considered view of the Falklands campaign. To which I replied that I wasn't born yesterday, whatever appearances at that moment might suggest.

At the Treasury my telephone rang steadily. An early caller was my constituency agent, with the news that the honorary secretary of the local British Legion had announced – to the local press – that if I was going to put in an appearance at the annual church parade and service for the Mayor of Knutsford, which just happened to be due that weekend, then the British Legion would not do so. That spelled Trouble. Then there was a call from one of the senior Parliamentary lobby correspondents – to enquire whether my head was to be called for on a charger? Surely not, I replied: you surely could not be fired because somebody stole a private letter and passed it to the press? 'Don't count on it', was the encouraging response. 'I have the impression that the knives are out'.

Considerably shaken, I called some Ministerial colleagues. I was advised to seek an early meeting with the Prime Minister, at which I should offer up my cards – when with any luck the offer would be rejected. I did as I was told, and a meeting was duly arranged at No 10 that afternoon.

The Prime Minister was both generous and understanding. 'You write too much' she told me – a charge to which, in the circumstances, I could not do other than plead guilty. But she wouldn't hear of resignation. With the help of her Parliamentary Private Secretary, Ian Gow, I drafted a statement to the effect that the stolen private letter reflected no more than a passing brain-storm, and in retrospect I realised had totally misjudged the public mood. This was generally interpreted – understandably – as a craven climb-down. I was in no position to explain that my earlier published comments on the recapture of South Georgia would have left me with no choice even if Downing Street had not desired a public retraction of the views expressed in the stolen letter.

The mandarins were full of sympathy and understanding. So were almost all my Parliamentary colleagues, from both sides of the House of Commons. They knew, or could very easily imagine, what I was going through.

There was, however, one surprising sequel. Some ten days later the Finance Bill was working its way peaceably through its Committee stage on the upper floor of the House of Commons. We were due to be sitting late. The rest of the Commons had packed up early. So when I came down to the Members' dining room for a bite of food during the dinner-break, one of the larger tables in the middle of the dining-room was already full with my colleagues from the Finance Bill Committee. Otherwise the room was almost empty.

Convention in the Members' Dining-Room has it that unless you have a special reason to dine in solitude you usually join colleagues at a table where a place is available. Immediately adjacent to the door was a table with a solitary diner: Edward Heath.

So far as I could recollect, we had not exchanged a sentence since the summer of 1974. Yet he was now staring at me. So I asked if I could join him. 'By all means': he sounded almost welcoming.

'And how did it come about', he asked me as soon as I had taken my place, 'that your very sensible views about this Falklands affair found their way into the public prints?' I had to confess I could not enlighten him. He evidently had more important matters on his mind than a colleague's tribulations.

There was one further sequel which is perhaps worth recounting in the light of the current debate about the rights and wrongs of 'leaking'. In the autumn of 1983 I was bidden to appear on the weekly Parliamentary programme on Channel Four TV which at that time was hosted by Peter Jay, an old friend and colleague and sometime Economics Editor of *The Times*. The day before, *The Times* had published the statement made to it by Cecil Parkinson's former mistress, Miss Sarah Keays, which had effectively ended that minister's career. That was not the subject of our programme, but inevitably it occupied our attention while we waited to go on the air.

Peter Jay asserted that, had he been Editor of *The Times*, he would have told Miss Keays that if she had anything to say she should release it to the press in general through her solicitors, when he would consider publishing it down-page on page 4. 'And when your proprietor discovered – as he no doubt would – that you had been offered it exclusively', I challenged him, 'and that you had spurned it, he'd have had your guts for garters.' 'Maybe,' was Peter's magisterial reply. 'But that is still what I would have done.'

So would he have published my stolen letter? It turned out that the editor of the *New Statesman*, Hugh Stephenson, was an old friend of his – and that he had been consulted before Stephenson published it. His advice had been that Stephenson had first to satisfy himself on three counts. Was it genuine? Did it concern a matter of genuine public interest? Had he come by it lawfully? If he could give affirmative answers to all three questions, he would be fully entitled to publish it.

To have acted lawfully Stephenson would have had to have believed that either I – to whom the legal copyright belonged – or Sam Brittan had authorized disclosure of the letter. But then Peter Jay's own former newspaper had performed a similar role when it had published, not so long before, a copy of a private letter from Denis Thatcher to the Secretary of State for Wales.

Long before these events the Falklands affair had reached its triumphal climax. Ministers could not just breathe again: they could begin to plan the second Thatcher Government. And Whitehall swiftly adjusted its sights accordingly.

If I could not bask so comfortably in the reflected glow from Port Stanley, neither could the Treasury. It had to contemplate the bills. There was an open-ended commitment to replace the ships and aircraft lost and damaged in the battle; and this, and the cost – running to hundreds of millions of pounds a year for years ahead – of turning a remote bunch of islands in the South Atlantic into a suppliable fortress, had to be added to the existing projections of the defence Budget. Yet at the same time the Treasury was expected to draw back the share of national resources pre-empted by the State below the levels inherited in 1979. It says much for its departmental perseverance that the squandering of hundreds of millions a year on so curious a purpose did not lead to a complementary burst of spending on more electorally appealing causes nearer home. Not like the days of Lord Stockton.

11

Building Stately Pleasure Domes

In Xanadu did Kublha Khan
  A stately pleasure dome decree

Until some time in the autumn of 1982 the term 'freeport' conjured up, for me, a vision of some exotic oriental den of vice: an offshore island like Macão, where you could gamble all night and buy contraband and counterfeit Cartier watches by day. Not, I thought, the sort of watering-place for serious-minded Treasury ministers. I soon learned otherwise. The freeport saga proved a choice *vignette* of Whitehall manners and *mores*.

The Adam Smith Institute is one of those fringe institutions which sprang up in the early 1980s and rapidly contrived to achieve a quite impressive profile on a shoestring budget. In the summer of 1982 it had published a pamphlet extolling the virtues of the freeport concept: enclaves where enterprise could flourish beyond the reach of the dead hand of bureaucracy in general, and HM Customs and Excise in particular. Attention was drawn to the example set by Hong Kong, freeports in the United States, and, nearer home, the freeports of Hamburg, Rotterdam and Shannon. Why, it asked, was the Thatcher Government, supposedly so keen on free markets, so negligent in practice of this alluring opportunity?

The pamphlet earned some column inches and the odd approving editorial in the 'drier' reaches of the national press; and seemed thereafter destined for oblivion. Only it was taken up by the Parliamentary Select Committee on Scottish Affairs. This was almost as though the Central Committee of the Communist Party of the Soviet Union had placed the works of Professor Milton Friedman on the Russian school curriculum. For the Scottish Select Committee is not normally perceived as a champion of open-market economics. It is usually engaged in special pleading for preferential Scottish access to the Whitehall gravy-train.

It so happened, however, that in the autumn of 1982 the Select Committee was investigating what could be done to rescue Prestwick airport. Prestwick airport is, essentially, a memorial to the early years of transatlantic air travel, when aircraft needed to touch down at the nearest landfall. As the range of the transatlantic carriers had lengthened, Prestwick, a good 30 miles from Glasgow down the Ayrshire coast, had become increasingly redundant. Glasgow developed its own international airport at Abbotsinch, and Edinburgh had Turnhouse. Three Scottish airports with pretensions to international status were generally perceived, by the early 1980s, to be at least one too many. Prestwick had become a consistent drain upon the balance-sheet of the British Airports Authority, which was now scheduled for flotation in the private sector. Prestwick's days were all too plainly numbered.

But Prestwick had champions in high places. In particular the Secretary of State for Scotland, George Younger, who, by a happy coincidence (for Prestwick), happened to be the town's MP. So the enquiry by the Scottish Select Committee was knocking at an open door.

The Adam Smith Institute shrewdly seized its chance. For it so happened that Shannon airport, on the south-western coast of Southern Ireland, had many similarities with Prestwick. Many further miles from anywhere, it too had faced disaster when the transatlantic airlines no longer needed access to the closest landfall. So the Dublin Government had set up the Shannon freeport, and given Shannon a fresh lease of life. The Adam Smith Institute urged the members of the Scottish Select Committee to pay a call on Shannon – and Miami too, while they were about it. Select

Committees are seldom loath to travel, and they needed no encouragement.

They were duly impressed by what they had seen. On return from their travels they invited the Department of Trade to give them its reactions. The junior Minister responsible for airports and shipping at that department happened to be Iain Sproat, himself a Scottish MP and a vigorous, not to say buccaneering, advocate of free enterprise and deregulation. He assured them they were onto a good thing, and wished them Godspeed.

Customs regulation, however, was the business of the Treasury. So no sooner had the Committee enjoyed the blessing of my colleague Iain Sproat than they called for my attendance. The Customs and Excise formed up to brief me. I was not at all surprised to learn that they thought this was a rotten notion. My immediate reaction to them was unsympathetic. Here, once again, I thought, was the civil service performing the role of Philip Guedalla's 'inverted Micawbers, waiting for something to turn down'. But the more I studied their critique, the more I was impressed.

No doubt it was true that the impact of a clutch of British freeports, each needing service and policing, upon their scarce manpower resources (which we were for ever pressing them to shrink) overshadowed their reactions. They argued that Customs officers allocated to the supervision of freeports would be cost-ineffectively unemployed. When they themselves had appeared before the Scottish Select Committee, in advance of my own grilling, their estimates of the numbers which would be required to supervise such enclaves were challenged (and in the light of both the experience of other countries, and also our own experience since, justifiably challenged). But I was always sensitive to the awkwardness of charging them to undertake additional duties when we were calling for manpower economies.

They had, however, other and, so I was rapidly convinced, weightier objections. First of all they pointed out that the rules already operating made it perfectly possible for traders to conduct entrepôt trade – bringing in goods for onward transhipment to third markets outside the European Community – or, if they were so minded, to assemble imported components and to add domestically produced components to them before shipping them out again to third markets, free of liability to import duties. Secondly they pointed out that the rules of the European Community banned the release of imported goods from a freeport into the Community market without payment of the appropriate Community tariff. And thirdly they warned that while freeports such as those at Shannon and at Hamburg, whose existence antedated the Community, were allowed to get away with some – marginal – fiscal privileges, newcomers would not enjoy any such indulgences. They convinced me, in other words, that if we did establish freeports there was no obvious reason why traders should queue up to set up shop within them.

The official line, however, was that this was an interesting enquiry by the Scottish Committee, about which the Government had an open mind. Indeed it was, simultaneously, being pursued by the interested Whitehall departments. Moreover my colleagues George Younger and Iain Sproat, while staunchly professing open-mindedness, had left the Committee with the clear impression that they were all in favour. I, while also making the appropriate obeisance to open-mindedness, had not. I had, they suggested, been nobbled by the excisemen.

Select Committees regularly come up with exciting ideas for new Government initiatives, and they are as regularly given a genteel brush-off by Whitehall. So it might have been on this occasion. But the bandwagon was filling up. The Institute of Directors, which at that time under the leadership of Walter Goldsmith was far more closely attuned to Thatcherite politics than was the rival CBI, had joined the club vociferously. Furthermore Geoffrey Howe claimed pride of parenthood in the earlier enterprise zone concept, which had distinct affinities with that of the freeport. Enterprise zones were defined localities enjoying exemption from local rates and planning constraints, and a number had been established in the first three years of the Administration contiguous to the more deprived inner-city areas. Hence he was highly sympathetic to the freeport idea.

And so it was that, towards the end of 1982, I was suddenly told that I was to preside over an Inter-Departmental Enquiry. There would be officials from the interested Whitehall departments – Trade, Transport, Ireland, Scotland, and of course the Customs – together with representatives of the CBI, the Institute of Directors, the British Importers Confederation. We were to report in good time for the 1983 Budget just in case – you never knew – it turned out to be a winner after all, in which case enabling legislation could be included in the 1983 Finance Bill.

I approached this assignment with considerable trepidation. Inter-departmental committees can signify that a particular proposition is an idea whose time has come: a question which, my schoolmasters had taught me, required the prefix *nonne*. Furthermore, while the British Importers Confederation were what you might call Customs and Excise-friendly, and the CBI at least neutral, the Institute of Directors nominee, Grahame Mather, was a dedicated freeport groupie. Yet my scepticism, and that of the Customs and Excise, remained complete.

My trepidation proved amply justified. Shortly before the inaugural meeting of our Court of Inquisition, the Customs came to see me. I was aware, they assumed, that the Department of Trade was not just to be represented at official level and that Iain Sproat was coming too? I most certainly was not.

I went off in search of the Chancellor. This, I said, would never work. I could not possibly run a committee including outsiders from beyond the village with a Ministerial colleague in attendance who was more than likely to dispute the way I tried to run it. I was told it was all very difficult. The Department of Trade had strong views about the enquiry, and felt that it must defend its corner. I was urged to give it a try.

With great reluctance I agreed to do so. My worst fears were rapidly confirmed. I mapped out a work programme for the Committee, including scrutiny of existing Customs procedures, visits to the existing freeports at Hamburg, Shannon and Rotterdam, and an invitation to all interested parties to submit views and evidence. Iain Sproat vigorously contested every proposition. We adjourned in some disarray.

I departed once again in search of my boss. I could not, I

told him, carry on the committee on this basis. Iain Sproat must withdraw. Geoffrey Howe promised to have a word with Iain's departmental leader, Arthur Cockfield. In due course I was told that it had been agreed that Iain would in future only be an occasional visitor to our deliberations. No, I said. Either Iain withdrew altogether, or I did. Finally I was advised to sort it out directly with Arthur Cockfield. I did. Iain withdrew.

It might be thought that the Department of Trade at official level would, at such a moment, have been battling staunchly on their junior Minister's behalf. That was not my impression. Indeed the officials of the Department of Trade seemed to be scarcely less *empressé* to see their Minister depart than were the Customs. But then in all Whitehall departments junior Ministers are expected to know their place. Iain Sproat never did. He was a Minister after my own heart.

In his absence we got down to work. We were shown how bonded warehouses work, and how Rank Xerox assembled and repackaged photocopiers with bought-in components from Taiwan and points east, and reshipped them under Customs clearance to Latin America. We learned how entrepôt traders in the Port of London were far more put out by the expensive life-style of their registered dockers than they were by Customs formalities, and why they doubted that a freeport would be much use to them unless – which seemed unlikely – it somehow contrived to escape the dock labour scheme. We were regaled with eager bids from local authorities and local development corporations in every corner of the land. We heard from one British commercial property company which had been vigorously engaged in US freeports. We were handsomely entertained at Rotterdam, Hamburg, and Shannon. At Hamburg it transpired that the bulk of business was done with eastern Europe; Rotterdam turned out to be a freeport in no more than name; and at Shannon we learned that while the freeport flourished, it had virtually nothing to do with the airport, which had pulled itself up by the bootstraps by selling visits to the leprechauns to the American Irish. As mentioned earlier, my Assistant Private Secretary acquired a scarf, and I acquired a coffee-table book about the Port of Hamburg, and gave it back to constitute a prize for the Treasury sports day.

Eventually our travelling was over. Even Grahame Mather found it difficult to point to specific and tangible benefits which traders within a freeport would enjoy, denied to those outside it so long as we conformed to Common Market rules. But it was clear we could not very well report that the whole idea was barmy. If Whitehall set up a Committee to investigate the case for launching building plots on the dark side of the moon, building plots on the dark side of the moon would be recommended. Moreover since it was also apparent that the Customs' estimates of staff numbers needed to police these entrepôts of enterprise had been overstated, any costs to the Exchequer should be modest.

So we did our duty. Having pointed out that the rules of the Community debarred us from proposing any very tangible benefits to accrue to those who joined a freeport, we waxed suitably lyrical about the mystical appeal – to footloose Yankee traders, the wily Japanese, who knew? – of freeport status, and recommended that some trial sites should be designated. I argued that a couple would be quite enough to be going on with; after strenuous argument no specific number was identified. But we were very stern about the need to ensure that 'commercial viability' must be the sole criterion for selection. Freeports could not be adjuncts to regional policy, and it was not a blind bit of good establishing them at the behest of local development authorities which could not produce the evidence of trader eagerness to enter them. The representative of the Northern Ireland office warned us fairly that his masters were unlikely to be swayed by such crude commercialism. His point was taken: we could, after all, only recommend the course of common sense. We could not guarantee it would be followed.

To nobody's surprise, it wasn't. Our report served as the green light for a flood of applications. No self-respecting municipality from Fermanagh to the Shetlands could afford to miss the boat. Sir Clive Sinclair, maestro of the matchbox television set, wrote to *The Times* to point out that if Dundee could only be a freeport he would be able to import components from the Far East free of the Community's seventeen per cent duty, build them into consoles and ship them to the continent on payment of the modest five per cent which was charged on the finished product. We felt bound to inform him that, sadly, he was wrong. No matter. The bids continued unabated.

Of all the representations which we had received during the course of our enquiry, the one that had impressed me personally had been that from Aberdeen. Aberdeen is the centre of the North Sea offshore oil supplies business. Owing to some quirk of Community rules, offshore supplies are treated as though destined for territories outside the Community's customs wall. It seemed to me that a freeport at Aberdeen might indeed have considerable attractions to offshore traders.

Eventually a choice of six experimental freeports was announced soon after the 1983 Election, by which time I was once more outside the system. Needless to say Aberdeen was not among them: for Aberdeen was thriving, and in a classic piece of Whitehall village trading the freeport concept had been hijacked by the regional assistance lobby. There was to be one for Scotland – Prestwick, obviously; one for Wales – near Cardiff; one for Northern Ireland, at Belfast airport; one for Liverpool; one for Southampton and one for Birmingham airport.

The only choices that seemed to have any apparent commercial logic were those at Southampton (which, in the event, was promptly hamstrung by the dockers) and – conceivably – at Birmingham. To the time of writing, progress has been very near invisible. Liverpool has made the greatest headway, with an enterprising Pakistani processor of duvets and a handful of warehouses. Southampton has staged a showdown with its dockers, and may, belatedly, be getting somewhere. The operators of the Belfast freeport complain understandably that the last thing Belfast needs just now is empty warehouse space. Otherwise the scheme has proved something of a frost. But it has cost the Exchequer little. We must be grateful for small mercies.

12

Steering the Economy

The range of tasks a Treasury Minister is confronted with from day to day seemed daunting. But the key inducement to accept the job in the first place had been the opportunity to play a part in 'steering the economy.' Hitherto, as a backbencher and a journalist, I had been a critic, mostly sniping at the way in which – or so it had often seemed to me – the central business of the nation had been mismanaged. The Thatcher Administration formed in 1979 was the first since I had been involved in politics which appeared to me to be aiming at the right objectives, and to be prepared to see them through. When I had had to notify the *Daily Telegraph* that I had been 'summoned by bells', one of the elder statesmen of that newspaper had, so I was told, commented that it was perhaps about time that I vacated the comfort of the stalls to experience life on the other side of the footlights.

Like the Church of England, the Treasury operates by calendar. The seasons follow as a seamless garment. The two public feast days of the modern Treasury year are Budget Day, which used to be in April and is now in March, and the Autumn Statement, towards the middle of November. On Budget Day the Chancellor announces how he plans to pay the bills. The Autumn Statement, revealing the outcome of the annual public spending negotiations (a recent innovation from the 1970s), spells out how the bills are expected to arise. In reality, however, both processes are more or less continuous. The composition of the Budget starts as soon as the Autumn Statement is delivered, and the annual haggle over public spending programmes begins before the Finance Bill, giving legislative form to the Budget changes, has completed its passage to the Statute Book. Besides, both sides of the balance sheet undergo regular adjustment. An apposite cartoon of the late 1970s depicted Mrs Thatcher, as Leader of the Opposition, and her Shadow Chancellor, Geoffrey Howe, staring with distaste at a figure of Denis Healey, the substantive Chancellor of the moment, surrounded by hoards of squalling infants each marked 'mini-Budget'. They proved less carelessly philo-progenitive in office. Indeed the Tory Government since 1979 has yet to be obliged to unveil one of those 'emergency packages' which had marked the sixties and the seventies. Yet corrections, unheralded and not infrequently unnoticed, continue to occur.

As with the Church, Advent marks the beginning of the Treasury's year. No sooner is the Autumn Statement delivered to Parliament than the machine embarks upon the 'Budget starters'. This is the material part of which will form the stodge of the following year's Finance Bill. Much of it, at this early stage, will consist of items which Customs and Excise or – predominently – the Inland Revenue had hoped to get included in the previous Budget or the one before that: items like the legal entrenchment of discretionary wavers to existing tax laws.

For the best-laid schemes of the Parliamentary draftsmen gang aft agley. The revenue departments discover in the course of duty that laws have paradoxical effects, which they had not intended, and of which Parliament is blissfully unaware. So they exercise discretion in favour of potential taxpayers. The taxpayers concerned are, by definition, unlikely to challenge the revenue departments in the Courts. Still, you never know, and as conscientious officials they are keen to regularise their behaviour and put it beyond legal challenge.

A second category of 'Budget starters' at this stage consists of changes in the tax laws rendered essential, or at least desirable, by directives from the European Community. A third, and more contentious, category will include (usually complex and lengthy) provisions for the closure of potentially expensive loopholes exposed by previous Finance Bills. Throughout most of the time I was at the Treasury there was a running battle over the Inland Revenue's attempts to restrict the diversion to offshore havens of corporate taxes, to which the Revenue reckoned it should be entitled, as a result of the abolition of exchange controls. Inevitably the multinationals based in London argued fiercely that the Inland Revenue was seeking to lay its hands on profits which lay properly beyond its jurisdiction, thereby putting them at a disadvantage *vis-à-vis* the international competition. A favourite ploy, which they did not hesitate to use, was the charge that the Inland Revenue ran rings round the Ministers, and drafted laws to suit their vindictive purposes which they got the Ministers to rubber-stamp. Needless to say we bridled at such allegations and insisted, as Ministers always do in such circumstances, that laws were of our own personal selection in each and every case. We were not believed.

Around the turn of the year occurs the first of several conferences in the office of the Chief Secretary (who will, in due course, take charge of the Ministerial team which transacts the Finance Bill, since the Chancellor, having produced his Budget, leaves his colleagues to complete the job). The Chief Secretary opens the meeting by complaining that already, with three months to go to Budget Day, the Finance Bill is getting out of hand. Every year he wants a shorter Bill. The Parliamentary Business Managers hate long Bills, and the longer the Bill, the greater the scope for Parliamentary trouble.[1] Then the horse-trading starts. Each of the attending Ministers has been forearmed with briefs, from his out-stations in the Treasury, designed to demonstrate that the world will fall apart unless their pet projects are, this time, allowed to pass. And the officials are in attendance to try and put backbone into Ministers who show signs of backsliding. Nevertheless, even at this early stage, some items fall by the wayside to be pursued another year; while others are down-graded so that they are almost certain to be

[1] The complexity of modern Finance Bills tends to insulate them from controversial politics (particularly for a Tory Government: City, accountancy and legal know-how on the Tory benches makes for a rougher passage for a Labour Government's Finance Bills). But they can be hamstrung for extraneous reasons. The 1984 Finance Bill, though not rich in subjects of political contention, ran into a prolonged filibuster provoked in part by a display of *machismo* from the Opposition Whip (for internal Labour Party reasons and to delay more contentious legislation pending. The shorter the Bill, the less the scope for mischief.

jettisoned before the Finance Bill goes to the printers. Little of the material at this stage carries political clout: the politically appetising items will be added later. Furthermore the wise Chief Secretary aims off for the near-certainty that he will be confronted, towards the end of February, with an irresistible demand from one or other of the revenue departments for inclusion of a hitherto unconsidered trifle, running to half a dozen clauses and supporting schedules, without which the Exchequer will be cheated of hundreds of millions of anticipated taxes.

Then, in mid-January, comes the 'Chevening weekend'. Chevening is a handsome country house situated just beyond London's south-eastern suburbs in Kent. The ancestral home of the Earls of Stanhope, it was left by the last Earl of Stanhope at the end of the 1960s for the use of the Prince of Wales, or, if he did not wish to use it, for other specified members of the Royal Family, or, failing them, members of the Government starting with the Foreign Secretary. In due course it had passed – *faute de mieux* – to Tony Barber as Chancellor of the Exchequer in the Heath Administration. The Inland Revenue unfortunately informed him, however, that it stood to be taxed as a perquisite of office. Since then it has been placed in commission, with no regular occupancy, although the Foreign Secretary is recognised to have the prior claim when he needs it for fulfilment of his official duties.

Geoffrey Howe secured its use as a Treasury retreat for one weekend in January in 1982; and it has been used for this purpose each year since. All the Ministers were bidden, together with about half a dozen of the most senior mandarins, and our three political advisers. Wives are also invited (on payment of a fee of, I think, £20 per head, to keep up the proprieties).

The contrast with the Spartan simplicities of our normal working environment in Great George Street could hardly have been more stark. The atmosphere was that of a country house weekend of almost Edwardian splendour. Chevening is a handsome early Georgian house, superbly furnished and set in splendid landscaped grounds. Our first visit happened to coincide with a heavy fall of snow, followed by days of brilliant sunshine, and by night the moonlit view across the lake was magical. The food, prepared and served by a team of local ladies who looked as though they had just come in from walking their dogs or following the guns, was Lucullan. This was the only occasion when we had a chance to meet all the wives of our colleagues, since all, or nearly all, accepted the invitation.

We assembled, in country tweeds, on Friday afternoon, and gathered for a first working session before dinner on Friday evening. After dinner there was a second working session, with another on Saturday morning. On Saturday afternoon we were released to walk the grounds (or, for those like the Chief Economic Adviser to the Treasury (Sir) Terry Burns, who were so minded, to watch football on television). Saturday evening dinner was a social occasion, followed, for the majority, by bridge – supplanted nowadays, so we are told, by charades. On Sunday morning we had a final working session, followed by another tremendous lunch, and departure.

In January 1985 the 'Chevening weekend' was somewhat rudely disrupted by the outside world. The Chancellor and his colleagues were confronted when they came down for Sunday morning breakfast by headline stories in the *Sunday Telegraph* and *Sunday Times* revealing that the pound, which had been sliding steeply *vis-à-vis* the dollar in recent weeks, was on its own. 'Sources close to the Prime Minister' were reported to be entirely relaxed about the exchange rate. Should it slump to parity with the dollar – and it was getting precious close to it – the Government would, it seemed, lie back and enjoy it.

What had happened, as very soon emerged, was that the Prime Minister's press spokesman, Bernard Ingham, during his regular Friday 'off the record' weekly briefing for the lobby correspondents of the Sundays, had been asked about the weakness of sterling, and had responded, as is his wont, in somewhat forthright terms. For some considerable time – certainly dating back to the period when I was in the Treasury – Bernard Ingham's propensity to indulge in 'lobby briefing' about matters which the Treasury regarded as its own exclusive concern, matters which were far too delicate to be left to rude mechanicals from 10 Downing Street, had been a source of much contention. This time he had gone Too Far.

The telephone wires from Chevening waxed hot that Sunday morning. By lunchtime the Chancellor was explaining, *urbi et orbi*, that the reports in the Sunday press totally misrepresented the viewpoint of Her Majesty's Government. Of course they had a view about the exchange rate, and that view was that it was far too low.

It took a sharp hike in interest rates to turn the tide of sterling sales, and the Treasury left no-one in any doubt that Bernard Ingham ought to go. He didn't. As one senior Cabinet Minister explained, 'Bernard can do no wrong'. Sterling, in time, recovered. But the 'Chevening weekend' will never, perhaps, be quite the same.

We suffered no such unsavoury disturbances. We received Terry Burns' latest update on the economic outlook, and discussed the hazards that we faced. Would oil prices, so crucial to our revenues and the exchange rate for sterling, behave themselves? Could the Budget help to turn the tide of unemployment? What did the Tory backbenchers expect of us on Budget Day, and where were the potential points of trouble with the disaffected? How were we to cope with the impact of President Reagan's 'supply side economics', creating a huge budget deficit and sucking in the savings of the world to help finance it? Were we to take at face value the performance readings from our monetary speedometers, or had what the jargon called 'noise' got into the cables, to give misleading messages?

It was a weekend for reflection and debate. We didn't aim to reach conclusions, or even to define the choices. Indeed it was not clear to me that our deliberations had any tangible impact on the formulation of the 'Budget judgment' in the weeks that followed. But undoubtedly we returned to London on the Sunday afternoon refreshed in mind and body.

The remaining weeks of January, and the first half of February, were much given over to the reception of the lobbies (see Chapter 9) – not that *they* made any identifiable difference to the emerging Budget strategy either. What did make a difference, by contrast, was the feel we got of sentiment on the Tory back benches at Westminster. In the spring of 1981 – before my arrival – the decision, imposed by the Treasury and 10 Downing Street in the teeth of what was probably majority Cabinet opinion at the time, to raise taxes by the non-indexation of allowances to offset the rebuff suffered by Prime Minister and Chancellor over public spending programmes in the previous autumn, had caused considerable strains on the back benches. The Treasury had been forced by back-bench resistance to cut the intended increase in the tax on derv, and to recoup it from tobacco instead. So in 1982 in particular there was much attention given to back-bench consultation.

We received the officers of the Tory back-bench Finance Committee. They were, in fact, regular visitors, since it is a prime function of the Committee officers in the Tory Party to alert 'their' ministers to the waves of Westminster opinion. Inevitably the views expressed are liable to be subjective. When I was in the Treasury – and this was normal – the officers reflected a broad cross-section of Tory private members' attitudes. The Chairman of the Committee, and one or two of the other officers, were staunch 'loyalists', while one or more of the officers were outspoken dissenters. Hence they were liable, when they came to see us, to disagree with each other more than they disagreed with us.

The Whips would also contribute their – more dispassionate – assessment of the opinions of their flock, and select a small stream of individual (and, for the most part, disaffected) foot-soldiers to be given the benefit of individual sessions with the Chancellor. In addition, in 1982, selected groups of back-benchers, carefully bunched to match dissenters with loyalists and floaters, were farmed out for attention by the other Ministers. We took them out to lunch in the company of a mandarin or two, and one of our political advisers, and listened closely to their wisdom.

In 1982 there was one clearly identifiable product of this consultation process: a reduction of 1 per cent in the National Insurance Surcharge, the per capita tax imposed on payrolls, ironically by Denis Healey in the late 1970s when the International Monetary Fund was snapping at his heels. Some of us within the Treasury argued fiercely against this expensive surrender of revenue, on the grounds that it was far more likely to be passed straight on in extra increments for existing employees than to assist in the (at that time necessary) restoration of profit margins, let alone the stimulation of labour recruitment which it was supposed to generate. Four years later, at the time of writing, it is a reiterated complaint of the Prime Minister that this is precisely what happened. But in the early spring of 1982 it was deemed to be an irresistible demand. The leaders of the CBI had convinced themselves that this was what their members wanted from the Government, above all else, and had then gone on to convince the Tory back benches that this was what the nation expected.

This was not the only respect in which, as Budget Day approached, the range of choice became pre-empted. Admittedly one self-imposed restraint – the Medium Term Financial Strategy (MTFS) – proved to be, in practice, fairly uninhibiting. The MTFS, drawn up by Nigel Lawson as Financial Secretary in 1980 was supposed to set the flare-path by which, over the period of the Parliament elected in 1979, we would reach the promised land of stable prices via shrinking budget deficits, falling interest rates and shrinking monetary growth. In the event the severity of the recession in 1980–81 had led to a huge rise in Government borrowing, justified *post facto* on contra-cyclical grounds; and the Treasury – or perhaps more accurately its Ministers – had learned by harsh experience that our interest rates were at the mercy of international pressures, since if US prime rates soared towards the high teens, as they did in 1981, sterling would fall further and faster than was deemed to be acceptable unless we followed suit. So it cannot be said that we pondered long and hard about adherence to the original, 1980 flight-path. What mattered, essentially, was to be heading in the right direction.

Fortunately there were always ways and means. The last update of the MTFS, at the time of the previous Budget, might have pencilled in, for the year confronting us, a range of 6–10 per cent growth in our £M3 lodestar, and a Budget deficit of £9bn, equivalent to 3½ per cent of the national product. And that might, come February of the following year, look too ambitious for our comfort. But if we could by then assert – and we usually could – that in the financial year drawing to its close £M3 looked like growing by 13 per cent, instead of the 7–11 range set for it, and the Budget deficit looked like turning out at £12bn, or 4¼ per cent of gross domestic product, instead of the £10bn/3¾ per cent of gdp figure given by the Chancellor last Budget Day, then we could make a virtue of our iniquities. Brushing aside our past intentions, we would boldly repeat the previous year's 7–11 per cent range for £M3, and estimate the coming year's deficit at £10bn, or 3½ per cent of gdp (which would have grown meantime), and emphasise the progress this would constitute, not against the previous year's intentions (which would be consigned to the memory hole) but against our latest expectations of the previous year's performance. Travelling hopefully, after all, is what matters.

Inflation predictions could prove somewhat more intractable. The 'Red Book', published by convention on Budget Day, containing all the small print which the commentators pore over, gives the Treasury's forecast of what they think will happen to prices over the ensuing 18 months. Since, for all the spread of 'realism' in wage bargaining since 1979, there was a nasty suspicion that both managers and men took close account of what the Government was supposed to think would happen in the year ahead to prices, it was deemed crucially important that the figures which would eventually emerge in the 'Red Book' should be pointing in the right direction.

Here too, fortunately, there is room for constructive arithmetic. This centres on the sheer magnitude of the variables. Suppose the going annual rate of price inflation when the Budget sums are being done is 6 per cent. If the soothsayers can come up, when due account is taken of the conventional Budget increases in excise duties, with a forecast of 5½ per cent – or even, *in extremis*, of 5¾ per cent – for the year ahead, result happiness. We are heading in the right direction. Should they come up with 6 per cent, or worse still 6½ per cent, result misery. Yet the percentages involve statistical 'rounding'. If the soothsayers confront you with 6½ per cent, there is nothing to be done. But if they confront you with 6 per cent, which actually represents 5.94 per cent, then why not shake hands on 5¾ – or even, if you are really minded to be wicked, 5½? The arguments are strenous, and even mildly absurd. Ministers want at all costs to maintain appearances, the statisticians to maintain their reputations for impartial accuracy. Yet both know well that all sorts of unforseen eventualities will make a monkey of the forecasts anyway.

It is always open to the Government to make the figures move. Take a point off VAT and, with a time-lag of some months, but well before the winter, the 'headline' figure for the retail price index will fall. Cut the excise duties, and the impact on the rpi will be almost overnight. Partly, no doubt, because I happened to be answerable for VAT, and therefore particularly conscious of the resentments provoked by the virtual doubling of the VAT rate in 1979, I was always keen to advance the case for a cut in the rate to lower inflationary expectations.

I might as well have saved my breath. I was up against two insurmountable obstacles. The first was that the quantum leap in VAT in 1979, which had taken the standard rate from 8 per cent to 15, had – not without considerable pain – achieved a major and overdue correction of the balance between direct and indirect taxation. This was not lightly to be thrown away. The second was that reductions in indirect taxation (increases, for that matter) have a bizarre effect on expectations of inflation in the pipeline. The first impact, in year one, is all that the heart could desire. Come the second year it is a vastly different matter. If a cut in VAT shrinks the growth of the rpi from 6 per cent per annum to 4 per cent in September of year one, then unless it is repeated in the following budget, September of year two will produce a corresponding deterioration in apparent price performance. This seemed to me, and still seems to me, Mad Hatter mathematics. But it is the way we live. The villagers know a lost cause when they see one. As I pressed for a reduction in the VAT rate, they averted, sensibly, their gaze.

Not that the impact of indirect taxes on the rpi is ignored. On the contrary, it is studied with the greatest care. Back in 1972, when I was an officer of the Tory Finance Committee, sweets, which had been made liable to VAT when the tax had been introduced the previous year, were suddenly zero-rated. At our regular monthly meeting with Chancellor Barber soon after the Budget, I protested vigorously. Having at that time two small children of the sweet-consuming age, I told the Chancellor that I found it crazy that we should thus encourage our offspring to wreck their teeth. Tony Barber was sympathetic, but unyielding: 'it's worth a whole point off the rpi', he explained.

As inflation gained momentum in the middle seventies, however, indexation became the rage. Government was obliged, by the so-called 'Rooker-Wise amendment' to raise tax allowances automatically at Budget-time by the inflation rate over the previous 12 months. (Although by a further amendment to 'Rooker-Wise', carried by the advocacy of a Tory backbencher called Nigel Lawson, they could apply an override to leave allowances unchanged providing they obtained specific Parliamentary sanction for so doing – which is precisely what the Treasury team, including Financial Secretary Lawson, had duly done in 1981). So by way of compensation Government slipped discreetly into the practice of assuming that indirect taxes would be similarly 'valorised'. Instead of bearing the odium of having to announce that duties on cigarettes or drink or petrol would be increased by ten per cent, or whatever, they trained Parliament – and the relevant lobbies – to assume that they would normally rise to recoup the erosion of their value over the previous year (the tax-take from VAT, an *ad valorem*, or percentage, tax, rose with the inflation rate in any case). Then Chancellors could – and do – take credit for increasing the specific duties by less than the rate of inflation. Except for the taxes on tobacco, that is. Here – such is the influence of the anti-smoking lobby – credit may be uniquely sought by increasing taxes *faster* than the inflation rate.

This process of 'valorisation' has had one little-noticed consequence. April used to be the Budget month. By then the Chancellor would have a full year's estimate of how the previous Budget forecast of the deficit, or Public Sector Borrowing Requirement, had worked out in practice. He would also have the benefit of the Treasury's regular spring economic forecast. But since up-rating of the tax allowances, although announced in the Budget, would not take effect until the tax year began, whereas 'valorisation' of the specific duties takes effect immediately, it came to be perceived that by shifting Budget Day to March the Chancellor could enjoy a full month's extra revenues, and in times of high inflation this was not to be sneered at. Chancellors even came to put their ignorance, in March, of how the dying financial year's PSBR would work out, to advantage, by 'rounding up' the Treasury's best estimate so as to flatter by comparison the target they had picked for the year to come. Inflation may have shrunk, but Budget Day has not gone back to April.

As February progresses, the Budget preparations gather momentum. The conferences of the junior Ministers, with Inland Revenue, Customs, and the Parliamentary draftsmen in attendance, at the office of the Chief Secretary become a weekly function. As the prospective girth of the Finance Bill becomes daily more distended, secret deals are struck. The Chief Secretary grabs the colleague with responsibility for the Customs for a *tête-à-tête*. 'Do we really *have* to have this brand new scheme for collecting tax on one-armed bandits this year?', he asks. 'It's two clauses and three whole schedules – and what's it worth? £25m in a full year? No, really, it must wait'. The colleague has been advised by the Customs that without this pet new scheme all sorts of rogues and vagabonds will get away with murder: they have set their hearts upon it. So sometimes it may be that the colleague will agree that, having fought the good fight on behalf of Customs in their presence at the plenary session, he will back down gracefully. Such are the ways of the village that the Customs will very likely be forewarned that the battle has been lost. But appearances will be observed, and the charade carefully played out. For Customs, in any case, will be scheming for a quid pro quo at the Inland Revenue's expense.

The real innovations – or so it seemed to me – emerge at a surprisingly late stage of the whole process. It was even said that Jim Callaghan was sold the Selective Employment Tax in 1966 to plug a yawning gap in his expected revenues *after* the Cabinet had had its final say. We never got as late as that. But the decision to index capital gains tax was not taken many days before the 1982 Budget. It is worth a short detour.

The Tory Government came to power in 1979 committed by its manifesto, and assorted pledges made in Opposition, to alleviate the tax treatment imposed by the previous Labour Government on capital accumulation. Essentially capital taxes had three flavours. There was Capital Transfer Tax to take the place of Death Duties, and claim a percentage on the value of an asset when it passed by gift at death, or between the living. There was Capital Gains Tax, levied on the appreciation in value of an asset between the time of purchase and the time of sale. And there was the Investment Income Surcharge, a sumptuary rate of income tax applicable when the income derived from investment rather than from employment (or approved pension schemes).

We were pledged to 'draw the teeth' of Capital Transfer Tax, and to eliminate Capital Gains Tax on 'paper profits from inflation'. Our commitments with regard to the Investment Income Surcharge were vaguer, although stern denunications, in Opposition, of loose talk about 'unearned income' – always to be spoken of as 'income from savings' – implied that we would do something.

The gums of CTT had been rendered gappy in successive Budgets, by substantial increases, well above inflation, in its starting-point, by increasing exemptions for lifetime gifts, and by concessions for the transfer of business assets (the biggest concession of all – albeit more accurately a deferment – had been Denis Healey's total waiver of the tax on transfers to a surviving spouse). But nothing had been done about Capital Gains Tax (or, for that matter, Investment Income Surcharge).

As so often happens with the plans of politicians in Opposition, exonerating 'paper profits from inflation' had turned out to be unexpectedly tricky. Everyone – the Inland Revenue included – readily agreed that snatching 30 per cent of that part of the appreciation in the cash value of an asset which reflected nothing more substantial than the depreciation of the currency was, if not wrong, at least indistinguishable from a Capital Levy. But the Inland Revenue darkly warned that if the taxpayer were allowed to write down the value of an asset by the level of inflation since its purchase, the tax would be hardly worth the trouble of collecting; and that if you simply gave it up altogether then clever men in EC 1 would find a myriad ways of transforming income into capital. Worse still, the Chancellor would catch the bills twice over. For when Jim Callaghan had launched the long-term Capital Gains Tax back in 1965, the then Labour Government's credit rating had been such that willing lenders did not exactly grow on trees. So the Treasury had persuaded him to grant a special exemption from Capital Gains Tax to anyone who bought his gilts and held them for a year or more. Scrapping, or emasculating, CGT, would remove this special privilege of gilt-edged funding overnight.

This particularly exercised the Bank of England. Confronted, in February 1982, with clear indications that the Chancellor was contemplating fulfilment of his Party's pledge on CGT in the forthcoming Budget, the Bank of England acted. Once again, as when faced with the unwelcome prospect of decontrol of access to indexed gilts (see Chapter 6), they made our blood run cold with predictions of a 'funding strike'. Mine, in particular. Since I was responsible for funding policy, and they were its executants, I argued that we could not lightly disregard such awesome warnings. But then I did not regard Capital Gains Tax as a high priority anyway. It was the Investment Income Surcharge, with its crude discrimination against personal investment, which seemed to me a far more suitable case for treatment.

My fears were swiftly swept aside. For the Treasury, at that time, had a secret weapon. Arthur Cockfield, our Minister of State. Arthur Cockfield was a gamekeeper turned poacher. He had originally made his name as an Inspector of Taxes, and he knew the Inland Revenue inside out. Lesser men and Ministers would be fazed by the sheer complexity of Inland Revenue arguments against a contemplated course of action – such as the indexation of Capital Gains Tax. Not so Arthur.

So the die was cast. Arthur would fix it. And he did. Come Budget Day the Chancellor announced that we had promised to terminate the iniquity of taxing citizens on the impact of inflation on their asset values, and now we would do precisely that.

Ten days later I was called upon to take a City seminar about the Budget. In due course a senior partner from Price, Waterhouse got to his feet. He recalled the Chancellor's announcement, and then added 'but he has done nothing of the sort'. Assets bought in – let us say – 1968, which had borne the heat and burden of the hyper-inflationary 1970s, would still bear Capital Gains Tax on all the paper gains of those locust years. Oh no, I assured him, he had got it wrong. 'I'd check that, if I were you' was his less-than-comforting response. I promised to do just that.

Next morning I called in my Private Secretary and asked for a short memo for the benefit of Price, Waterhouse, to put them in their place. Alas! When it materialised, the memo informed me that Price, Waterhouse had got it right. What we had decided was indeed that CGT would be indexed. But for the future. Not the past. Oh dear me no.

That did not precisely tally with my recollection. I checked my recollection with the Chancellor. He shared it. Nevertheless, when the Finance Bill shortly made its appearance, the gentleman from Price, Waterhouse turned out to be right.

> 'The Cabinet rises and goes to its dinner,
> The Secretary stays and gets thinner and thinner,
> Scratching his brains to record and report
> What he thinks that they think that they ought to have thought'.

And not just the Cabinet, or the Cabinet Secretary.

A more perennial bone of contention concerns the tax treatment of charities. It involves both the revenue departments, Inland Revenue and the Customs and Excise, as well as the Ministers at play.

Every year when I was in the Treasury the run-up to the Budget was marked by a strenuous campaign by the charities lobby to secure release from VAT on their purchases. In 1982 one of the most respected and popular of the charities, the Spastics Society, ran a series of advertisements displaying the VAT-men as armed gangsters hijacking charity donations. The advertisements caused great offence to the Customs, and they were quite misleading, since they implied that VAT was deducted from charity donations, which, of course, it isn't. The source of grievance, however, was that charities, just like other 'final consumers' (i.e. the general public), are charged VAT on purchases, and cannot reclaim it unless they are also traders (which some of the largest, such as Oxfam, are).

The Customs pointed out that zero-rating charities would cost £70m a year, or more, in revenue foregone. But they didn't rest their case on that. They argued that the European Community would object; that there would be substantial manpower consequences resulting from a huge burden of processing claims (at a time when we were always on at them to reduce their payrolls); and that most of the benefit would go to unexpected causes: Eton, for example, would benefit a lot more than the Royal National Institute for the Deaf. They wished us joy of explaining that Eton was a more deserving cause than, for example, the Royal Shakespeare Company, which had been campaigning for years, with the aid of most distinguished champions, for relief from the obligation to pile VAT upon their tickets. And there were many more controversial beneficiaries than Eton.

Against this we were dedicated, as a Government, to the promotion of voluntary involvement. It was absurd for us to champion self-help, and then tax it. Moreover the Brussels Commission was prepared to give clearance to a scheme for reimbursement of VAT on purchases made by non-trading charities which they had worked out. And the manpower calculations of the Customs were (not for the first time) suspect.

The problems of definition nevertheless seemed to me well-nigh insurmountable. The major charities suggested that we could apply a *de minimis* rule: the little local voluntary welfare funds would hardly, if at all, notice their exclusion. A likely story, or so it seemed to us. We had visions of streams of letters from MPs protesting furiously about the disallowances of claims from the Friends of their local Cottage Hospitals. OK, said the charities, let's do a sheep and goats operation, with Mencap and the Spastics on one side of the line, and the Moonies and Eton on the other. This was, if possible, even worse. Exclude the public schools from access to a VAT refund benefit, and you would pave the way for withdrawal of the charitable status of their endowments. It did not take much imagination to foresee the trouble that would cause in the shires. Besides, charity is in the eye of the donor: what right has Government to decree that monies donated to the Moonies cannot be spent without VAT liability so long as the Moonies are deemed to be a charity? I was also impressed, through experience, by the force of the argument that VAT concessions for what most of the travellers on the conventional Clapham ominbus would regard as underserving causes would make it far harder to resist claims for corresponding treatment of the 'performing arts' – or, for that matter, the performing professional football clubs.

Yet such considerations threatened to be overrun, particularly in 1982, by the strength of back-bench feeling on the charities' behalf. In the end we worked out a 'charities package' consisting of zero-rating for specific items of paramedical equipment bought by charities for the disabled and suchlike. The Budget was well received overall by our backbenchers, and the steam went out of the VAT challenge.

It swiftly returned. Another source of grievance to the charities was that a home – for mental defectives, for example – run by a local authority escapes VAT on its purchases, whereas a similar home run by a charity does not. This is because from the word go VAT had not applied to central or local government institutions, since its application would have been pointless: the tax revenue thereby collected would simply be recycled in higher public spending. But we were now anxious to encourage hospitals and local authorities to 'contract out' ancillary services: and VAT was a barrier. For if, for example, a hospital carried out its laundry 'in house' no VAT arose; whereas if a private contractor took on the laundry service it would have to charge VAT on its bills to the hospital. It was therefore decided that such 'contracted-out' services should also be zero-rated. I foresaw a renewed outcry from the charities at such enhanced discrimination against them in favour of the public sector.

It did not materialise – not least because the 1983 Budget in which the zero-rating of contracted-out services was introduced was immediately overshadowed by the General Election of that year.

In the 1986 Budget, however, Nigel Lawson gave short shrift to the Customs' warnings and the scruples of the Revenue. He not only extended considerably the range of items free of VAT when bought by charities to include services such as non-classified advertising. He also lifted the ceiling on tax relief for charitable donations, and introduced a new scheme for tax-deductible charitable donations out of PAYE by employees. This was balanced by a bland reference to the planned restriction of tax relief 'only to money which is used for charitable purposes'.

Behind this aside lay a long battle waged by the Inland Revenue against the abuse of charitable status for purposes of tax avoidance. In the early 1980s investigations into the affairs of one of the leading tax consultancy businesses which had sprung up in the high tax climate of the 1970s had revealed the crucial role played by 'charitable' trusts in the effectiveness of some ingenious schemes. Subsequently the Inland Revenue had pursued one charitable trust through the law courts. Unfortunately its victim had not been well-chosen: the Courts found that the particular trust's income had indeed gone to charity. So now the Revenue planned to have a more comprehensive bash at what it perceived as bogus charities.

All hell broke loose. Lord Goodman, doyen of the charities lobby, reacted to the VAT concessions just as the Customs had always warned it would. 'The Budget', he wrote in the pages of *The Observer,* 'demonstrates how specious is the time-honoured argument that it is impossible to exercise discrimination in the imposition of VAT on select causes.' So the Chancellor should do the decent thing and extend parity of treatment to 'the theatre and other performing arts'. Even more serious was the allegation that in seeking to catch the bogus charities, the Inland Revenue was threatening to put the National Trust, and even the Church Commissioners, out of business. Treasury ministers protested at the base ingratitude of the charities lobby, and talked of trying to redefine charitable status. But at the time of writing it rather looked as though they had wandered into a minefield.

If so they did so essentially for two reasons. First, they discounted the evidence from experience of the hazards of creating exposed salients in the tax base. Second, and by contrast, they failed to probe sufficiently the fall-out from a classic Inland Revenue raid on tax avoidance. They bounced the Customs, and were themselves in turn bounced by the Inland Revenue.

To revert. As Budget Day approaches, and life becomes more hectic, half the papers in the Ministerial boxes come to bear the magic slogan 'Budget Secret', in fat scarlet letters, and Ministers and mandarins must log their private conversations. Yet the final days resemble mobilisation for the Kaiser's War. The troop trains are embarked, and you cannot stop them. There may be scope for pennies here and there on the fringes – a small reduction in the projected whisky tax to placate the Scots, for example, or an extension of VAT to previously zero-rated mousetraps. But the time has long gone by to challenge the ingredients of the 'Budget judgment' (if, indeed, it ever genuinely exists).

Even so, almost every other year several cats do contrive to escape the bag. In 1984, for example, *The Guardian* carried extensive – and, as it proved – embarrassingly accurate forecasts of the Chancellor's plans to tax insurance policies ten days in advance. The life offices were working round the clock to cope with demand. Being, by then, back in private life, I was myself among the tens of thousands who felt it wise to take the hint. When my policy was duly delivered some days after the Budget, my agent innocently enquired if I had had prior information. 'Only *The Guardian*', I was able to reply.

Chancellor Lawson, like all his predcessors in a similar predicament, was vastly unamused; and in 1985, by all accounts, mandarins and ministers were virtually locked up for weeks before the Budget. Yet in that year apparently well-authenticated rumours of his plans to broaden VAT and tax the life offices themselves led to a massive, and ultimately successful, lobbying campaign.

How do these leaks occur? Attempts to trace them back to source are seldom known to be successful, since inevitably a fair number of people, not only in the Treasury, but also in the revenue departments and the Bank of England, as well as some senior mandarins in the spending departments, are in the know; and obviously the journalists are not going to split on their informants. Sometimes it is no doubt a matter of 'careless talk'. Sometimes it may be the work of consciously disaffected villagers. But perhaps most often it results from an intentional strategy, on the part of ministers or mandarins or both, to 'soften up' the reception of the Budget. When there are fears that a particular item will be badly received, whether in the markets or at Westminster, then a discreet trailer may be used to break the shock. It is a delicate operation, and not infrequently it backfires. Yet it is also worth reflecting that when a true surprise is sprung there is often great recrimination about the 'failure to consult'. The introduction of a 5 per cent tax on 'American Depository Receipts' in the 1986 Budget is a recent case in point (see Chapter 6). The Treasury was charged with having entirely failed to grasp its repercussions; and it had to be withdrawn subsequently for redrafting. There is no way of pleasing everyone.

With a few more days to go, much anxious thought is given to the 'balance' of the Budget. Is it open to attack as too generous to the leisured classes? Or insufficiently 'business orientated'? If so, is it possible, by piling a number of individually cheap and trivial concessions to 'enterprise', small businesses and professional partnerships one on top of the other, to produce an 'enterprise package'? Or, by performing a similar labour of love with community and youth work schemes, to create an 'employment package'? The effect upon the overall arithmetic may be marginal, but it all helps to 'make the medicine go down' on the day in Parliament, and to improve reception in the public prints. Or so ministers and mandarins will fondly hope.

Also at this stage the Chancellor will place the broad outlines of his intentions before the Cabinet, and take the voices. From outside the Cabinet this exercise appeared to be conducted largely for the sake of form. If the Chancellor offered a comprehensive draft for discussion, his colleagues might complain that he was pre-empting their opinions.

Besides, there was 'Budget secrecy' to think about (not to mention the risk that one or other of his proposals might encounter insurmountable resistance). So it always seemed that he listened more than he spoke. Truth to tell the colleagues rather like it that way too. It enables those with ideas about 'alternative strategies' (Anthony Crosland in the 1970s, Peter Walker in the 1980s) to get them off their chests. The Chancellor receives their counsel much as Mr Gladstone used to receive a Message from Windsor: respectfully, if impatiently. It usually seemed to me that Tory back-bench preoccupations were taken more seriously (although admittedly the two might largely coincide).

There is one other input which cannot possibly be ignored: that from 10 Downing Street. Every Prime Minister takes a close and abiding interest in Budget-drafting. Harold Macmillan, for example, was annually convinced that the Treasury, left to its own devices, would plunge not just the United Kingdom but the whole western world into slump: he attributed to Great George Street powers of almost mystical malignancy. Under Tony Barber in the early 1970s we sometimes formed the impression on the back benches that the Budget had been taken over lock, stock and barrel by the Prime Minister and his indispensable Man Friday, Sir William Armstrong.

Mrs Thatcher certainly had her views, and made sure that they were known within the Treasury. There was one memorable occasion when, following a luncheon at 10 Downing Street in the spring of 1982 at which we had been in attendance, Peter Middleton, Terry Burns and I were asked to stay behind. We were treated to a lecture about the contents of the Budget currently in preparation. Terry Burns, greatly daring, ventured to dissent from some of the suggestions offered. He was fiercely reminded that a ministerial reshuffle was in the offing, and that the Ministry of Defence would be becoming vacant. It was a position made to sound like the proverbial Siberian power-station for an erring Chief Economic Adviser. We were also reminded of the title on the front door down below: 'First Lord of the Treasury'. There were times, we were told, when the Prime Minister was tempted to take it literally. Perhaps, I suggested mischievously, she might indeed do that, and present the Budget Speech herself? Indeed she might was the stern reply. Peter Middleton looked horrified that I should have put such ideas into her head.

Nothing came of that interesting proposition. But on one subject 10 Downing Street was unshakeable. For years the Treasury, despairing of its ability to remove the anomaly of the special tax relief for interest on mortgage borrowing, had done its best to ensure that it 'withered on the vine', by failing to uprate the ceiling of permissible relief and leaving inflation to take its toll. The Prime Minister found this increasingly irksome, never failing to point out that to maintain the real value of the concession originally introduced by Jim Callaghan in the 1960s the ceiling would need to be raised from the £25,000 level the Tory Government had inherited in 1979 to £60,000 or more. By 1982 she was determined that it must move at least some of the way.

The Treasury was ineradicably opposed. This was an issue on which mandarins and ministers stood shoulder to shoulder. Politically we found it hard to defend an increase in tax relief for home buyers when subsidies to council tenants were being steadily reduced. Moreover any increase in the ceiling would inevitably lead to increased borrowing and thus enhance the strains on monetary targeting. We fought a desperate rearguard action. But as Budget Day approached it was plain that we were losing. I pleaded for permission to put the case for leaving well alone on monetary grounds to the Prime Minister myself. I was told that it would be a waste of time. Nevertheless, I argued, I should like to feel I had done my bit. Permission was refused. The ceiling on mortgage interest relief went up to £30,000.

So, finally, the Budget Speech goes into production. It takes, in all, about ten days, and passes through at least a dozen drafts. Nowadays tradition demands at least five separate sections. First there is the review of the financial year just ending, both at home and abroad. Then comes the outlook section, leading to the 'Budget judgment', giving the broad order of magnitude of the total changes, in taxes, allowances and public spending programmes (for although these have been unveiled the previous autumn, some adjustments at Budget time are invariably reckoned to be called for). Then there is a 'monetary' passage, giving the Chancellor's forecast of the size of the Budget deficit in the year ahead – 'after the changes which I shall shortly be announcing' – the range of percentages deemed acceptable for the monetary indicators, and such ancillary items as the target for National Savings.[1] Next comes the details for which Parliament and Press Gallery will be waiting: the headline figures of 'pennies off' and 'pennies on'. And then the peroration, reaching for – albeit not always achieving – the slogan by which the Chancellor would like his Budget to be known: a 'Budget for jobs', or a 'Budget for industry', or, most hazardous of all, a nautical phrase such as 'steady as she goes', much favoured by ex-Petty Officer Callaghan, and usually preceding brutal contact with the rocks.

Some Chancellors – Roy Jenkins perhaps, Nigel Lawson certainly – do a lot of personal rephrasing. Others of a less literary bent, like Geoffrey Howe, rely heavily on the mandarins, and the speech-writing talents of their political advisers and ministerial colleagues. Far more time is spent on polishing the felicitious phrases and the presentational surprises than on the substance of the Speech, since this is already pretty well set in concrete. Besides, presentation can make a vast difference to reception. Nigel Lawson, for example, has proved a master of the misleading preface to wrong-foot the Opposition (as when, in 1986, he announced that there was no scope for a reduction in the standard rate of tax . . . (pause) . . 'beyond a penny.') Trivial tricks, no doubt. But they do disconcert the Opposition, and by the same token delight the Government supporters.

The Budget spawns a mass of paper. On Budget Day itself there are lengthy Treasury press notices, spelling out the details of the tax changes, and also offering detailed guides

[1] Rather endearingly, in 1986 Nigel Lawson skipped this section, on the ground that Parliament finds it far too boring, and reserved it for a City audience one month later. It is a safe rule of thumb, though, that when Chancellors leave features out – as Tony Barber left out his PSBR forecast in 1972, it is because they do not feel them fit for too close scrutiny.

to any new taxes unveiled in the Budget. There is also the so-called 'Red Book' (because of its scarlet cover) or Financial Statement and Budget report. This is a major source-work for the learned commentators, containing as it does all the figures which composed the Chancellor's sums. Although it appears over the signature of the Financial Secretary, it is essentially a village production, and its 'strict regard for truth' is jealously guarded by the villagers. The Chancellor may get away with some judicious fudging of the risks which he has made up his mind to run. Somewhere in the 'Red Book' there will be perceptible a footnote or a table, for those equipped to search. Much agonising goes into almost every phrase in the Red Book, with the Bank of England tipping in its – by no means always welcome – three ha'porth of judgment and prediction. Particular attention is paid to concordance between one year's Red Book and the one that went before it, since if – for example – the Government's monetary policy is said to be designed to 'bear down' on inflation (a phrase from the labour ward which has enjoyed a considerable vogue in the Treasury in the 1980s) in year one, and to be 'consistent with the consolidation of progress against inflation' in year two, the learned commentators will prick their ears up, and sharpen their quills. But the phrase that eventually goes in will have to be one that the mandarins can square with their consciences and what they think the auguries are telling them.

Some three weeks later comes the Finance Bill, designed to give legal form to the Budget changes, a depressingly weighty tome these days running usually to more than 100 clauses and schedules (and in some years to nearer 200). Suffice it to say here that the Bill that receives the Royal Assent in early August will have undergone quite far-reaching changes: some the result of backbench and Opposition amendments, but many more a result of second thoughts within Whitehall, after the accountants and the lawyers have made their representations.

The Bill is entrusted to the care of the Chief Secretary and the junior Treasury Ministers, together with the pundits from Treasury, Inland Revenue and Customs, leaving the Chancellor and the senior mandarins free to run the gamut of the almost endless modern round of Select Committee inquisitions and international gatherings, the Summits and the meetings of 'G5' (top countries' finance ministers and bank governors) 'G10' (a somewhat wider circle), the European Community and the OECD, which follow one another in bewildering succession as spring merges into summer. The modern Chancellor – the modern mandarin, for that matter – does not only need a thick skin and a ready tongue. He must also have, or acquire, a capacious stomach and an ability to sleep in aeroplanes. A Chancellor like Derrick Heathcoat Amory, who would not venture out as far as Paris if he could avoid it, would find the life a misery today.

The next major date in the Treasury's calendar, though, is the public spending Cabinet shortly before Parliament departs for the beaches and the grouse-moors. This will have been preceded by the completion of the midsummer (unpublished) economic forecast. For reasons so far as I know as yet unfathomed this forecast gives the first indication, more often than not, that there are storms ahead. It is true that the last sterling crisis prior to the time of writing blew up in January, in 1985; and that there might easily have been an another one in early 1986 but for some deft footwork by the Bank of England. So perhaps the climate is changing. But traditionally British Governments have run headlong into major economic trouble towards the end of the summer holidays. So the midsummer forecast is liable to be awaited in the Treasury with some trepidation. Moreover even if it finds not a cloud in sight it will still form the background to the July Public Spending Cabinet (although in that case the Treasury will bowdlerise it to ensure that spending Ministers do not seize upon it to back up their claims for extra cash).

Thus begins a stately minuet that lasts from around the end of June to mid-November. The Treasury mandarins take their partners from the spending departments, and find themselves confronted with 'bids' for indispensable increments in their Budgets for the following year, and the years thereafter, running into billions of pounds apiece. They know, and their partners know they know, that these 'bids' will contain judicious padding intended to protect their real core ambitions from the Treasury's dread axe. The first round of attrition takes place immediately, and by the time the Cabinet foregathers several billion pounds of padding will already have been bargained away.

At this stage it is mostly shadow-boxing, but both sides owe it to their *amour propre* to play up and play the game. The first result, logged at the Public Spending Cabinet, is almost drearily predictable. The Chancellor reminds his colleague that in the previous autumn they agreed a global figure, and individual departmental budgets coinciding with it, amounting to X hundred billion pounds for the following year. Unfortunately it now transpires that they are apparently hell-bent on spending X plus £4bn, or plus £6bn, or plus £10bn, as the case might be. This is wholly unacceptable, and threatens the whole fabric of society, not to mention the balance of payments, sterling, and inflation. So after a couple of hours of heart-searching he persuades his colleagues to re-endorse the original targets of the previous year and the last Budget Day.

That is the easy part. For both the Chancellor and his colleagues know quite well that this is no more than a collective Midsummer resolution. To be sure the Chancellor will take it down and seek to use it in evidence against them as the real battle moves towards its climax in the autumn. They know it is a conditional – a very conditional – agreement. When we really get down to the figures, they say to themselves, well primed by their mandarins, he will have to concede that *my* case for extra pennies is quite unanswerable. Furthermore my preparedness to make concessions to the Treasury will depend on the corresponding preparedness of my colleagues. If the Treasury allows them to get away with murder, then they are certainly not going to stop me getting away with petty larceny.

In theory, this is where politicial philosophies ought to make a major difference. A Labour Government, which is supposed to have an inbuilt bias in favour of public provision, should always have the Treasury running scared. A Tory Government, invariably elected on a rhetorical tide of commitments to 'good housekeeping', rewards for enterprise, and 'getting Government off our backs', ought to be a pushover. There is precious little evidence that it works that way in practice. For Labour Governments almost invariably find themselves fairly soon in trouble with the international markets. Whatever the Party manifesto may say, a Labour Chief Secretary soon finds himself in a strong position to say 'no' to the spending departments to keep the International Monetary Fund at bay. Whereas precisely because a Tory Government is much less likely to be having trouble with the markets, a Tory Chief Secretary's ability to scare his spending colleagues into abstemiousness is sharply diminished.

Admittedly Tory Governments almost invariably don hair-shirts on taking office, just as Labour Governments reach for the cheque-book. But for both the first fine careless rapture swiftly fades. Labour Governments begin to find the cheques are bouncing (see Joel Barnett's blow-by-blow description); whereas Tory Ministers are soon taught the skills of empire-building in Whitehall. Very occasionally a Tory Minister does try to keep his hair-shirt well laundered. Keith Joseph was such an exceptional Minister *par excellence*. He consistently argued, both at Industry and at Education, that overall budgetary disciplines applied to his own (as opposed to other people's) departments. The village regarded him as a freak. A sincere – indeed, by universal consent, almost a saintly – man. But quite simply not attuned to the rough realities of Whitehall's battle for survival. At Industry his 'Sir Humphrey', Sir Peter Carey, would dig in remorselessly until Sir Keith, with shaking head, gave way. Education was not so successful in obliging him to see the errors of his ways.

So regardless of the colour of the Government, the Treasury knows it has few allies as the annual public spending round begins in earnest, when the Ministers depart with Parliament for their chosen watering-holes. That section of the Treasury concerned with public spending, and their counterparts around Whitehall, embark upon a much-loved and familiar season of horse-trading through the dog days. By the time the Ministers return, the battlefield has narrowed. Usually by around one-third. It is time for the Chief Secretary to embark on his 'bilaterals'. One by one the Ministers from the spending departments, sustained by vigilant minders from their departments, are called in for individual haggles. These are supplemented by person-to-person arm-twisting between the politicians on the same lines as the arm-twisting within the Treasury which takes place over the drafting of the Finance Bill. The parties are programmed: if they make concessions beyond the chosen limits of their mandarins, Whitehall marks them down as men of straw.

With all this jousting going on it is inevitable that the Chief Secretary and his colleagues invariably emerge with a large gap remaining to be bridged between the Treasury's ambitions and those of the big spenders. In good years it may be £1bn, or even less. In bad years it may be £5bn or more. So the brave contestants nowadays pass on, as you would expect, to a Conciliation and Arbitration Service, presided over by – who else? – Lord Whitelaw. It was given the soubriquet of the Star Chamber: and it has stuck. What past Governments did without it is hard to imagine.

By this late stage both Treasury and the spending departments are starting to throw dancing girls to the wolves. The officials have had ample time to judge the clout (it is usually described as 'political clout', but it is more often, even at this late hour, 'mandarin clout' in reality) behind the items in contention. The Chief Secretary will be advised to go quietly on some; the spending ministers on others – and a rough dovetail will have been contrived at official level.

The Star Chamber assembles. Its membership – apart from the obligatory Lord Whitelaw – includes some *parti pris* such as the Scottish Secretary, and also some non-spenders such as the Leader of the Commons, John Biffen (presented in some quarters as a Treasury trusty – little do those quarters know him). The Treasury puts the case for the prosecution of the outstanding would-be overspenders, and they put the case for their defence. The Star Chamber does its best to arbitrate. But everyone knows that there is a right of appeal – to full Cabinet. Everyone also knows that he or she will get short shrift for digging in on what is deemed to be a peripheral issue; and everyone has to make an individual judgment about the relative sympathy of Star Chamber and full Cabinet to a particular cause. Not that Ministers will necessarily accept the verdict of Star Chamber because they think they would be bound to lose in Cabinet. They may decide that they owe it to their careers to be seen to stand by their standard to the bitter end. Or again, their mandarins may decide so for them.

The Treasury has more complex sums to do. As the Star Chamber completes its work it will see that it is still £½bn or, if it has been unskilled or unlucky, £1½bn, wide of the global figured reconfirmed in Cabinet before the summer holidays. It faces three choices. It can settle for what it has got. It can go for what it is missing in Cabinet – and run the risk of being routed in whole or in part, and worse, being seen to have been routed. For spending departments, and particularly spending Ministers, are not renowned for magnanimity in victory. Or it can creatively account.

The choice it makes will depend on its judgment of the Chancellor, Chief Secretary, and Prime Minister it is saddled with at any given time. When Harold Macmillan was Prime Minister it presumably went quietly, since it knew that it was beaten in advance. But unless it has a dedicated foe in 10 Downing Street, to go quietly would be a betrayal of territorial obligation, and not to be contemplated. So the choices must normally shrink to two.

However 1981 had been a horrible experience. The Treasury had fought through to Cabinet, vigorously encouraged – not to say whipped on – by No 10, only to be routed humiliatingly. That was to be avoided at all costs.

The next major confrontation threatened in the autumn of 1982. The Star Chamber had completed its arbitration, and left a yawning gap. The Secretary of State for the Environment, Michael Heseltine, was threatening a Rambo imitation; others were promising to be more discreetly macho at the Treasury's expense.

Yet all was sweetness and light. The final public spending Cabinet passed smoothly. From the sidelines within the Treasury – public spending was not my patch – I could see no sign of concessions by the big spenders of the scale required to approach our target. Yet when the dust had cleared the Chief Secretary was modestly announcing that he had scored a bullseye, and accepting generous plaudits from every side. What had happened?

What had happened, of course, was that the Treasury had fallen back upon its third option. It has two pieces of elastic in its pending tray. One is called the 'contingencies fund'; the other is called 'shortfall'.

The 'contingencies fund', as its name implies, is there to cope with the unexpected. The Falklands War was a classic call on the contingencies fund. It was an unpredictable expense; and the fact that it could be paid for in the year in which it occurred out of the fund reflected the Treasury's prudence (the fact that year one's bills were but the first of many was hardly the Treasury's fault). In practice the fund is also called in aid for the expected. Thus the Treasury, having secured acceptance through Whitehall of a cash-limited increase in provision for departmental payrolls – an increase which reflects its aspirations for the ensuing pay-round rather than its expectations – will seek to insist that where the eventual pay settlement exceeds the provision, the excess must be recovered through additional economies, whether in manpower or in services provided. But it knows full well it will not succeed in every case. In some politically emotive instances – the nurses, for example, or the police – ministers will feel obliged to honour a pay settlement which substantially exceeds the cash-limited provision without seeking to claw it back through economies. The excess will then be carried on the contingencies fund although it can hardly be regarded as an unforseen contingency. The great thing, though, is that unless so many claims are made upon it in the course of a year that the fund is exhausted, the agreed total of public spending will still not be exceeded, since the contingencies fund issue is included in that total.

This means, however, that it is always capable of adjustment. Furthermore in recent years it has become the custom for the Treasury to write in an increased sum for the fund as its estimates project into the future: thus the fund may be put at £3bn in year one, £4bn in year two, and £5bn in year three. When year one has elapsed, and year two becomes year one, then the fund can be scaled down to £3bn with propriety, on the grounds that the imponderables diminish as the time-scale shortens.

This process also gives scope for massage, though. Should

the outcome of the annual public spending review fail to live up to Treasury expectations, then it is always open to the Chancellor to conclude that, with inflation falling or public spending firmly in his grasp (or for any other reason which can be made to carry plausibility), the contingencies fund can with prudence be reduced by £1bn or whatever figure is required to make the sums add up to the figure the Treasury had first thought of as its target.

'Short-fall' is a more speculative affair. It represents the amount by which the Treasury calculates that spending departments will, in practice, underspend their approved budgets in the year ahead. When cash limits were applied to getting on for half of Government expenditure in the 1970s, departments underspent their departmental allocations by billions of pounds. Cash-limits had the impact of novelty; departments were scared stiff of being pilloried for infringing them. So it was not unreasonable for the Treasury to complete its sums with an assumption of substantial under-spend.

By the early 1980s this was becoming a lot more hazardous. Falling inflation was making it easier for departments to calculate their spending accurately; and they were learning to live with cash limits. Furthermore they had discovered that defaulters were not, in practice, burned in boiling oil. Their misdemeanours were indeed reported back to Parliament. But in small print, which Parliament was effectively debarred from debating anyway. Hence familiarity with cash-limits, like familiarity with the breathalyser, bred contempt.

Nevertheless, 'short-fall' remains available as an aid to the presentation of the Treasury's public spending target. In the autumn of 1982 both the contingencies fund and short-fall were called in aid. Nine months later both adjustments were looking sufficiently suspect to provoke the Chancellor to bounce his Cabinet colleagues into a series of out-of-season cuts in spending programmes. But by then there was a new Chancellor, and a new Chief Secretary – and, indeed, a new Parliament. Sufficient unto the day.

Budget Day in March, and the Autumn Statement in November, are the two fixed feast-days in the Treasury's calendar. But economic steering is a continuous process. In recent years the exchange rate for pounds sterling has come to play a major role in the wheelhouse – albeit a role which, for the most part, 'dare not speak its name'. In 1979, 1980, and the early months of 1981 the exchange rate was treated as almost an irrelevance. Inherited monetary incontinence had to be staunched, and that required high rates of interest. If, at the same time, external funds chose to flow into sterling, whether because their owners wanted to be where the oil was following the second 'oil shock', to receive the benefit of our interest rates, or to display their confidence in the determination of the Thatcher Government to conquer inflation, that was neither here nor there. So sterling soared to $2.40. Industry cried out that it was being squeezed to death. Whitehall told it to stop complaining and get to grips with its costs.

By the time I reached the Treasury in the autumn of 1981 the tune was undergoing subtle transformation. Professor Alan Walters, in his recent book, *The Renaissance of Britain*, has implied that this transformation, and the sharp retreat in the pound/dollar exchange rate that accompanied it, were more or less directly attributable to his success, on moving into Downing Street as the Prime Minister's personal economic adviser that spring, in convincing her that monetary policy was far too tight and had to be relaxed. He may be right. It didn't look that way at the time from down the road. For as soon as I arrived I discovered that the mandarins were telling us that our chosen dial, sterling M3, was delivering an uncertain reading. If it were to be believed, interest rates should rise again, since it was sailing cheerfully above the range fixed for it in the 1981 Budget. Moreover the financial markets had been shoving in the direction of higher interest rates since late July, and the exchange rate had been sliding since the spring. Yet the Bank of England had been holding out against dearer credit.

Was this the response of the Treasury to the arrival of Professor Walters, calling for what was known in the trade as 'monetary base control', and the jettisoning of sterling M3? Or an instance of great minds thinking alike? It may have been: as noted elsewhere, the Treasury always has to keep its eyes skinned for change of mood at No 10. Yet it didn't feel that way. It felt as though the village was essentially reacting to the fierce invective trained upon it for having allowed the exchange rate to soar in 1979 and 1980. In retrospect it was – whether justifiably or not – pleading guilty, and anxious not to sin again. Its chief concern, by the autumn of 1981, seemed to be the achievement of a 'more competitive' exchange rate. It certainly did not want the pound to go into free fall – indeed when that began to happen as soon as I arrived (though not, I trust, for that reason) – it rapidly conceded not one, but two, jumps in the rate of interest. But a further gentle slide in sterling was entirely welcome. In the ensuing months I was never left in any doubt that my personal concern over the continuing exuberance of sterling M3 was out of date – unless sterling also fell out of bed. The guiding star, even though we did not talk about it (and indeed, with a strict regard for truth, frequently denied it) was the exchange rate. Cheaper, but not too much, and above all not too fast.

So we continued to be criticised for trying to live by monetary policy alone. Yet not only was the village paying far more attention to the exchange rate: it did not, in practice, sneer at fiscal fine-tuning, that chosen instrument of the Keynesians we were so keen to repudiate.

By the late summer of 1982, while the Chief Secretary was preparing to do battle with the spending ministries, we were being warned that actually they were not spending nearly fast enough. The latest message from the entrails was that 'the PSBR was going to undershoot substantially'. Now since this, the Budget deficit, is always identified as the most wayward of predictions, representing as it does the difference between some £130bn or more of spending, and some £130bn or less of revenues, and since huge overshoots had been – rightly – taken in the Treasury's stride the previous year, why worry? Because, we were solemnly assured, our 'wet' critics on the Tory back-benches would give us hell. And we solemnly agreed. So the public-expenditure wing of the Treasury, without, so far as one could tell, a moment's loss of sleep, embarked simultaneously on the penultimate round of axemanship upon the 1983 spending programmes, and the stimulation of faster spending in 1982. The Prime Minister was even induced to berate the local authorities for failing to spend as they should be doing on housing repairs.

That was not all. Why not, we were asked, get rid of hire purchase controls? The motor car manufacturers had been clamouring vigorously that summer for HP freedom (though only in respect of cars: the last thing they wanted was to have potential customers frittering away their credit on videos and washing machines). I expressed measured doubts: there was enough credit sloshing around as it was, I suggested. But the village had a foolproof answer to such qualms. HP controls, they pointed out, were really quite anomalous. They only applied to the great unbanked. Sophisticated souls like mandarins and Treasury ministers went to their bank managers for their credit needs, and paid a cheaper rate of interest to borrow to their hearts' content. It was indefensible to limit access for a small minority of citizens who were made to pay through the nose for the privilege anyway. Besides, such rationing was wholly inconsistent with the free-market philosophy which we were supposed to be so keen upon. The logic proved irresistible.

With benefit of hindsight the critics of 'Thatcherism' have since claimed that this late summer 'package' proved them right after all – recovery from the slump of 1979–81 had indeed involved a rise in spending programmes and a fiscal boost, as they had always said it must, although we continued to deny it; and also that we were cynically stoking up a pre-election boom.

Both claims are much exaggerated. Unlike the classic pre-election boom this one continued, and indeed – allowing for the distorting effect of the miners' strike – gathered momentum long after the votes had been safely garnered. Moreover both the spur applied to spending programmes and the scrapping of HP controls were modest as fiscal stimuli go.

Yet there is something in it. I was surprised to find, on looking up the figures, how large the boost to HP trade resulting from the scrapping of controls had been. Not as significant, in terms of the overall economy, as the signatories of the memorandum of the 364 economists, scrapping around for explanation of the post–1981 economic growth which they had dismissed as impossible, sought to claim.

But a lot more significant than we had expected at the time.

And here's the point. If we stoked up a pre-election boom I am sure we were not aware that we were so doing. We were simply pushing the PSBR back on course, and scrapping some boring old anomalies. If the villagers perceived more considerable consequences, they did not let on. Not, I am sure, because they were desperate to see the Tory Government re-elected, and thought we might be embarrassed by encouragement to buy the votes. Maybe because, deep down in the village soil, the Keynesian roots still ran?

The sequel, at any rate, was that the PSBR turned out in April 1984 not to have 'undershot' at all. It overshot, substantially. And the Tory Government went on to win the Election. Though not, I think, for that reason.

Modern Ministers of State, however, cannot devote their waking hours exclusively to the steering of the ship of state. They must also play at being engineers down in the boiler-room. Ever since the Heath Administration arrived in Whitehall in 1970 trailing plans, culled mainly from the United States, to enhance the 'cost-effectiveness' of Government, visitors to the Whitehall village have been expected to get to grips with Management.

The 1970 Government embarked on a series of initiatives described by stylish initials. There were 'PARs' – standing for 'Programme Analysis and Review' – and there were 'PPBS', or 'Programme Planning Budgeting Systems'. In layman's language the basic idea was that Ministers and mandarins should pull selected spending programmes up by the roots and put them under the microscope. What were they supposed to be achieving? Were they achieving it? Was it needed anyway? Were there better/cheaper ways of doing it? Could they be 'hived off' – not necessarily into the private sector (privatisation was much less fashionable in those days), but perhaps into a separate agency to be treated as an independent cost-centre and run as a private-sector business look-alike?

The fruits of this exercise amounted to a modest crop. Activities such as the management of Whitehall's vast property portfolio, and procurement for the Ministry of Defence, were indeed 'hived off' into semi-autonomous agencies. The performance of these agencies was mixed. At any rate the 1979 Tory Government was not tempted to pursue that particular route.

What did eventually ensue was a far-reaching programme to shift assets from the public to the private sector. For the Whitehall village that was a task like any other. Some other initiatives impinged much more directly. One was the target set, with the Prime Minister's personal imprimatur upon it, for contraction of civil service numbers. The second, the exercise master-minded by Sir Derek (subsequently Lord) Rayner of Marks and Spencer to identify Whitehall economies. The third, a series of new financial management initiatives within departments.

The contraction in civil service numbers was achieved in part as a by-product of the privatisation programme, since those employed in services displaced to the private sector disappeared automatically from the head-count. That was the painless part. The more painful part was the reduction of manpower in services retained. The Treasury, particularly after the restoration of its responsibility for management of the civil service in late 1981, had to set a good example to the spending departments, and the 'bleeding stump syndrome' was much in evidence. The civil service unions, understandably no doubt, regularly complained that the approach of the politicians was a mite selective. We positively boosted manpower to track down abuse of the welfare system; yet at the same time we insisted on economies in the policing of VAT and tax evasion. To which the honest answer was that there was widespread public concern about abuse of social welfare; whereas there was not the same belief in generalised abuse of the tax system. Yet, again, understandably perhaps, the mandarins themselves, and especially the managements of the Inland Revenue and the Customs, tended to sympathise with the Unions' resistance, while doing their best to make progress toward the targets set by the politicians. After all it was their empires we were curtailing, and the economy drive went high up the scale. It was not only the Customs men at Dover whose numbers might be shrunk, but also the ranks of the Deputy Under-Secretaries in Whitehall. Nevertheless, the target set by the Prime Minister in 1980, of a civil service payroll reduced to the levels of the 1940s within the lifetime of the Parliament, was in fact achieved.

The 'Rayner scrutinies' played a crucial role in this. Sir Derek was no stranger to Whitehall. He had been recruited by Ted Heath to assist in his drive for efficiency and cost-effectiveness in the early 1970s. Under Mrs Thatcher his role was more specific. Together with a small team of seconded civil servants he was to crawl over specific activities nominated by the Whitehall departments, and identify economies. Each department was required to nominate at least one major activity for a 'Rayner scrutiny' each year. When the task – which lasted about six months – was completed, the Rayner team compiled a checklist of specific economies, and the savings which were reckoned to ensue. This list was returned to the department for acceptance, deferment or rejection, of each specific recommendation. It was then passed on to Ministers, who knew that Sir Derek had direct access to the Prime Minister, and that if he felt we had acquiesced in the unreasonable rejection or deferment of his team's suggestions, we would have some explaining to do.

I was impressed. We were confronted with a list of perhaps 60 specific recommendations, each costed for economy. Perhaps 50 of these would have been accepted before they came to us. But among the ten outstanding there were likely to be one or two of the largest, in terms of potential saving. We had then to adjudicate on the case presented to us for rejection.

An example may illustrate the process. One 'Rayner scrutiny' which came to me concerned the management by the Department of National Savings of its deposit accounts. The Rayner team had discovered, among other things, that the DNS had a limit of (if I remember rightly) £10 on withdrawals by customers without reference to head office. They pointed out that the clearing banks operated a £50 limit, and suggested that the DNS could do the same, thereby achieving substantial economies. The DNS had rejected this suggestion, and they argued vigorously that a £50 limit would lead to additional fraud on a scale which would more than wipe out any savings.

It was an argument incapable of proof on either side. I finally backed the Rayner team, and the limit was duly raised to £50. So far as I know the fraud feared by the DNS has not materialised.

Perhaps, though, it was not quite as easy as it seemed. A recent (March 1986) survey by the National Audit Office has found that little more than half the economies identified by Rayner and his men in the first five years of investigation – judging by a sample check on three Whitehall departments – have actually materialised to date; and only about two-thirds of those promised by the departments concerned. There is evidently a risk that the scrutiny, once processed through the system, will thereafter be forgotten. Ministers have quite enough to do without digging up past scrutinies and finding out what has happened to them.

They have, for example, also to cope with 'Financial Management Initiatives'. These are rather different animals. Their prototype was the 'Minis', or 'Ministerial Information System' developed by Michael Heseltine at the Department of the Environment. 'Minis' got a lot of press, and was credited, at any rate by its inventor, with responsibility for an impressive run-down in the head-count of that department. Basically 'Minis' was supposed to enable the Minister to find out what each man-Jack (and woman-Jill) in his far-flung empire was up to, and whether it was needed or superfluous. Other departments (including the Treasury) were somewhat sceptical. But the Financial Management Initiatives, launched around Whitehall from 1982 onwards, had a similar purpose.

Unlike the Rayner scrutinies, they took some grasping. Sometime after midnight one would be confronted with a massive tome, running to several hundred pages, in which was set out staff complements, and the numbers in position, in out-stations of one's territory of which one would be but dimly aware. There were, I learned, seventeen copy-typists (Grade H8) and five accountants (two Grade A9 and two Grade A7) in the Newcastle office handling claims against the Department of National Savings. Outside Blackpool, where Ernie picked the lucky winners of Lord Stockton's Premium

Bonds, by contrast, there were but eleven copy-typists (Grade H8) and one accountant (Grade A7). Did that mean there were too many ladies tapping and gentlemen auditing up in Newcastle? Or too few in Blackpool? It was a nice conundrum, to which I did not find an easy answer. The tome came back time and again for further thought, since we were sternly lectured about the vital importance of Ministers achieving a 'positive input' to keep the mandarins upon their toes. The process, as I recall, was to culminate in a brainstorming session encompassing all the ministerial team, together with the mandarins, followed by a working 'overview' at Chequers. The 1983 General Election burst upon us before this work could reach its consummation. After which, presumably, it was resumed. Fortunately, perhaps, I was no longer there.

13

Reflections

Access to the Whitehall village comes by summons from 10 Downing Street. Egress comes in several forms. Once again, the call may come from 10 Downing Street, perhaps with a request to 'make way for a younger man' (who not infrequently turns out to be older). A face no longer fits. The Minister has proved too accident-prone in the House of Commons for the Whips to tolerate. Or he has paraded dissent within the Cabinet once too often. The sack may be inflicted without warning. Or it may be trailed for months before: the dismissal of Peter Rees as Chief Secretary, in September 1985, had been almost universally predicted for six months before (and there had been no discouragement of the predictions from Whitehall). Normally, nowadays, ministerial reshuffles are signalled well in advance, usually to coincide with the victims' return from their summer holidays. Potential victims – and potential beneficiaries – spend anxious hours beside their telephones.

Or, of course, the visitors depart en bloc. Their party has gone down to defeat at the hustings. Occasionally the party is successful, but the Minister is not. If he is deemed to be sufficiently important, his party may bust a gut to contrive an early by-election to bring him back to Parliament, keeping his portfolio warm for him in the interval. But modern precedents are not encouraging, and in all probability those who lose their seats when all around are keeping theirs will console themselves as best they may with a peerage (if they are offered one). There is one further, although not common, door marked 'exit'; and that is the one I found myself conducted to in 1983.

Every ten years the Boundaries Commission, an independent arbitrary body dominated by members of the legal profession, redraws the Parliamentary map in an effort to ensure that constituencies do not get too far out of touch with population movements. My constituency of Knutsford had a lengthy history. But the Commission is no respecter of tradition. It was sliced into six pieces and portioned out around adjacent territories.

Knutsford had the reputation of being one of the jewels in the Tory crown. It boasted more than 4,000 paid-up members, and its record of fund-raising and financial support to the central Party machine had few rivals. The constituency activists therefore too easily assumed that, while the constituency might die, its traditions would live on. Since the adjacent constituencies into which it was to be apportioned could not remotely match its organisation, that organisation would assume control of them.

They had different ideas. The town of Knutsford, and its surrounding area, rich in paid-up Tory members, was to be conjoined with the neighbouring towns of Northwich and Wilmslow. Northwich had precious few paid-up Tory members, and no organisation to speak of. Yet the management of the new constituency was to be determined purely on the basis of population; and on that basis Knutsford found itself hopelessly outnumbered. There were old scores to be settled. Knutsford was to be put firmly in its place. And that, as I rapidly discovered, included me. Tory Central Office had laid down that sitting Tory MPs were to be consulted at every stage of the reorganisation. Here again, the 'adjacent hunts' had different ideas. Parochial debts were paid, and I departed. It was by then too late to take up my carpet-bag and search for electoral new pastures: the 1983 Election was almost upon us. Besides, I reckoned my travelling days were over. So as the nation carried Mrs Thatcher back to Downing Street upon a Parliamentary landslide, I bade the village a discreet farewell.

In the three years that have supervened since my departure, the Whitehall village has passed through interesting times. Two civil servants have been prosecuted under the Official Secrets Act for 'leaking' information to the press, one to be sent to prison, the other to be acquitted; a third has been charged with selling official documents to Fleet Street, and found guilty. The Government has decided to ban Trades Union membership at one of its out-stations, the secret communications centre at Cheltenham, and found itself confronted with continuing resistance from the Unions. There has been much anxious debate about the 'politicisation' of the higher echelons of the civil service, balanced by calls for more overt 'politicisation' than we have already. The mandarins' own Trades Union, the First Division Association, has called for a charter of civil servants' rights of conscience. The extraordinary Westland saga has thrown a new – and lurid – light on in-fighting in Whitehall, with civil servants seemingly manipulated to protect the reputations of their masters.

The only real novelty in this catalogue is the Cheltenham affair. The motivation for the Government's decision to ban Union membership at GCHQ remains a subject of debate. So does the wisdom of the decision to impose a ban when none had hitherto existed, and still more to turn down out of hand the Unions' offer of a pledge of non-disruption. Certainly the attempt to buy out Union rights with £1,000 for those who agreed to surrender them looked remarkably cack-handed. As it has proved to be.

There is nothing very novel about the other bones of contention. As I have argued above, 'leaks' have always been a feature of the lives of Governments, and no doubt always will be; and some are made by Ministers and mandarins on behalf of Government or for their own honour and glory, just as some are made against them, and become the object of – usually fruitless – investigations. Nor is there anything unusual about civil servants being manipulated to protect their masters – or masters being manipulated to protect their civil servants for that matter. Although I suspect that, over the years, the Ministers are the commoner puppets in that process.

It is alleged that, over the past three years, the villagers' loyalty has been sorely tried by the propensity of Ministers to 'lie in public' – or, even worse, to make them lie on Ministers' behalf. But Ministers – and civil servants – do that all the time. No-one seriously disputed, for example, that in the days of fixed exchange rates, when devaluation of the pound was seen to be inevitable and imminent, both Ministers and mandarins were quite properly entitled to lie like troopers when confronted with enquiries about their intentions, since the speculators would have had a field-day had they not. It is true that Chancellor Callaghan professed to feel that the public stance he had taken against devaluation up until the day that it occurred in 1967 made it desirable for him to move to pastures new. But few seriously believed that this was why he wished to move: or that he would have had his 'lies' tied round his neck had he chosen to carry on.

'Lies' seldom come as stark as this. More often it is a matter of *suppressio veri* – and *suggestio falsi*: or, more simply, tangled wires. A pristine example of the former was the treatment of oil sales to Rhodesia by South African subsidiaries of Shell and BP during the period when such sales were forbidden to British companies by sanctions legislation. BP and Shell knew what was going on, and convinced the Foreign Office that they were, in practice, powerless to prevent it. Forms of words were found to enable the Foreign Office Minister responsible, George Thomson (now Lord Thomson of Monifieth) to assure the House of Commons that British companies were not breaching sanctions legislation. Appearances were thus preserved, although the officials concerned were perfectly well aware that Parliament was being consciously misled. None of them felt their conscience outraged thereby: but then their Minister was doing his duty to his department.

When Ministers told Parliament, following the Falklands war that the Argentinian battleship *Belgrano* had been seen sailing towards the British expeditionary force when it was torpedoed, and it subsequently transpired that it had in fact been sailing in the opposite direction, Clive Ponting of the Ministry of Defence felt impelled by his conscience to impart the information to Labour MP Tam Dalyell, who had been seeking for months to try and prove that the *Belgrano* had been sunk simply in order to sabotage peace negotiations. Nothing has emerged to sustain that charge; nor does it seem improbable that the Cabinet was unaware which way the Argentinian battleship was sailing when the authorisation for the torpedo attack was given. But it surely required a degree of tunnel vision to believe that the loyalty of civil servants was strained beyond endurance by Ministerial statements to Parliament, which subsequently turned out to be erroneous, about the direction of an enemy warship in the middle of an armed conflict with British lives at stake. In this case if Parliament was consciously misled – and that is not proved – it was misled in defence of a Ministerial, as opposed to a departmental, position. But historians of our epoch might conceivably be driven to conclude that hypocrisy over sanctions against Rhodesia was more heinous than confusion over the precise circumstances surrounding the sinking of an enemy battle-ship in time of war.

What, then, of the Westland affair? The Westland affair was unusual, in the extent to which it exposed the unarmed conflict which is, in truth, a feature of the village culture (as I hope this book may have suggested) to public gaze. An episode of 'Yes, Minister' which depicted the Downing Street press spokesman selecting bits from a letter from the Attorney-General criticising one of Hacker's Cabinet colleagues, for immediate transmission to the Press Association by Hacker's departmental press office, would have been treated as caricature. Yet I find it perfectly believable. Mandarins, like lesser mortals, do become emotionally engaged, and their engagement sometimes warps their judgment. Bernard Ingham is not the first to whom this has happened: and he will not be the last.

An instance of the 'politicisation' of the senior village denizens? Hardly. A mandarin who started life as a Labour councillor and progressed to service as press adviser to Mr Wedgwood Benn was surely an improbable candidate for preferment to 10 Downing Street on grounds of political patronage. Nor is his unquestionably fierce protectiveness towards his current employer that unusual. Joe Haines played a not dissimilar role under Harold Wilson (and the historically minded might reflect that Lord Melbourne's advice to the young Queen Victoria was injudiciously flavoured with romanticism on occasion) in the days when the relationship between the Crown and Ministers was somewhat more akin to that between the Ministers and civil servants nowadays.

All this has, however, served to fan the flames of debate about the Official Secrets Act. Few subjects provoke more inconsistencies of attitude. At least since the prosecution brought against Jonathan Aitken (now a Tory MP) and the *Sunday Telegraph* at the time of the Biafran War in the late 1960s, the 1916 Act – or rather Section Two thereof – has been pronounced an Ass.

Section One, which covers the transmission of official information to a foreign power, is not controversial. It is Section Two, the catch-all provision, which lays a civil servant (or a minister, for that matter) open to prosecution for divulging any information which has come to him in the course of his or her official duties to an 'unauthorised person', which provokes dismay.

Politicans out of office pledge themselves to abolish it, or at least to restrict its impact to the transmission of material which is genuinely damaging to state security or the requirements of commercial confidentiality. Some politicians out of office, and some mandarins in retirement, go further, and espouse the cause of a 'Freedom of Information Act', which would place the onus upon Government to show cause why material should not be made automatically available to enquiring spirits. Politicans in office, and mandarins in harness, never get around to either.

It is, in truth, not hard to see why. What to those in exile seems a 'cover-up' becomes, in office, that necessary confidentiality without which the business of Government cannot be carried on. Moreover the dividing-line between the harmless and the harmful turns out, on closer inspection in Whitehall, to be remarkably difficult to draw. The Westland affair is regularly cited as proof positive of the absurdity of an Official Secrets Act which was plainly flouted by all concerned, day in and day out. It could equally well be argued – to my mind a good deal more cogently – that the Westland affair demonstrated the impracticality of carrying on effective Government at all when the rules of confidentiality between Government departments break down. Nor is the complexity of demarcation lines just a Whitehall smokescreen. I have participated, since leaving Whitehall, in debates across the airwaves in which Gerald Kaufman, currently the leading Opposition champion of freedom of information, has cited the confidentiality of ministerial engagement-books as a classic example of the folly of the present law. Yet it is a sad fact of modern life that there are plenty of terrorists around who would be delighted to have access to ministerial engagement books.

I am not seeking to suggest that official secrecy is not abused, or that confidentiality is not attached to material that does not require it. Indeed I have already argued (Chapter 6) that the slogan 'secret' slapped unnecessarily across a document may in practice serve to make it *less* secure, not more. But from my brief experience of Whitehall I have no doubt that 'more open' Government would not necessarily be better Government: it might very well be worse. Issues – far removed from state security, and yet of major consequence for the citizens – which cannot be argued back and forth within the corridors of Whitehall in confidence, will not be discussed at all.

Furthermore the opposite is also true: what is available to all is liable, in practice, to be of interest to none. Sir Douglas Wass, now a paid-up leader of the Freedom-of-Information pressure group, used sometimes to speculate, when we were in the Treasury together, that if we released a batch of documentation setting out the pros and cons of, let us say, changing the chosen instruments of monetary policy, to every Fleet Street newsroom, not one would print a word.

Nor is Section Two of the Official Secrets Act the bogey it is made out to be. Too often it seems to be discussed as if prosecution is indistinguishable from conviction. A civil servant who divulges to a newspaper that his Minister is colour-blind may be in formal breach of Section Two: a Government which prosecuted would simply be asking to be made to look a fool. Even when material has been divulged which was calculated to be a serious embarrassment to Government, it may well prove impossible to secure conviction – as the Ponting case ought to have reminded us. Nor is it unusual to have upon the Statute Book an Act which is not infrequently unenforced, or unenforceable. We do not scrap the speeding laws because the citizenry flouts them daily with impunity.

To many critics of the present Government, however, a propensity on the part of the Civil Service to leak, and resentment at the way in which the Official Secrets Act has occasionally been used to face them with the consequences, are no more than symptomatic of a more profound malaise among the villagers. The archetypal mandarin of the 1950s and early 1960s, Lord Plowden, and his Top Salaries Review Body, warned in 1985 that their morale was 'exceptionally low'. The inheritor of Lord Plowden's mantle in the late 1970s and early 1980s, Lord Bancroft, who had retired early after losing a long and bruising battle with the Prime Minister and Sir Derek Rayner to preserve the Civil Service Department, told the London School of Economics at the end of 1983 that 'the civil service ethos . . . has taken one and a quarter centuries to build, but could be destroyed in a decade'. He left little doubt in the minds of his audience that in his judgment it very likely would be if Mrs Thatcher stayed that long.

There are several strands to this perceived collapse of self-esteem. Grahame Turner summed it up in a review of Whitehall sentiment in the *Sunday Telegraph* in June 1985: 'Pay, of course. And the impression Mrs Thatcher had created that working in the public service had something parasitic about it. They sometimes wondered whether she'd prefer them to leave and set up hairdressing salons . . . There was also a general feeling that their own bosses, the Permanent Secretaries . . . had become a great deal less independent. They were now "merely courtiers", "faceless men".'

Now it would be pointless to deny that this Administration came to office with a determination to 'reduce the bureaucracy': a determination in which (so far) it has never wavered. And no human institution delights in shrinkage. But it is important to set the process in perspective.

No post-war Administration was more 'mandarin-friendly' than that of Mr Heath. Essentially a chief of staff by inclination, he found it easier to work with mandarins than Ministers. And they were handsomely rewarded. In particular in 1971 the public service as a whole was endowed with index-linked pensions. At the time the inflation rate, though high, was still falling, and it no doubt seemed like a good idea. But as inflation rapidly accelerated, and stories began to circulate of senior civil servants receiving pensions way above their own rates of pay at retirement, and even in some cases substantially above the going rate of pay for their successors, resentment began to fester. Private industry, which, for the most part, could not hope to guarantee the real value of its pensions (and indeed was liable to have schemes to do so disallowed by the Inland Revenue) became increasingly vociferous. Stories of generous arrangements to enable officials posted overseas to see their sons through Eton added fuel to the flames. Nor did it escape notice that throughout the 1970s the public service was the fastest-growing employer in the country. It was inevitable that a Tory government coming into office in 1979 would be committed to reversal of the trend.

Most Administrations, however, in time 'go native'. It is one of Mrs Thatcher's unusual qualities that she never has, and never will. She regularly talks about her Government as if she did not belong to it. She is also incapable of comprehending – no doubt wholly unaware of – the fact that many mandarins, perhaps the majority, are quite used to dealing with male politicians who test their stamina from time to time with stridency. But nothing in their training has prepared them to cope with such handling from a lady. Those who have adjusted, as many of them have, have invariably discovered that she readily appreciates robust dissent.

At any rate I hope this book may help to dispose of the *canard* that the topmost mandarins have been transformed into 'merely courtiers'. If they have I did not meet them. Nor did I see much evidence of incapacity among the villagers to defend their own. On the contrary. The way in which the Cabinet was induced to approve the large and contentious pay rise for the senior civil servants in 1985 (on the curious grounds that a shrinking civil service was leading to too much competition for the topmost prizes) hardly suggested that the villagers had lost their cunning.

With one possible exception – and that not in the Civil

Service – I saw no instance where the real or imagined political allegiance of alternative candidates played any part in their promotion prospects either. Assuredly the present Prime Minister is no friend of 'Buggins's turn': yet even Bugginses still have their day. Certainly there has been nothing to compare with the calculated insult inflicted on the Treasury by Lord Stockton when he called back Sir Roger Makins from the Embassy in Washington to take charge of it. Maybe the Prime Minister does have a preference for appointment to the most senior echelons of officials whom she has come to know and respect. But so have most, if not all, of her predecessors.

This leaves the charge that the provision of a service to the public has taken second place to the pursuit of streamlined numbers. There must be something in this. But a Government which believes, whether rightly or wrongly, that the wealth-creating sector of the economy has been overburdened with bureaucracy must be presumed to will the end of some reduction in the range of official services provided. Were cost-effectiveness the sole, or even the principal, consideration by which tasks were allocated within the system, the reduction in numbers could no doubt have been achieved with less impact on the range of services on offer. But the villagers are not unique in our polity in cherishing labour-intensive activities.

All Governments are disappointed, and this one is no exception. Indeed precisely because its ambitions – or at least its rhetoric – have been unusually 'radical', frustration at the comparative meagreness of its achievements in certain directions has been all the greater. No-one, perhaps, has voiced frustration with the ways of the Whitehall village more trenchantly than Sir John Hoskyns. His charge-sheet, and his recommendations for reform, deserve analysis.

John Hoskyns is a quondam regular soldier who left the army to set up his own computer software business which he subsequently sold for a substantial sum. In the late 1970s he offered his services to Keith Joseph, and became one of the Shadow Cabinet's principal advisers on policies to restore enterprise to the economy. Following the 1979 Election, he was appointed head of the Policy Unit, or 'political Think Tank' (as opposed to the then still extant Central Policy Review Staff) at No 10. Three years later he departed, more than somewhat disillusioned, and in due course became Director-General of the Institute of Directors. From there he has produced a steady stream of provocative – and thought-provoking – critiques of the management of Whitehall.

Sir John attributed a not insignificant share of responsibility for the poor performance of the British economy over several generations to the Whitehall village and its entrenched traditions. He regards the villagers as incurable 'generalists', with little or no understanding of the needs of a modern industrial society, invincibly resistant to radical change. He is distressed by the way in which Prime Ministers are obliged to pick their Ministers overwhelmingly from what he regards as the quite unqualified and narcissistic membership of the House of Commons, and furthermore to pick them on grounds which have little or nothing to do with either competence or experience. Once picked, he sees them rapidly overwhelmed by the sheer volume of work to which they are subjected, and hence quite incapable of ever sitting back and taking stock, or lifting their eyes above tomorrow's or – at best – next week's crisis.

None of these charges is original, and it may have emerged from this book that there is substance to virtually all of them. Strenuous efforts have been made in recent years to encourage cross-fertilisation between Whitehall and the world of commerce and industry, but with strictly limited success. Civil servants loaned to industry usually find the rewards much more attractive, and do not often come back. Business-men are all too often loaned to Whitehall because they will not be missed by the firms from whence they came. There has been some success in recruiting late entrants into the permanent civil service from the private sector – the Chancellor's official chief of staff at the Treasury when I was there had, for example, spent the bulk of his career as a chartered accountant – but not much. Similarly the number of recruits to the senior echelons of Whitehall from the universities – so much a feature of the American system – can at any given time be numbered on the fingers of two hands (although the

Chancellor's Chief Economic Adviser is almost always one of them).

It may also have become apparent that Ministerial selection is, indeed, a fairly random process. Apart from the Lord Chancellor and the Law Officers, no Cabinet Ministers are picked on the basis of professional qualification; and when a conscious attempt is made to widen the selection, by implanting experienced businessmen by Tory Governments, or real live Trades Union leaders by Labour, the House of Commons can be relied upon to do its best to reject them.

It would also be hard to dispute that Ministers are in permanent danger of submerging beneath their workloads. I used to reckon I worked something like a one hundred-hour week when I was in the Treasury. Attempts *are* reqularly made to lift horizons, with day-long seminars at Chequers (and I suppose the annual Treasury weekend at Chevening falls into that category). But it has to be confessed that these are usually regarded by most of those involved as a waste of time they can ill afford. Some Cabinet Ministers in every Government endeavour to perform their proper role by entering into debate on matters far removed from their departmental responsibilities. They are seldom thanked by their colleagues for so doing. A week is, as Harold Wilson said, a long time in politics. A month is an eternity. Five years ahead is out of sight and out of mind.

So what are we to do about it? Sir John Hoskyns has advanced a number of suggestions. He has toyed with the idea of enabling the Prime Minister to recruit Ministers from right outside the Parliamentary arena, who could speak in either House without the right to vote. He has advocated something akin to the American 'spoils system', by which an incoming Government brings with it a small army of political appointees, who provide a top layer of more or less politically advice and support above the permanent bureaucracy.

His latest proposition is more modest. Instead of the American system he has taken the French as his model. He suggests that each Cabinet Minister should have a personal *cabinet* of six to eight people, consisting partly of 'high-flyers' from within the village, and partly of sympathetically-inclined temporary recruits from the outside world. They would subsume the role hitherto performed by the Ministerial 'Private Office'. But in addition they would work on longer-term issues, keep the Minister abreast of work emerging from private research institutions and the like outside Whitehall, make sure he was fully briefed on items on the Cabinet agenda beyond his departmental remit, and also relieve him of some of his constituency work.

This is not a proposal which has found much favour with the mandarins. Lord Bancroft told a BBC programme in 1981 that he did not 'think it would be a good idea in our present system . . . to have the Minister of the day warned off from his department by a *cabinet* of people who were especially chosen for their political affiliations.' Five years later he had evidently not changed his mind. He told the Treasury and Civil Service Select Committee that he was 'apprehensive . . . in case it walls off the Minister from his department'; and the First Division Association was 'fairly suspicious about it as a panacea'. The Secretary to the Cabinet and Head of the Civil Service, Sir Robert Armstrong, damned it with faint praise: he thought it 'could be made to work'.

The Select Committee was undeterred. It recommended a 'Minister's Policy Unit', including 'a number of special advisers, together with a number of career civil servants and his Parliamentary Private Secretary. The advisers would be there to keep the Minister in touch with his party organisation and to give policy advice. The civil servants would be there to keep the Ministers in touch with his department and to give advice. The PPS would be there to keep the Minister in touch with his backbenchers.'

The Select Committee balanced this proposal with others more calculated to appeal to mandarin taste. They thought 'the Prime Minister should . . . formulate and publish guidelines for Ministers which would set out their duties to Parliament and responsibilities for the Civil Service'. They filled this out by quoting, with evident approval, the terms for such guidelines offered in evidence by journalist Mr David Lipsey, to include 'the duty to give a fair hearing and a considered response to civil service advice . . . and not merely to overrule them on political whim; the duty to ensure that the official who speaks his mind is not thereby disadvantaged . . .; the duty to ensure that influence over appointments is not abused for partisan purposes; the duty not to ask civil servants to act in ways which are immoral; the duty to be fair with regard to terms and conditions of service; and the duty to treat civil servants with personal consideration'.

They also bowed to the wisdom of Lord Bancroft and two previous Prime Ministers, Ted Heath and Jim Callaghan, in advocating the restoration of 'a single Minister for the civil service', to match the Minister for Sport and Children's Playgroups, together with the restoration of the position of a Head of the Home Civil Service with nothing else to do.

Other propositions currently on the table were not considered by the Select Committee, since they hardly came within its chosen remit. Former Labour Trade Secretary Edmund Dell, anticipating Sir John Hoskyns, advocated the freedom of Prime Ministers to recruit talent outside Parliament; but he was also in favour of a more 'presidential' system of power involving 'a stronger central control on matters such as the level of public expenditure', balanced apparently, if not self-evidently, by 'more open government' and proportional representation. Sir Douglas Wass, late of the Treasury, in his 1983 Reith Lectures, produced two positive, though cautious, suggestions of his own. One called for the secondment of a select coterie of mandarins to staff the Shadow Cabinet. To prevent political infection their secondment would be limited to five years, after which they would return to mainstream Whitehall, where they would apparently undergo a period of quarantine 'away from the political stage'.

His second suggestion was that there should be a Central Analytical Staff which would, in ways not very precisely explained, contrive to avoid 'the failure and disappointment of the Central Policy Review Staff' (Ted Heath's Think Tank), to which it bore a notable resemblance. 'To make absolutely sure that it was in touch with departmental business, it would have to be involved closely in the annual public expenditure survey, and it should be represented at all the meetings between the Treasury and the spending ministers', producing its own alternative report to Cabinet at the end of the exercise. One dreads to think what Sir Douglas would himself have had to say had he been confronted by such a proposition when he had been in service. Distance lends enchantment.

The more radical of these proposals for reform would require constitutional change on a scale of which their proponents seem to me to show scant awareness. Our Government emanates from Parliament in a way that those of the United States and France do not. Until the Great Reform Bill, or thereabouts, Ministers were genuinely the appointees of the Crown, and the monarch, like a modern French or American President, could choose at random (although from well back into the eighteenth century the Chancellor of the Exchequer had been required to be a Commons man). If the choice should fall upon a citizen who lacked a seat in Parliament, he could always be elevated to the Lords, or a borough-owner could be persuaded (in return for Crown favours) to produce a rotten borough. Modern Prime Ministers can similarly elevate a – strictly limited – quota of non-Parliamentary placemen, like Harold Macmillan's Percy Mills, or Mrs Thatcher's David Young, to the Upper House. But unless some fundamental changes were induced, the large majority of the membership of any British Government must consist of members of the House of Commons.

The Commons does have a somewhat childish propensity to bully imports like Labour's Frank Cousins or Ted Heath's John Davies. But critics like Sir John Hoskyns or Edmund Dell too easily dismiss the central role of Parliamentary accountability and experience in our system. The imports may bring great wisdom and awareness of the 'real world' outside. But they cannot, by definition, have been subjected to long years of attrition on the doorstep which – like it or not – is the essence of *parliamentary* goverment.

It was precisely because de Gaulle distrusted this attrition that he required the Ministers under his Fifth Republican constitution to have surrogates to replace them in the National Assembly upon elevation. We could adopt a similar 'reform'. But Ministers in the Fifth Republic – like Cabinet members in the United States – are chosen by a Head of State who has himself been chosen by nationwide election. That is not a form of democratic authentication available to us (unless our domestic reformers have more far-reaching designs upon the Crown than they have mentioned). It is also significant that de Gaulle not infrequently required his chosen, non-elected Ministers to submit themselves to popular election (notwithstanding the fact that, having been elected, they would be required to pass their mandates to their surrogates). Nor should it be overlooked that when, in 1968, de Gaulle's Fifth Republic was confronted by insurrection on a scale which threatened to destroy it without prior warning, many French politicians attributed this unnerving shock to the inadequacy of the connections between Ministers and grassroots sentiment. No such accusations can be laid against the US constitution, since the President and his hand-picked Cabinet can only propose, and it is for a separately, and independently, elected Congress to dispose. Here again we would have problems in fitting such a division of the powers beneath the concept of hereditary monarchy.

If we are thus condemned to selection of the majority of our Ministers from the Parliamentary club, could we at least improve the quality of its membership? Parliament, in the considered view of the erstwhile boss of the Ministry of Defence, is 'a public disgrace', and he is certainly not the first to deplore its collective calibre. Within the Tory Party – and it is not unique – strenuous efforts are made to persuade the 'selectorate' to give a preference to candidates of proven excellence or obvious potential. The selectorate has other thoughts upon his mind. The Hon Samuel Slumkey may be 'Cabinet timber'; but if it is the considered judgment of the selectorate that the dim but worthy Mr Horatio Fizkin is the lad to wow them in the back streets of Eatenswill, then Fizkin it will be. And who is to say that the selectorate is wrong, however much it may displease Sir Frank Cooper and Sir John Hoskyns by its choice? The Slumkeys of this world are frequently rejected by the voters, and selectors are in the business of choosing local winners rather than gentlemen to be the next Prime Minister but three.

Besides, there is a more fundamental misconception at work. It is the misconception that Ministers are, or ought to be, in the business of 'management'. 'Management' is offered to us in two guises. The first, and more harmless, involves 'management' of the public service.

Sir Frank Cooper, whose own last Minister when he was in service, Michael Heseltine, had been frequently exposed to view (by himself as well as others) as the paragon of political management in the Village, told the conference called by Sir John Hoskyns at the Institute of Directors in May 1986 to 're-skill' Government, that in his view:

'the idea that Ministers can manage is a nonsense; none of them is trained to manage anything; they are not interested in it; they have got so many other things to do . . . If one is in business' – an area to which Sir Frank has clearly taken as a duck to water – 'and has a . . . non-executive chairman, one has a professional managing director . . . This is a role which ought to be fulfilled by civil servants . . .'

Now like it or not, Sir Frank's own last Secretary of State has indeed been 'trained to manage' something, albeit a group of magazine publishers, and he was not unique, at any rate in a Tory Government. Nor is it true that all Ministers 'are not interested' in the management of the civil service: apart from Michael Heseltine, Ted Heath was arguably obsessed with it. The real problem, to which Sir Frank Cooper did not refer, is that Ministers, whether trained or interested (and assuredly he is right to assert that most of them are neither), simply do not have the instruments. A manager in the private sector lives with continuous updates of the budgets and the profit forecasts of the profit centres for which he is responsible. A Whitehall Minister, as I have reported from my own experience, is presented very late at night with a sheaf of manpower figures on which he is expected to adjudicate without the smallest point of reference. It may be that Michael Heseltine's 'Minis' initiative worked wonders, first at Environment and then at Defence (although the former Permanent Secretary at Defence does not make it sound that way). If so its special magic clung to its inventor: it certainly did not come our way in the Treasury. So I agree with Sir Frank that the concept of the 'managerial Minister' is a will o'the wisp, even if I come to that conclusion by a different route.

It is, however, I submit, the second guise of 'Ministerial management' that enjoys the more fashionable following. This is the concept of 'Great Britain Ltd' (or rather, to be truly up to date, 'plc'), endowed with far-seeing business politicians, attuned to 'the real world' outside Westminster to run it, like Japan Inc. or perhaps France, SA.

There are difficulties, within our constitutional system, about the recruitment of businessmen to Cabinet which I have already touched upon. There are, though, more fundamental difficulties. The businessman is after 'market share' and 'bottom line' for his corporation. So are Ministers. But in our Parliamentary form of Government, unlike that of Japan Inc, or perhaps that of France, SA, their 'market shares' and 'bottom lines' are fundamentally different. Both consist of voters to be garnered.

Throughout most of the critiques of the way in which the Whitehall village is managed runs a strong vein of impatience with the propensity of Ministers to indulge in pork-barrel politics. A passage in the Crossman diaries, in which that enthusiastic student recorded Cabinet calculations about the number of marginal seats traversed by a hopelessly uneconomic railway line in Wales, is quoted repeatedly in tones of horror. But if ICI's share price were determined by the number of marginal constituencies in which that great corporation contrived to operate, its boardroom would be motivated similarly. Mrs Castle's decision, in 1966, to give the go-ahead for a Humber Bridge which lacked then – and indeed still lacks – any vestige of commercial logic is frequently cited, justifiably, as a classic of misdirected investment. But it was promptly followed by the Labour victory in a Hull by-election for which it was designed. And this by-election victory persuaded a cautious Harold Wilson to risk a General Election which gave his Party another four years of the fruits of office. No-one can prove that Mrs Castle's bridge had anything to do with it (indeed the connection between vote-sweeteners and votes cast is tenuous to non-existent). But the dividend was spectacular.

If, like the French, we severed Ministers from their electors, they might be more prone to concentrate on higher things.

And like the French we might experience more high-minded Government, tempered regularly by revolutions. But it seems to be naïve to believe that we could somehow find a better breed of political managers, rich in industrial experience, who would fix fine eyes on the markets of the world in our existing constitutional environment. Or that, if we did, they would last for many months.

Which brings us to another hazard of our system: the temporary nature of political office. Senior executives of major corporations can normally expect to hold their jobs for five years or more. Long enough for their chickens to come home to roost. Eighteen months on a single job is well above per score for the politicians. It takes a pretty energetic chicken to make it back in time.

A classic example of UK Ltd at play was the 'investment' of rather more than £80m of the taxpayers' cash in the de Lorean car enterprise in Northern Ireland, between 1978 and 1982, most of it ending up in numbered bank accounts in Switzerland and on the ski slopes of Colorado. The original 'investment' was made by Labour's Roy Mason and Don Concannon. Within six months they had been deposited on the Opposition benches by the electors. In their place came a Tory team led by Humphrey Atkins, which topped up Roy Mason's generosity. And departed. By the time Mr de Lorean had made contact with a drug-pusher from the FBI and the enterprise went bust there was yet another Ministerial team, led by Jim Prior, faithful unto death, in charge.

Sexual aberration – of a nature practised by the majority of their fellow citizens – is the unforgivable offence for our political managers. Proven incompetence often leads to promotion. And even when, as in the case of de Lorean, the incompetence is so flagrant that Parliament feels obliged to notice it, retribution is automatically ruled out if – as in this instance – both the major Parties are involved. But in any case the perpetrators have almost always moved on – or out to the back benches – before the skeletons appear.

The same is true, albeit to a lesser extent, of the mandarins. The Public Accounts Committee, given the task of conducting a post-mortem into the de Lorean affair (the PAC, by tradition, does not cross-question Ministers) was told that 'no heads had rolled'. Senior civil servants who can be shown to have proferred what turned out to be terrible advice to Ministers may, in Whitehall jargon, 'have their cards marked'. They will assuredly not be fired.

When I was in the Treasury I had to deal with one official (the only one, I hasten to add) who appeared to me to be manifestly inadequate. Eventually his superior came to see me. The superior said he had formed the impression that I was not happy with his work. I admitted that this was indeed the case. 'Yes', said his superior, my predecessor had shared my unhappiness. And he agreed that our dissatisfaction was understandable. But just at that moment there was no available siding for the individual in question to be shunted to. One of the consequences of the Prime Minister's drive to slim down the civil service, one was led to understand, was that sidings were in rather short supply.

In the private sector the executive who acquires a can of worms usually departs, as does the branch manager who falls down on the job. Their departure is sweetened by a handsome (even in the case of the executive a monster) golden handshake. But his fate does not pass unnoticed. It is surely crying for the moon to expect that Ministers or mandarins will 'manage' like their counterparts in private industry while the penalties of failure are, to all intents, non-existent. To which the Village might legitimately reply that the rewards of achievement do not compare with the private sector either. The sad fact is that managing Whitehall and managing the private sector are, as Charles I said of subject and sovereign, 'clean different things'.

If we want the assets managed by the Whitehall Village to be managed as they would be in the private sector, then that is where we had better put them. Which is what this Government is doing.

So let us turn to another section of the charge-sheet: the need for the visitors to the Village to be better equipped for their task. If it has to be accepted – as I believe it has to be – that their selection from within the Parliamentary club is bound to be fairly random, can we ensure that, once selected, they will at least be endowed with the wherewithal to make the best fist that they can of the cards that happen to have been dealt to them? Would this be achieved by restoring a 'Central Analytical Staff' to the Cabinet, and by endowing individual Ministers with individual *cabinets à la française*?

At the risk of sounding like Guedella's inverted Micawber, I doubt it. In its heyday, the Central Policy Review Staff (which by any other name is what Sir Douglas Wass is calling for) got dangerously involved in politics. Its *patron*, Lord Rothschild, reported in 1973 that, having spent the first 18 months of its existence alerting Ministers to where they had been diverted from the course set out to the electors in 1970, the CPRS had since become engaged in a search for areas where Ministers had *not* been diverted though they should have been. To some of us it appeared at the time to have been notably successful in this second role. But it is not an appropriate constitutional role for villagers, however eminent. In the years of its decline under Wilson, Callaghan and Thatcher, the CPRS became something of a fifth wheel to the Whitehall buggy. But that is not presumably what Sir Douglas has in mind.

As to Ministerial *cabinets*, here again I take leave to doubt. The difficulty with the concept of Ministerial *cabinets* is, perhaps, more speculative. That Ministers are both overloaded and ill-equipped to address the issues which lie beyond the scope of their individual departments is not in dispute. Unfortunately it seems to me that endowment with a *cabinet*, at any rate along the lines so far suggested by its proponents, would be far more likely to enhance the load than to ease it. Sir John Hoskyns, for example, envisages that the *cabinet* would, among other things, keep abreast of research in the private and academic sectors. The imagination boggles at the thought of the extra midnight boxes *that* would throw up. Nor is there any real prospect, as Sir John and others have suggested, that the members of a *cabinet* could in practice take some of the load of constituency duties off the Ministerial shoulders. Only those who have never served in Parliament can envisage that constituency activists would be content with an official substitute for the presence of their elected Member.

The *cabinet* might, it is true, send its *patron* off to meetings of the other Cabinet better equipped to play a role in collective decision-making over non-departmental items on the agenda. But supposing – and as I have already mentioned, this is by no means an unusual aspect of the Whitehall culture – the department at official level has agreed to put its Minister up to back another Whitehall kraal in Cabinet on the 'cutlet for a cutlet' principle, and the *cabinet* advised him to oppose the plans of the other kraal on broad grounds of public policy, it really is not difficult to predict which side would win the argument. Not, I think, the *cabinet*.

Besides, it has to be admitted that, for all the current talk at the time of writing about a 'restoration of collective Cabinet decision-making' the modern Cabinet would very soon seize up altogether if all 23 or 24 members had their three-penn'orth to contribute on most of the items on the agenda. Under every modern Government the wise departmental Minister seeks to sell his case to the Prime Minister in *tête-à-tête*. If that has been successfully achieved, the argument, except in rare instances of acute controversy and political sensitivity, is largely over; and another Cabinet member not directly involved who seeks to air his implanted wisdom on the subject might as well save his breath.

Sir Douglas Wass's other important proposal is the endowment of the Shadow Cabinet with official staff on secondment. It is rather difficult not to detect in this the ambition of the Whitehall village to begin the process of domestication of its 'masters' before they even take up residence. Assuredly Parties in Opposition do saddle themselves with commitments which they – and their officials – have every reason to regret when they have an opportunity to fulfil them. But such hostages to fortune are usually given in expectation of electoral reward; and against that calculation warning words from seconded civil servants would surely carry little weight. The Tory Shadow Cabinet in early 1979 did not really need seconded civil servants to warn it against the dangers of promising in advance to honour the awards that Labour's Comparability Commission would come up with: some of its own backbenchers did so, vigorously. But in vain. There were, we were reminded, 'five million votes at stake'.

Nor is it difficult to predict the calbre of civil servants who would be selected by their peers for a stretch in exile: those who 'never would be missed'. Those with a real future would surely reject the poisoned chalice anyway.

A much more radical suggestion than any hitherto discussed has been advanced by Lord Stockton's erstwhile Private Secretary, Sir Philip de Zulueta (in correspondence to Sir John Hoskyns): the wholesale streamlining of Whitehall by the elimination of departments. That would indeed reduce the workload of the Cabinet, and give its members more time to consider strategy. But unfortunately, as Sir Philip himself recognises, it is not going to happen, since the vested interests are too strong. It is indicative that Sir Philip's first candidate for euthanasia is the Industry Department. Sir Keith Joseph went there in 1979 with just that aim in mind. Industry made a successful take-over bid for Trade instead.

What, then, could be feasible and desirable? One modest suggestion that would do something to ease the workload of Ministers would be to release them from the obligation to act as the cheapest form of lobby-fodder for the Party Whips. No doubt the back-bench infantry needs to see the mighty sharing in its nightly vigils. But it is grotesque that Ministers should be ordered home from far corners of the globe, often in the middle of tense negotiations, to swell a Government's majority which is not remotely in danger.

It also occurred to me to wonder, as I watched my nightly homework being bundled up in my Private Office at the Treasury about the time that the rest of the world is putting on its slippers, whether there is not something wrong with the Whitehall daily timetable. It is obviously convenient for the village to keep the politicians out of mischief in meetings and receipt of delegations during daylight hours, and then to present them with the results of the day's toil to mull over into the small hours. But 2 or 3 a.m. is not necessarily the best of times for Ministers to face up to choices on which the well-being of their fellow-citizens may depend.

Beyond the bulging boxes and what in other walks of life would be called the 'unsociable hours', Ministers in Government, regardless of its colour, who seek to carry out their constitutional duties must frequently ask themselves 'but are there other choices?' Whitehall presents them with Option A or Option B to choose from, occasionally Options A, B and C, and often makes it clear which is the proper answer. But is there an Option D lurking in the woodwork unexposed?

The advocates of Ministerial *cabinets* would have us believe that this is precisely where the beefed-up Private Office would come in useful: it would second-guess the departmental brief and dig out the third or fourth alternative. I have a nasty suspicion that it would soon find itself in trouble if it did. The village has its little ways with Ministerial advisers who trample on the village culture.

I sometimes considered whether Ministers might not get a better glimpse of the whole terrain if we moved in the opposite direction altogether, by eliminating the Private Office filter between the political visitors and the residents. The Minister who is any use will argue through the reasoning behind a proposition with his mandarins if he is unsure. But the scope of the debate has been pre-determined by the submission filtered through the Private Office. Supposing – just supposing – I had been allowed to participate in the debate that had gone on below the surface between officials of the Treasury and officials of the Bank in which they had sought (not invariably successfully) to reach a common front before they brought their work to me? It will not happen: that would be a grievous assault upon the culture indeed. But I retain a suspicion that if the politicians ever really wanted to analyse the full range of alternatives before arriving at decisions, this is the way that they would need to move. Fortunately, perhaps, most of them have better ways to spend their waking hours.

There is, though, a more fundamental question-mark about the way in which the Whitehall village goes about its business: the collegiate ethos. I was bemused by the jealousies and rivalries which dominated the working relationship between the Treasury and the Bank of England. These have not diminished since I departed. They have palpably increased. Nor are they unique, although they are currently high profile. Semi-public conflicts, between the Departments of Industry and Employment over responsibility for 'deregulation', between Environment and Agriculture over the so-called 'green' issues, and most recently between Employment and the Treasury over profit-related wages schemes, serve as a regular reminder of the state of territorial conflict which is the blood of Whitehall life.

It is fashionable to complain that we suffer by comparison with our neighbours from 'adversarial politics', and the violence of the change which is said to come about when a Tory régime takes the place of Labour, or a Labour Government comes to office. This can be overstated: arguably the more fundamental changes of direction in recent years have taken place out of phase with changes in the composition of the House of Commons: from deregulation to planning in 1961; from laxity to restraint in public spending in 1966, and back again in 1971; from the imposition of monetary targets in 1968 to their abandonment in 1971, and their reimposition in 1976. The 'adversarial politics' within the Whitehall village, with each department perpetually fighting in defence, or where possible for the enlargment, of its territory, is surprisingly neglected. Yet the way in which the enhancement of the departmental budget, both absolutely and, still more, relatively to its rivals, is treated as a test of collegiate machismo, impacts upon the allocation of national resources regardless of the choices of elected Government. The rare politician like Keith Joseph or Nicholas Ridley who challenges the empire-building propensities of his mandarins is letting down the side. Nor is the tension between departments otherwise constructive: indeed when it reaches the pitch of current quarrels between the Bank of England and the Treasury it seems markedly destructive.

Such habits are deeply engrained, and it is not obvious how they could be eradicated. It is theoretically conceivable that a new-style Central Policy Review Staff could contrive to knock the departmental heads together, although it takes a degree of optimism to believe it would in practice: the last one certainly did not. It is, however, open to the visitors from Westminster to challenge departmental priorities and to arbitrate between them. They very rarely do.

They very rarely do, of course, because to challenge those

priorities adds substantially to the working day – and night. Acquiescence with the departmental strategy requires nothing but a signature. Dissent involves lengthy argument. As a result it resembles Dr Johnson's analogy of the dog walking on his hinder legs for the woman preacher: 'it is not done well; but you are surprised to find it done at all.' Yet the Minister who does not at least occasionally challenge the departmental priorities abdicates his constitutional function. It is a function that no other mechanism is likely to fulfil.

It is, however, a far cry from these strictures to lay the blame upon the Village for the relatively disappointing performance of Great Britain Ltd over the past 100 years. That is hardly more logical than to blame the janitor for a school's record in exams. It attributes to Government a capacity for harm which may reflect some politicians' expectations of its potential for improvement, rather than the reality of its strictly limited influence for either benefit or damage. Moreover where decisions taken in Whitehall can be seen to have diminished national potential, the influence of the civil servants was rarely more than marginal.

In his 1985 Reith Lectures, for example, Dr David Henderson singled out Concorde and the power station building programme of the 1960s and 1970s as two of the worst investment decisions in recorded history. That may be a rather sweeping judgment: but there is at least an element of truth.

Now undoubtedly the obsession of the official Foreign Office to frustrate de Gaulle's ambitions for a 'third force' Euope by securing entry to the European Community contributed to the original Cabinet decision to embark on Concorde in 1961. But it was a relatively secondary contribution. Far more significant was the enthusiasm of the politicians to try and steal a march on the Americans, and in particular the *penchant* of the then Prime Minister, Harold Macmillan, for big-spending projects repugnant to the Treasury. Certainly the opposition of the official Treasury was at least as vociferous as the eagerness of the official Foreign Office – and far more cogently presented.

As to the endless procrastination and indecision which

dogged the power station programme, this reflected essentially the political desire to preserve an artificial market for the Coal Board and the miners. Officials did their best to persuade successive Governments to lift their sights beyond the coalfields, only to be frustrated by the instinctive loyalties of Labour and the timidities of Tories.

Or take the issue which appears to have contributed more than any other to the sense of frustration with the Village and its customs which Sir John Hoskyns took with him when he left 10 Downing Street: the reform of industrial relations law. Sir John felt that his personal enthusiasm for more radical changes was blocked by civil service obscurantism.

Now it is true that the Department of Employment, like the old Ministry of Labour which it replaced, is the Department for Trades Unions just as the Ministry of Agriculture is the Department for Farmers. It was sceptical and resistant. But then so was its Secretary of State, James Prior, throughout the time that Sir John was the head of the Downing Street 'Think Tank'. It might be argued that this was no more than a typical example of the politicans 'going native'. But it could also be argued that Jim Prior was more influenced by the experience of Ted Heath's attempt at root-and-branch reform in the 1970 Industrial Relations Act, and its nugatory results, than by departmental sentiment. What cannot easily be argued is that the Department of Employment would have been able to resist Sir John Hoskyns' impatience, shared as it was by the Prime Minister, had its political chief been an agnostic or a lightweight.

It might of course be claimed that had the Department of Employment had a different collegiate ethos – had it, for example, been subsumed into the Department of Trade with its bent for open markets, then Jim Prior's instinctive preference for gradualism might have been subverted. That is a rather different proposition. Even so, I doubt it. Politicians, like lesser mortals, tend to have their opinions shaped in the rough school of experience.

The conclusion, if there has to be a conclusion – and I explained in the introduction that this is designed to be a tourists' guide, and not a constitutional treatise – is that the Village has its territorial integrity; and that it takes both determination and application on the part of politicians to harness the considerable skills of the villagers to the achievement of the politicians' political goals. Most Ministers lack the determination and the capacity for application needed. But there is no obvious reason why they should be thus endowed. For it is not those qualities which secure entry to the political base-camp at Westminster. Charm, connections, plausibility, luck (and, in the Tory Party, an attractive wife): these are the ingredients of successful candidature. Nor are strength of character and an appetite for hard work the characteristics that secure promotion when the base-camp has been reached (although at this point they help). 'Usefulness', effective performance in the House of Commons, even trouble-making, but above all, perhaps, 'clubability': these are the qualifications which secure preferment when the vacancies appear. Administrative capacity is nowhere, since it can only be shown when the chance is given. Admittedly it may command recognition among those who have once made the Ministerial grade. Even then it will take second place to performance in the House of Commons.

So the critics are to that extent correct: Westminster is a clubhouse which promotes its own and repels the interlopers. But their strictures for the most part miss the target. It is somewhat academic to complain that the committee of the Athenaeum Club is composed of members of the Athenaeum. Accountants, or management consultants, might make a better fist of managing the Club's assets, and from time to time no doubt the services of a management consultant or accountant are enlisted. But only because he happens to be a member of the Athenaeum: an institution to which he is unlikely to have been elected for his professional qualifications.

So the quest for managerial Ministers is doomed to failure unless we contemplate much more far-reaching constitutional changes than the critics have envisaged. For those who believe that modern Governments ought to be equipped to make management decisions at the micro-economic level, this may be a judgment of despair. For those who believe that the capacity of Governments to transform the performance of a modern industrial economy, for better or worse, is marginal, it is a lot less apocalyptic. It suggests that Ministers would be well advised to concentrate upon the task – for which they ought to be professionally qualified, which is pleasing the electorate to the extent required to secure re-election.

They could, however, 'politicise' the top crust of the civil service, as do the French and the Americans. The skill with which the Village has tamed, or occasionally ostracised, the political advisers which have been imported on a more modest scale for 20 years suggests that they might be disappointed. But there is a more fundamental difficulty. The 'spoils' of the American 'spoils system' are distributed ultimately by a President who has had to cobble together a 'national' constituency. A British Prime Minister, by contrast, has had to cobble together a party constituency. He or she has then had to carry that party constituency to a national majority at the polls; nevertheless it remains essentially a party constituency. For this reason there is an element of substance to the claim advanced by the Whitehall village under all Governments: the claim of independent continuity, or 'keeping the show on the road', in the words of Sir Patrick Nairne, erstwhile Permanent Secretary of the DHSS.

The 'constructive tension' between the villagers and their passing political landlords leaves much to be desired. So do the alternatives. The radical reformers need to heed the advice of Sir Douglas Wass, most civilised of mandarins, in his Reith lectures: 'The evolutionary quality of our system of Government reflects our pragmatic and cautious approach as a nation to change and reform'. But above all they should reflect that reordering the engine room is no substitute for politicians on the bridge who know where they want to get to, and who have the nerve and application to select the course, and stick to it. Such Ministers, like the virtuous woman of Proverbs, may have a price 'far above rubies'. But they occur: and there is no substitute.

Index